Life and Times
of Dionysius
the Divine

Life and Times of Dionysius the Divine
website or the url is
www.careerandlifecoach-dionysiusthedivine-llc.com

Life and Times of Dionysius the Divine

and his Forty Year Journey in the Desert of Life

Dionysius the Divine

Copyright © 2011, 2016 by Dionysius the Divine, LLC.
Facebook: Dionysius Divine
Email: dionysiusthedivine@gmail.com
Twitter: dionysiusthediv
www.dionysiusthedivine.com
Library of Congress Control Number: 2011909265
ISBN: Softcover   978-1-4568-7573-2
               eBook   978-1-4568-7574-9

Print information available on the last page.

Rev. date: 01/14/2016

Published by Xlibris Corp,
1663 Liberty Dr, Ste 200, Bloomington,
IN 47403, USA

To order additional copies of this book, contact:
Xlibris
1-888-795-4274
www.Xlibris.com
Orders@Xlibris.com
568140

Life & Times of Dionysius the Divine
CONTENT

This book is dedicated to all the people on Earth.
Stop destroying the earth, and each other
Arm in Arm, no cultural or theological boundaries
God in us, with us, through us, by us, and for us.

Quintanilla Coat of Arms description:
First quarter—green with 3 Moors' heads; Second quarter—silver with poplar green leaves; Third quarter—blue with 3 gold stars; Fourth quarter—silver with 3 red bands over a base of wavy silver and blue bars; all with a read border and 8 gold towers.

PREFACE

This book is the result of over 50 years of work and study seeking answers to the meaning of life that no one could answer to my satisfaction. Born in extreme poverty, my inquiries into the meaning of life began as a teenager in the pursuit of knowledge, wisdom and universally applicable truth. So, this book is the result of this journey. For this I was born. We all have a purpose in life. What is your purpose in life?

In my pursuit of knowledge, I traveled the world, studied at/with numerous universities and pursued a long successful engineering career with many fine corporations.

In my pursuit of knowledge I pursued knowledge of life, religion and God through study with many religious faiths, romance, marriage, fathering children and helping my children find their place in life until I found my place, faith and value in the universe.

In my pursuit of knowledge I experienced success and failure, happiness and sadness, trials, challenges and tribulations. I have rejoiced, sorrowed and grieved. Through all of this, I prevailed and navigated from blind faith to knowledge faith. Perhaps you have traveled a similar journey through life. Have you written the story of your journey through life?

Toward my latter years, the same force that compelled me to pursue knowledge and wisdom strongly compelled me to write this book. The actual writing took me about three (3) years, and much thought and research. As a result of my research, I have quoted from many sources. These sources were revealed to me in a vision at the right time over a period of many years until it came time to do the actual writing. My initial writing was just notes, and I was overwhelmed because I knew that it would be an arduous task to write this book. But, I am grateful to my sister, Ada, who in 2009 volunteered to transcribe my initial notes. My sister's efforts gave me the impetus to begin my final writing.

In this preface I state that I navigated "**From Blind Faith to Knowledge Faith**". This is not to say that I see anything wrong with blind faith. Blind faith basically means hope for and of things we cannot see, or understand, and that our needs will be provided by a supreme being if we have the right beliefs and do the right things. I know of and have seen many successful people who are guided in success, happiness, health, knowledge and wisdom by "blind faith". My mother survived and raised her three children by blind faith in the principles of the Christian Bible. And, I was guided through many dark lonely times by the faith built into me by my Christian upbringing. But, Knowledge faith is not Gnosticism, which is a belief in spiritual redemption by strict self denial, knowledge of God, and that material things are evil. Knowledge faith is similar to blind faith, except more humbling with scientific knowledge of ourselves, the earth and the universe, such as I discuss in chapter 10 on Intelligent Design. With this scientific knowledge, we are astounded and in awe of the magnificent order and irreducible complexity of human existence, the creation of the earth and the universe, and how it all fits together, which intelligent design infers an intelligent designer.

In the process of my writing, circumstances compelled me to add chapters that I had not initially envisioned, chapters 8 through 15.

Chapter 9, America, a Christian Nation was based mostly on the book "Christian Life and Character of the Civil Institutions of the United States" Written by B.F. Morris and published in 1864 at the request of Charles Sumner, Senator from Massachusetts

"Christian Life and Character of the Civil Institutions of the United States" was digitized from the Harvard College Library by Google and was obtained at http://books.google.com. The family pictures in this book come from the archives of the Quintanilla Family Estate.

Finally, there is a hidden message in these writings, not specifically written, which I cannot tell you, and only the spirit within you can reveal to you.

PROLOGUE

This book is a compilation of the writings of Dionicio Quintanilla, Jr based on a lifetime of education, experience, study, his quest for truth, justice, knowledge, wisdom, and universally applicable truth.

This book has been over two years in the writing. Why am I writing this book? Because I feel that I must. It seems that I have been running away from stupidity all of my life. I do not have millions of dollars, and yet I am wealthy, with excellent health, excellent family relations, excellent intellectual & spiritual relations, and very nice retirement benefits. I have not given millions of dollars to charity, but I have given my life in service to God and country, my mother and father, my sisters and their children, the women I married, and the children I fathered, and industry. I am not an author of many books, but I have written much in my life about my experiences and beliefs from which to publish. I am not a re-known speaker but I am an accomplished speaker. I have not been the CEO of a large corporation but I have served many large corporations. I am not a famous pastor of a large church, but I have attended and studied in many churches, including Baptist, Lutheran, Presbyterian, Methodist, Episcopal, Catholic, Mormon (where I was ordained a Deacon in the Aaronic Priesthood in 1962), Church of Christ, and Greek Orthodox. I am not an accomplished published scholar, but I have studied in numerous universities and earned numerous degrees and certifications.

So, who could possibly be interested in my book? I have pondered this question for about a year before beginning my final edit. Then the answer hit me. I am strongly compelled to write this book precisely for the person I am not, because of the simple person I am, unrecognized and unheralded, and because of my quest for survival, achievement, accomplishment, success, learning, education from numerous universities, and working for numerous large corporations to reach the peaceful, quiet, modest monastic life I enjoy today, **My Promised Land**, teaching Intellectual and Spiritual Enlightenment, and Enlightened Christianity. I call my life experiences **"My Forty Year Trek in the Desert of Life"** because that is approximately the span of time from 1960, when I started my university career at New Mexico State University, until 2002 when I retired.

Today I find that I can teach from what it took me a lifetime to learn. It also struck me that there are many like me that devote our whole lives to working, serving, learning just to survive from day to day and serve our destiny in the **Intellectual Dungeons of Industry**, while our task masters get rich by hiring and firing us. That is why I must write this book.

INTRODUCTION

The name Dionysius is the Greek version of the Spanish name Dionicio. The title "Dionysius The Divine" is used not because of the presumption of my divine nature, but because of my quest for divine knowledge and wisdom, seeking that which is good, wholesome and pure. The name Dionysius the Divine is not to be confused with Dionysus, the God of Wine in Greek mythology. Dionysius the Divine is a Warrior Monk. Do I look like a warrior or a monk?—no. Why warrior? Because I am and have always been ready for intellectual, spiritual and physical challenges. Why monk? Because my life is a quiet monastic life of study, prayer and service.

I am told by some that I exude an aura of wholesomeness that is apparent and obvious to many. Some call me "The Real Thing". Because of my quest for divine knowledge and wisdom I pray that my every thought, word and action be a prayer. I pray constantly to be good and do good. This is why I am a seeker of truth, justice, knowledge, wisdom, and universally applicable truth, and a Teacher of Intellectual and Spiritual Enlightenment, with no theological or cultural boundaries, and a teacher of Enlightened Christianity. Enlightened Christianity focuses on the spiritual nature of God and Heaven.

This quest began as a teenager when I first wanted to understand the Christian Bible. This quest further continued into later life as I sought to apply Christian principles in non-biblical terms without theological or cultural boundaries.

These writings then resulted from my many inquiries, over a period of many decades, into the wherefores and whyfores (a word I coined) of life. No, this is not a joke, and not a pipedream. This is the destiny to which I was born. In the pursuit of my 42 year career as an engineer, my journey in the desert of life, I knew in my youth that my career as an engineer was only a means to an end to prove myself, but I did not know what that destiny was to be, until I was about 65years of age. Then I realized that my destiny was to become Dionysius the Divine, and to write this book, and teach Intellectual and Spiritual Enlightenment, and Enlightened Christianity. In this destiny I believe that the purpose of life is to enjoy life, living and being alive by being good and doing good toward the purpose of achieving a balance with life, nature, the creator of life on earth and the universe. (Note: if there is a creation, earth, humanity, the flora and the fauna, the universe, then, there is a creator, God if you please)

Born in1942, I was named Dionicio Quintanilla, after my father and his father, of course. The name Dionicio is the Spanish (Spain) version of the name Dionysus, the Greek God of Wine. The name Quintanilla is a Spanish heraldic name, having the meaning of "one who comes from a house over the hill". In the days of knights, heraldic referred to being a herald, or representative of a monarch or king, and being generally represented by a coat of arms.

I have 2 sisters: Emma Maria De La Luz Quintanilla, born in 1943, and Ada Quintanilla, born in 1945. Thanks to our mother's tremendous efforts bringing us up from extreme poverty in San Antonio, Texas, and with the help of numerous fine friends, my sisters and I did well in life, university educations, marriage, careers, and retirement.

My inquiries into life began as a teenager, when I began seeking to understand the Christian Bible from a scientific point of view. Then as a young man in my early 20's, after going to college at New Mexico State University in Las Cruces, New Mexico to acquire my Bachelor of Science degree in Electrical Engineering, I set goals for myself. These goals were (1) understand the Christian Bible, (2) to be respected, (3) become an engineer, (4) become an intellectual, (5) find God, (6) find love, (7) find universally applicable truth, (8) conquer the world, (9) marry and have children. In these pursuits, I found many decades later that universally applicable truth is love, a small word with a very complex meaning. And, I conquered the world by taking everything the world had to dish out, good and bad, without by and large striking back. By and large I accomplished all of these goals, and then in my 60's I set new goals. My new goal was to write about my life, and become a teacher of Intellectual and Spiritual Enlightenment, and Enlightened Christianity.

I was born in San Antonio, Texas to Maria Teresa Guadalupe Morales Juarez and Dionicio Martinez Quintanilla, both very strong, bright, hard working individuals albeit individuals of very humble status, who immigrated from Mexico. My mother was born October 15, 1906 in Morelia, Michoacan, Mexico, to Placida Morales and Isidro Juarez, and died in 1986. My father was born January 26, 1915 in Piedras Negras, Coahuila, Mexico to Paulita Martinez and Dionicio Quintanilla, and died in 1996.

My mother and father were married in San Antonio Texas at the First Mexican Baptist Church on September 14, 1941. I will write more about them in a future edition. At this stage in my life, and looking back on my youth growing up in San Antonio, Texas, it astounds my sisters and myself what my parents were able to do with very little formal education. My mother spoke very little English, and did not drive an automobile, much less a huge gas guzzling SUV like today's very savvy immigrants, but her value was her charm, intelligence and her cultural education from her adopted mother in Mexico, Carmen Macias Fuentes. Because of my mother's cultural background, and my early life experiences, my culture is "old world European"; my intellect is "British"; and my work ethic is "German-Judeo".

My mother was orphaned about 1915 when her parents were killed in a civil war. The only thing I know about my mother's parents is that her father, Isidro Juarez, was a shoe maker. When my mother and her younger brother lost their home, she went knocking door-to-door to see who could give her work. One of the places she knocked at was an orphanage run by Carmen Macias Fuentes. This noble lady took my mother in and took care of her as her daughter until my mother immigrated to the United States in 1931. While growing up in Mexico City, my mother was converted to Protestant at about her mid 20's from the Catholic Church by a step sister before immigrating to the United States. Our mother was very religious, and she showed us the love and respect of God, as well, as a strong work ethic. Although we were poor growing up, mother always kept a clean home and clean clothes for us in a clean neighborhood, and we always had regular meals. My sisters and I never went to a school prom, but we never seemed to miss that. All of our life revolved around youth activities at the First Baptist Church of San Antonio, YMCA, YWCA, and for me Boy Scouts, and working after school when we were old enough.

My mother was brought to the United States of America, with permission of the American Consulate in Mexico City, as a governess for the child of a military family on 8 Sept, 1931. The only thing I know about that family was that the child's name was Porfirio. But my mother left that family because they gave her no money. When my mother left Porfirio's family, she searched door-to-door for families in the north side of San Antonio until she found families that would help her.

One of the people that helped my mother when she left Porfirio's family was a lady, who lived on College Blvd in Alamo Heights in San Antonio, and was a friend of my mother for many years until my sisters and I graduated from high school.

Another person who helped my mother when she left Porfirio's family was a lady, who lived on Kings Court in San Antonio for many years and was a lifelong friend of my mother and my sisters and I until her death in about 1975. When we had no home I remember showing up early in the morning at this lady's back door so we could have a meal and a bath. This lady's sister, Miss. Helen, who lived at the Lamar Hotel in Houston, and taught piano, was her life and sustenance, and I remember often going to her apartment on Christmas and Miss Helen would give my sisters and I each a $5.00 gift, which was a lot to us.

Another very generous and loving family who helped my mother when she left Porfiio's family was a doctor and his wife who lived at 102 E. Huisache in San Antonio (the house is still there). The doctor's wife, a retired teacher, with a master's degree in education from St Mary's University in San  Antonio, Texas, and whom I got to know as Ma Manes, actually gave my mother, and her three children, a place to live in a garage apartment and was very influential in my sister's and my early childhood, helping us to learn to read and write. This doctor attended to the birth of myself and my sister Emma at Baptist Memorial Hospital in San Antonio. My sister Ada was born at Santa Rosa Hospital in San Antonio, but her birth was attended by an unknown doctor.

Another very good family friend in San Antonio assisted and employed my father and mother for many years. In fact it was this family that helped my mother start her kindergarten as well as recruit students from affluent families for her.

With the help of these fine people, my mother was able to find odd jobs, working sometimes as many as three jobs at a time, until she was able to establish a small kindergarten to teach children of affluent families in San Antonio to sing and dance Mexican songs and dances. In this manner my mother was able to care for my sister's and I until my sister Emma and I graduated from college, and my sister Ada got enough college and career education to start her career in business. Residences that we lived at in San Antonio during the 1950's, but no longer exist, were 706 Brooklyn Ave, and 714 Brooklyn Ave.

In the 1960's my mother resided at 136 E. Craig Place, in the Monte Vista Historical District of San Antonio, across from Keystone Private

School, until my mother moved to Dallas with my sister Ada, my father, and myself as our family united. The house at 136 E. Craig is still there. It was at 714 Brooklyn and 136 E. Craig that my mother ran her kindergarten.

About 1950 Baptist Missionaries took my sisters and myself to the First Baptist Church of San Antonio and I still remember their names: Mrs. Brent and Mrs. Anderson. My sisters and I were baptized in that church between 1951 and 1953, by a famous Southern Baptist Pastor, Dr. Perry F. Webb, and my sisters and I attended the First Baptist Church of San Antonio until we graduated from high school. Dr Webb was a friend of our family until his death.

Thus living under the influence of many fine people in San Antonio, as well as under the influence of the fine people at the First Baptist Church of San Antonio, as well as the influence of the schools we attended in San Antonio, and especially Thomas Jefferson High School, a college preparatory school at the time, is the reason my sister's and I are who we are, and have done well in life, retiring to a comfortable life.

My father's father, Dionicio Quintanilla, was a rail road engineer in Mexico, but was killed in a train accident when my father was very young. My father never recovered from his father's death, and seemed to have a childish character the rest of his life, even though he was very strong and very intelligent. As a result, my father and his mother looked to his mother's brothers, Nickolas Martinez, and Fermin Martinez who eventually settled on adjacent farm property in Floresville, Texas. My father's mother, Paulita Martinez Quintanilla, used the death benefit from her husband's accidental death to raise my father and his older brother, Sam Quintanilla. Paulita moved to 208 E. 17th St, Port Authur, Texas, in the 1920's, where her brother, Nickolas Martinez and his family lived, and worked in the new oil fields, and where my father lived with his mother, and where he completed grade school, before they moved to San Antonio, Texas. Paulita died penniless in 1948, and Fermin died in the early 1950's, and Nickolas died in the early 1960's. Fermin was very gentlemanly, and my mother was close to him. My father was closer to Nickolas, who raised cows and planted peanuts, black eye peas, pinto beans, corn and watermelon.

My father was also very religious, although sometimes he strayed. He knew the Christian Bible from cover to cover, and was an itinerate Nazarene preacher in the 1940's in addition to other work. He became an Engine Cadet with the U.S. Dept of Commerce Bureau of Marine Inspection & Navigation on 7 Oct, 1937, and became a United States citizen on 27 Dec, 1938. On November 7, 1942, my father was promoted from General Helper, at Ft. Sam Houston, Texas, to Lithographer by Major General Donovan. Later, my father became a gun repairman on .30 and .50 caliber machine guns at the San Antonio Arsenal until 1946. Then my father served in the U.S. Army from June, 1946 to January, 1947, where he became proficient as an automobile mechanic and in driving trucks of all sizes. Then, my father worked for Zachary Construction, but lost his job in 1948 because of an eye injury. In 1950 my father started working for the San Antonio Transit Company as a bus driver. My father worked as a bus driver until about 1958, when he had to quit because of a death in an accident involving the bus he was driving. After that my father drove a dump truck, which I learned to drive, delivered and installed billiard tables and juke boxes, and operated gasoline stations until 1970.

In 1970 my father and sister Ada and her child of 2 years old, Deanna Kim came to live in Dallas, Texas where I was employed in my second professional engineering job. At that time my father and I ran a gasoline service station for American Oil until 1975, when the service station was converted to self service. After that my father operated other gasoline service stations until his retirement in 1982 at age 67.

In 1971 my mother came to Dallas to live with my father and my sister Ada and her child Deanna Kim. In that same year my father, mother, sister Ada, and Deanna Kim moved to a house in Mesquite, Texas that my father bought with his veterans eligibility, and with savings from Ada and my mother. At this time Ada had started working for Western Electric, and my mother had started doing baby sitting so they were able to save money to buy the house in Mesquite, where Ada and her husband still live.

My sister Ada married John McMullen in 1998, and my sister Emma married Curtis B. Hendricks Jr in 1967. Ada has one daughter, Deanna Kim Martinez, from a previous marriage, and Emma and Curtis have one daughter, Cynthia Belle Hendricks. Deanna Kim married Thomas Knoff in 1989 and they have four children, Joshua, Rebekah, Caleb, and Anna. Cynthia married Kevan Krysler in 1995 and they have 3 children, Trevor, Matthew, and Claire Marie. Both of my sisters and their husbands are now retired and doing well.

Nelda and I married on February 25, 1967, in Mobile, Alabama, with no one in attendance, except Pastor Fred D. Brown, one week after my sister Emma and Curt Hendricks were married in Oklahoma City. Nelda and I later divorced on 2 July, 1971 in Dallas, Texas. I was a young Electrical Engineer when Nelda and I met in Mobile, Alabama in 1966 where I was working at the Mobile Shipyard on an aircraft carrier's communications systems. Nelda was a registered nurse, but our marriage never had a chance for survival because of the difference in our ages, cultures, and personal differences. However I loved Nelda very much and tried hard to provide for her and her three children by a previous marriage. Nelda and I had one daughter, Nelda Denise, born in 1968 in Dallas, Texas. I am still grateful for my marriage to Nelda for my growth and learning and the happiness we had for a short time.

Linda and I were married on March 19, 1983 at the First Presbyterian Church in Mesquite, Texas, by Rev Thomas Wilbanks, and we divorce in August 1985. Linda and I met at work, where we both worked as Software Engineers. This marriage was also doomed from the beginning because of our cultural and personal differences, but I loved and admired Linda very much, and tried hard to meet her needs. Linda and I had two children, Dionicio IV (Dion)—born in 1983, and Elizabeth Loraine (Lorrie)—born in 1985. I am of course grateful for my marriage to Linda for my growth and learning and the happiness we had for a short time, and the two beautiful children we had.

Denise married Mark Edmondson in 1999 and they divorced in 2006. At the time of this writing Denise has a son, Aidan Carlin Edmondson, and a daughter born in 2010, by the name of Tara Maria Grace Quintanilla-Sutton. Dion and Kimberly Hayden were married on July 19 of 2008, and their son William Martinez Quintanilla was born in 2009. Elizabeth and Christopher Wells were married on June 2, 2007, and their daughter Catherine was born August 8, 2014.

Now, back to our education. I have degrees and certifications from the following universities: New Mexico State University, Bachelor of Science Electrical Engineering, 1965; University of Texas at Arlington, Master of Science Electrical Engineering, 1975; University of Texas at Dallas (12 hours graduate studies in Computer Science—1981); University of Texas at Austin, Software & Systems Engineering Institute Master's Certification, 1995; Richland College, Associate Degree Computer Networking—Novell, 1998, and an Associates Degree in Computer Networking—Microsoft-NT,

1999; Texas Tech University, Master of Engineering, 2000; Brookhaven College, Math Teacher Certification Course, 2003.

Dion has a few college credit hours, from Richland College, and Devry University, and he enlisted in the Army in 2003. Dion was discharged from the U.S. Army in 2011 after which he joined the Texas National Guard and worked in the oil industry factory maintenance for 3 years but was caught in industry wide layoffs. Dion is now studying for 7 IT certifications.

Elizabeth earned a Bachelor of Science Degree in Electrical Engineering with Highest Honors (equivalent to Summa Cum Laude), and has a Master of Science degree in Electrical Engineering. Christopher Wells earned a Bachelor of Science degree Cum Laude in Math and Physics in 2006, and a Master of Science degree in Applied Math in 2009.

Denise graduated from St. Edward's University, Austin, Texas in 2003 with a Bachelor of Liberal Arts Degree in Public Administration, but was mostly a stay-at-home-mom until she re-entered the workforce in 2009. Notably, Denise tenaciously worked at many odd jobs between 1986 and 1999 while pursuing her education at various colleges and universities, including Richland College in Dallas, Texas, Texas State University in San Marcos, Texas, and finally, St. Edward's University.

In a span of forty-one(41) years, from 1961 to 2002, I worked for numerous corporations. Denise is now a Professional Development Specialist Supervisor for a Head Start program (early childhood education). Elizabeth now works as a Principal Control Systems Engineer, and Christopher now works as a Sr Software Engineer. Dion continues as a Specialist in the Texas National Guard.

It is also important to state in this introduction, the accomplishments of my sisters, Emma and Ada, and their husbands, respectively Curtis B. Hendricks Jr, and John McMullen. We are a closely knit family, serving family, God and country, and we have helped each other along the road of live for many decades. Both John and Curt have attended family weddings, births, birthdays, deaths, and graduations, and are a very important part of our family.

Emma (aka Mimi) graduated from Thomas Jefferson High School, San Antonio, Texas, in 1963. Then Mimi attended college, and graduated in 1967 with a B.A. in Education. Mimi received her Teacher Certification and then taught Spanish in public school until her retirement in 2001. Mimi's attendance and graduation from college is another great tribute to our mother who provided financing for Mimi from the fruits of her kindergarten work. I also assisted Mimi and my sister Ada with college financing after I graduated from New Mexico State University in 1965. My sister Ada also assisted with financing, while attending college from from 1965 to 1966 by working at United Fund and at TG&Y, a Five & Ten store which type no longer exists with the advent of large corporate ventures like Walgreen's. Emma's career as a teacher was remarkable because she was not only a teacher, but for many decades, she was a beacon and a lighthouse of trust for many students, whom she knew, assisted, guided and worked with personally.

Now comes the remarkable education and career story of my sister Ada, another tribute to our mother and the fruits of her kindergarten work. Ada was tutored in algebra at Keystone Private School, and graduated from Thomas Jefferson High School, San Antonio, Texas, in 1964, and proceeded to attend Draughon's Business College in San Antonio for six successful months. Then Ada attended Southern Nazarene University from 1965 to 1966, and later studied accounting in 1972 at Eastfield Community College in Mesquite, Texas, while working for Western Electric. Ada's story is particularly remarkable because she did not speak English when she started elementary school at Breckenridge Elementary School in San Antonio, and had to repeat the first grade. At every grade, Ada was considered slow, comparing her with her older brother and sister, but she wasn't. Ada just kept quietly plugging away.

From here on, we never knew what Ada was up to because she never said much; Ada just kept on working and working and working. Witness—Ada's first job was with EODC-CEP (Economic Organization Development—Concentrated Employment Program) , a government program for poor people who wanted to improve their lives, from 1966-1967. Next, Ada worked for Air Lift International from 1967 to 1969. At ALI, Ada was the only employee requested to move to Miami when the company moved, but Ada stayed with her mother and went to work for LTV, San Antonio, Texas, from 1969 to 1970. After that, Ada moved to Dallas with her father and mother, and went to Work at Western Electric, in Mesquite, Texas (later Lucent Technology, and then Tyco) from 1970 until her early retirement in 2000. For the 30 years that Ada worked at Western Electric, Ada did project management and research in many areas, including Personnel Investigation, Accounts Payable, Accounting, Payroll, Shipping and Receiving, Materials Management, Customer Service, and finally, Purchasing from 1990 until 2000. And, we never knew what Ada was up to until she recently responded to my inquiry.

Then there is the very impressive career of my brother-in-law, my sister Emma's husband, Curtis B. Hendricks, Jr (Curt). Again, we never knew much about Curt, except that he was an attorney for Kerr-McGee, and occasionally took trips, sometimes overseas. Curt graduated from Oklahoma City's John Marshall High School. in 1959. Curt then was a student for three years at the University of Central Oklahoma, and volunteered for the U.S. Army serving 1962-1965. While serving with the U.S. Army, Curt was in the Army Security Agency with assignments at Ft. Leonard Wood, MO; Ft. Devens, MA; Ft. Meade, MD (National Security Agency); and two years posted in Hokkaido Prefecture, Japan. After returning from the Army in May 1965, Curt finished his B.S. in Business Administration (Management) graduating in early January 1967. Curt then went to work at Tinker AFB in Oklahoma City, but quit to go to school full time to study law at the University of Oklahoma. Curt then received his Juris Doctorate from the University of Oklahoma in 1972. After that Curt then worked for Kerr-McGee Corp. for 27 years until his retirement in 2000. At Kerr-McGee, Curt worked in the Law Dept. and also served as Director of the Industrial Relations Dept. reporting to the CEO. I also remember Curt solving many labor relations problems for Kerr-McGee. Curt also helped me in the early 1970's to understand that management were human beings too because I did not respect management at that time.

Now comes the remarkable career of my sister Ada's husband, John McMullen. I call John, Big John with an eagle eye that misses nothing. John and Curt enjoy playing golf every opportunity they get. John is a strong, gentle caring person, assisting many in church and community at every opportunity. John graduated from John Tyler, High school in Tyler Texas, in 1958. John then attended Tyler Jr College for 2 years earning an Associates Degree in 1960. John also attended Abilene Christian University, Dallas, in 1974. John's early work history is sparse gaining valuable work experience. Dallas Morning News in 1954; H.K. Knight Builder in Dallas summer of 1955 & 1956; Several used car lots in Tyler 1957-58; McMullen Janitorial Services 1959-60; Daniels & McMullen Garage in Tyler 1961-62. Then John served with the U.S. Air Force from 1962 to 1965 receiving an honorable discharge. After that John worked with GE A/C Division, Tyler Tx from 1965 to 1966. Then John worked as a Highway Patrol Officer with the Texas Department of Public Safety from 1966 to1979, and with the U.S. Army National Guard from 1970 to 1976, as Platoon Sgt (SFC) in a tank battalion. Finally, John worked as a security guard with Western

Electric, AT&T, Lucent, Tyco Electronics from 1979 until his retirement in 2009.

It is also important to include here the education of my sister Ada's daughter, Deanna Kim Knoff. Deanna attended Richland Community College in Dallas, Texas where she met her husband Tom Knoff. Deanna was mostly a stay-at-home-mom, but now works as a Teacher's Aide in the public schools in Mesquite, Texas. Tom Knoff also attended Richland Community College. Later in 2004 Tom earned a Bachelor of Arts Degree in Biblical Studies (Summa Cum Laude & H. Leo Eddleman Award for top of class) from Criswell College—a Christian college and divinity school in Dallas, Texas. Tom Knoff also earned a Master of Divinity Degree from Liberty Baptist Theological Seminary in Lynchburg, Virginia, via the internet. Tom has pastured several churches, and is now pastor of the Journey Bible Church in San Angelo, Texas.

It is also important to include here the education of my sister Emma's daughter, Cynthia Belle Krysler. Cynthia earned a Bachelor of Arts Degree in Education (Magna Cum Laude), received her Teacher Certification and then taught Spanish in public school until she married Kevan Krysler. Then, Cynthia became a full time stay-at-home-mom. Kevan has a Bachelor of Arts Degree in Accounting, and is now a vice president in a large accounting company with world-wide coverage.

This introduction is not complete without a tribute to Curt's parents, Curtis and Belle Hendricks. Curtis served in World War 2, and, as a wounded veteran, was awarded many medals, including a Purple Heart for bravery in combat. Curtis and Belle were very important friends in Emma's and Ada's lives while they attended college, and continue being a friend to all of us to this day. Curtis worked as a supervisor at CMI Oklahoma for 21 years until his retirement in 1965. Belle has been a very faithful stay-at-home mom serving her three sons, Curtis, Jr, Allen, and Dwight. Curtis and Belle have both faithfully served their church for many decades, at Piedmont Church of the Nazarene. Fortunately, at the time of this writing, Belle are still with us, although ederly in her 90's. Unfortunately, Curtis Hendricks Sr died 11 July, 2010.

Returning to my life, when I was in my 30's, life was really a struggle after a 2nd marriage & divorce, to Mary Alice, changing jobs three times, and after the birth of my first daughter, Nelda Denise Quintanilla. At this stage in my life, although at the age of 33, I obtained my first Masters Degree in Electrical Engineering, I was a long way off from meeting the goals of my youth. During this time and into the1980's, I struggled to develop my career, a third marriage and divorce, to Linda, and caring for my youngest children, Dionicio IV (Dion) and Elizabeth Loraine (Lorrie), and providing for my daughter Denise, from my first marriage. Denise was kidnapped from my home in Mesquite, Texas, by her mother about the age of four years old in 1972, but I obtained custody of Denise when she was 7 years of age, and again when she was about 11 years of age. When Denise was 14 years of age she returned to Atmore, Alabama, of her own free will, to live with her mother until she returned to live with me in Mesquite, Texas after she graduated from high school in 1986. This was a very difficult time for me because of the expense of providing for Denise, Dion and Lorrie, and my struggle to survive. So during this time I was not optimistic about meeting my youthful goals.

Because I was not optimistic about meeting my youthful goals in the 1970's, I started calling myself "Semi-Distinguished", "Pseudo Sophisticate" and "Quasi Intellectual". This characterization of myself lasted through the 1970's until about the mid 1990's, and bothered my family. But, nevertheless, that is who I was, and represented who I wanted to be.

In the early 1980's, I returned to college to study graduate Computer Science at the University of Texas at Dallas (UTD), and change careers. With the help of a professor of Computer Science at UTD, I found employment in 1981 as a Software Engineer after my rocky career as an Electrical Engineer and Technical Sales. I will include a chapter about my career experiences in this book. Then about the mid 1980's, after my 3rd divorce, I was invited By John Hoelzel Sr to join a bible study at work. John Hoelzel was one of my supervisors at work and subsequently became a lifelong friend, and helped me considerably to cope and stabilize emotionally after my separation from Linda in 1984.

Then I joined a Liturgical Bible study at work, which split from the first open discussion Bible study. This time was a time of awakening and self realization for me as my career stabilized somewhat, and I was no longer changing employers, although I changed groups and assignments many times. During this time I began to gain the scientific understanding of the Christian Bible that I had so desperately sought as a youth 34 years earlier. Toward this end I also owe much to both John Hoelzel and to other engineers. Because of my experience with these bible study groups, I then also began to lead in bible studies.

Then in 1994 I returned to college study again until the year 2000. I returned to college study because I realized that my education was outdated. From 1994 to 2000 I earned 97 college and university credit hours with a

GPA of 3.6. My life time GPA with a total of 284 college and university credit hours is 2.926. It was during this time frame that I realized I was no longer identifying myself as "Semi-Distinguished, "Pseudo-sophisticate", "Quasi—Intellectual". Now I was characterizing myself as "Full grown, mature male of the specie, battle scared and weathered, with the tenacity of bulls, and the compassion of angels".

With the technology I acquired from 1994 to 2000 I was able to do many newer technology tasks like migrating from the HP computers to Unix operating systems; transition from structured software engineering to object oriented software engineering; transition from single platform computers to client server computers; and into process science.

Then late in 2001, I was given one too many assignments with broken down equipment and software, and wrong information, and I just shut down mentally, although I could have done the work. I just seemed burned out, discouraged, abandoned and isolated, while the younger engineers continued to get the well supported tasks. So, I announced to my management at work that this task exceeded my level of expertise. After that I was given odd jobs until I was laid off in March 2, 2002, with a nice severance package. However, even as I was ushered out, I was still passing important information to my manager that he needed for his responsibilities. Grieving, and with my head bowed in sorrow, I never stopped serving and helping.

After March 2, 2002 until September 2002 I bridged my time to retirement with severance pay and unemployment compensation. From September 2002 until I started collecting Social Security in May of 2004, I bridged my time with retirement pay, savings and working as a substitute teacher in grades 6 through 12. I continued to work as a Substitute Teacher until the time of this writing. My substitute teaching has been an eye opener, extremely educational, and has transformed me as I learned to work with students and teachers.

Eighty percent (80%) of my work as a substitute teacher in the public schools is psychological, insofar as getting and keeping the students attention, maintaining discipline, keeping the students focused on their subject matter class work; ten percent (10%) of my work as a substitute teacher involves assisting students with their lessons; and ten percent (10%) of my work as a substitute teacher involves executing teachers' lesson plans and providing complete reports to the teachers I substitute for.

Also, in November 2005 just before Thanksgiving, a vision (like a bolt of lighting) hit me to run for "Garland City Council, Place 1. I did not win the election, but I gained many friends, and became well known to Garland City Council, Garland City Management, and many citizens of Garland. The person that won the Garland City Council election for Place 1, Douglas Athas, and I became good friends, and he subsequently appointed me to the Housing Standards Board, where I served from October, 2006 until I resigned in March of 2007. The Housing Standards Board served to hear Residential Code Compliance cases of non compliance and to assess abatement and/or condemnation time frames. I resigned from the Garland Housing Standards Board in 2007 after contributing significantly to the City Attorney's Office to rewrite the Housing Standards Board Rules and Procedures and because the Residential Code Compliance Department needed no advisement or oversight.

Then, in 2009 I was inspired by a vision to run for Garland City Mayor because of the problems I saw in the 2007 elections for Garland Mayor. Again, I did not win the election but I learned a lot, and became even better known to Garland City Management, Garland City Council, and the citizens of Garland. Mayor Ronald Jones, with whom I took considerable issue, won the Mayor's election in both 2007 and 2009 with a very solid block vote. In 2007, only about 8% of the 100,000 plus registered voters in Garland, Texas voted, and in 2009, only about 5% of the registered voters in Garland, Texas voted. The voter turnout in both 2007, and 2009 was not good enough for a break from the political establishment in Garland. Douglas Athas and Ronald Jones were both well established in the Garland political establishment.

It was during this transition period that I reached my next level in life. Both the substitute teaching and running for city council were extremely eye opening and life transforming experiences for me. I met many students and people in these pursuits. Because of these experiences, combined with my 40 plus years working industry, and my extensive college and university education I realized that I had become a metaphysicist and an *Ecologist of the Human Fabric* (not Social Ecologist, people and the ecology of mother earth), and a teacher of Intellectual and Spiritual enlightenment, and Enlightened Christianity. Enlightened Christianity focuses on the spiritual nature of God and heaven using scripture references from the Christian Bible.

I coined the title of *Ecologist of the Human Fabric* to mean the study of the ecology of holistic human nature, protecting the *human fabric* in the economy of community, business, government, industry, education and religion. By holistic human nature, I mean considering the whole human being in terms of mental, intellectual, physical, spiritual, social and religions needs as they function in symbiotic and synergistic relations in the interrelated economies of community, business, government, industry, education and religion. I strongly believe in preserving human fabric and the efficiency of human relations which can best be done by the utilizing the *Ecology of the Human Fabric*. Although social sciences and psychology are involved in the Ecology of Human Relations, the Ecology of Human Relations is not about the social sciences and psychology.

I use the term *metaphysicist* to designate my use of logic to navigate through the cause-effect relations of the principles of engineering and mathematics for the solution of technical and engineering and computer science tasks. In my Software Engineering work, I found that many software engineers used logic to navigate through the cause-effect relations of the principles of engineering and mathematics for the solution of technical, engineering and computer science tasks, but they didn't call themselves metaphysicists.

So far in this introduction, I have mentioned a little about my marriages and divorces, my parents, my religious experience, career and education experiences, growing up, but nothing about my experiences in courts of law. In courts of law I gained much experience in family law in dealing with divorce and custody issues with my three children. I also gained much experience in Civil Rights and even represented myself as a Pro Se Litigant at the Fifth Circuit Court of Appeals, and the Supreme Court of the United States. I gained my experience in Civil Rights through my discrimination law suits. Although I did not prevail in my law suits, I learned much that I would not have otherwise been able to learn. I have also represented myself as a Pro Se Litigant and prevailed in my law suits against insurance companies to recover damages to my automobiles suffered in accidents with the insured, in which I was not at fault and the insurance companies refused to compensate me for the damages to my automobiles because of their age.

I must also pay tribute here to the many university professors and instructors that guided me through many decades of education, none-the-least of which was Dr. Murat Tanik, now a Professor of Computer Science at the University of Alabama. I remain forever indebted to Dr. Tanik for my awesome transformation, through the knowledge, wisdom and foresight of the educational programs Dr. Tanik directed at work through the University of Texas and Texas Tech University from 1995 to 2000. I continue to benefit tremendously from those educational programs, including my Software and Systems Engineering Institute Master's Certification, and my Master of Engineering Degree, and will for the rest of my life.

This first edition will include writings about my religious experiences, career, health, education, America, a Christian nation, Intelligent Design, and quotations to live by, both those that are legend, and those defined by me, as well as Intellectual and Spiritual Enlightenment, and Enlightened Christianity. And now, lest I boast of my modest accomplishments, it was not I, but the God in us, with us, through us, by us and for us that brought me across my 42 year trek in the desert of life to make me what I am today, Dionysius the Divine. This is my story. Have you written yours? If you are young, what are your goals in life? If you have run the race of life and finished, what have you accomplished and what have you learned, and what can we learn from you?

I press toward the mark for the prize of the high calling of God in Christ Jesus (Philippians 3:14). Thanks be to God.

CHAPTER 1

Education

Early Years through High School

In the introduction to this book I referred to my mother and father. I refer to them again now because our parents, and our home are the first component of our education. The second component of our education is the church, whatever the denomination, where hopefully we have community and learn about love, faith, morals, and respect for men and the laws of man (government). The third component of our education is of course school, Kindergarten through grade 12.

Thanks to our mother's tremendous efforts bringing us up from extreme poverty in San Antonio, Texas, my sisters and I did well in school, university educations, marriage, life, careers, and retirement.

Our mother was very religious, strong and intelligent. She was converted to Protestant from the Catholic Church by a step sister before immigrating to the United States. Our mother showed us the love and respect of God, as well, as a strong work ethic. Although we were poor growing up, mother always kept a clean home and clean clothes for us in a clean neighborhood, and we always had regular meals. My sisters and I were baptized in the First Baptist Church of San Antonio, where we attended until we graduated from high school. This of course was the very important second component of our education. Whatever the church said was right and wrong, true or false, that is what we went by until we left home. When we left home we had to learn new principles to live by in the outside world.

To raise us, my mother worked up to 3 jobs at a time until she started her kindergarten in San Antonio for the children of affluent families teaching them Spanish singing and dancing. With the home environment my mother provided, my sisters, Emma and Ada, and I were able to peacefully, although modestly, attend school from elementary to junior high school and to high school. Our grades were modest, but credible A's, B's and C's, and sufficient for us to enter college.

My father was also an important component of our education, even though many times he was absent in our lives. My father was also very strong and intelligent. In our pre-school years, in the 1940's my father drove us in an old car to churches he was assigned to pastor by the Mexican Nazarene Institute in San Antonio. My father's favorite topic to preach about was love, and he knew the Christian Bible well. These were memorable, although hard times for us. My father and mother were assigned to pastor abandoned churches first in Carrizo Springs, Texas, and then in Laredo, Texas. These were very hard times for us because the people didn't have money to give for offering. And sometimes my father would go to Piedras Negras, Cohuila, Mexico, where he was born, leaving us alone. The people did give us food and animals, but that was not enough. So my parents had to quit their pastoring assignments to do other work back in San Antonio.

I remember the long drives to Carrizo Springs, sometimes in the thundering night, and I could hear my father's powerful voice over the thunder singing "There's Power in the Blood" in Spanish. In Carrizo springs, the pastor's home had a leaky tin roof and the water came through the roof when it rained. In the hot summer, the house got very hot, and my sister Emma had a stroke. This is when my mother and her 3 small children returned to San Antonio one night on a bus. I don't know where my father was at that time.

Arriving in San Antonio my mother searched late at night for some church people where we could stay the night. That night, in the dark of night we found a place to stay in the projects of west San Antonio with someone she knew from church. At this time my mother and father returned to the Nazarene Institute briefly where I first attended an elementary school nearby for the first grade. What I remember about this was that I carried my lunch in a tin lunch box, and singing America the Beautiful.

After this, my mother and father gave up their efforts with the Nazarene Institute of San Antonio and we went to live in the garage room of a doctor friend and his wife at 102 E. Huisache in San Antonio. The house and garage room are still there. My mother returned to doing other types of work, and my father went to work for Zachry Construction. At this time I started in the first grade at Travis Elementary School attending school with the children of many affluent families. The School is still there. I remember that I was the only child that went to school happy while all of the other children were crying for their mother.

Elementary School

By now the year is 1949, and living with the doctor and his wife was very opportune. The doctor, I called him Paw Doc, attended to my birth at Baptist Memorial Hospital years earlier in 1942. I remember the doctor's wife, I called her Ma Manes, helping me with my school lessons every day, and giving me cookies and milk when I came home from school. This is where my British Intellect came from. Ma Manes had a Master's Degree in education from St. Mary's University. The help Ma Manes gave me the 3 years we lived in her garage room empowered me, and my sisters. During this time, my mother worked as a custodian at Bonham School in the San Antonio School District. Early in the morning she would go to work and take my sisters to the Carmelite Catholic School while she was at work. I remember, I would wait for the milkman to deliver the morning quart of milk, make myself breakfast of a glass of milk with egg and sugar and vanilla. Then, I would walk to school, and of course walk home every day by myself.

When I was in the third grade, my mother moved to a rent house close to Breckenridge Elementary School. This school is no longer there. This was our first home. At this time I took my sister Emma to be enrolled in the first grade.

At Breckenridge Elementary School I remember 3 significant teachers. These teachers were my 3rd grade teacher, my 5th grade, and my 6th grade teacher. I remember that my teacher in the third grade used to make fun of me because I always liked to answer questions. My 3rd grade teacher used to tell me, "I can find someone to beat you", and she did, a boy I would later know at high school and church.

Then, in the fifth grade, my teacher was very caring toward my sisters and myself. This teacher loved Indian and Mexican children.

Then, in 1954, my 6th grade teacher had a big impact on my sister's and myself. My 6th grade teacher was very strict. I remember she was very upset when the school desegregation law was passed. But this 6th grade teacher had a bigger impact on me when she read us Walter Farley's story of "The

Black Stallion". This started my phase of reading every book I could find about horses and dogs (The Call of the Wild). This reading became another component of my education, and continued into my college years and further. While in high school, I read books about space science fiction, the Three Musketeers, and others. In college I started reading western novels. Then in the 1970's, as I traveled in South America, I started reading romance novels. In the 1970's I started a book collection, at considerable expense, which continues to this day, and the books number in the hundreds.

Another big component of my early education was while I was in the third grade at Eleanor Breckenridge Elementary. I enrolled in a boys military organization that met after school and was led by high school ROTC (Reserve Officer Training Corps) students. This organization was called "Junior Yanks", where I wore a uniform, and learned to march and salute. This organization was probably started because of the Korean War.

Another thing I remember about elementary school was that we could pray in class before the days of civil rights, and before an atheist put an end to prayer in our schools.

YMCA

Another big component of my early education while I was in the third grade was when my mother enrolled me at the YMCA (Young Men's Christian Association), and yes, I would walk myself to and from the YMCA on days for my age group. At the YMCA I learned crafts, swimming, and my participation with the YMCA lasted for a couple of years. I also learned not to gamble my lunch money at the pool tables with boys that were experienced pool players.

Music Study

And yet another important component of my early education while in the third grade was that I started studying the accordion. My mother paid for me to study accordion and my two sisters to study piano at the San Antonio School of Music. I studied accordion until age 12. I became quite accomplished at playing the according, and I played on a radio program with my accordion teacher. From age 12 to age 15 my mother hired a piano teacher to come and give my sister's and me piano lessons.

At age 15, my mother sent me and my sisters to study in Mexico during the summer. I studied piano with a conservatory teacher, and then went to study Spanish literature and short hand writing. After age 12 I rarely touched the accordion, and after age 15, I rarely touched the piano, although I became quite good learning to play such music as the "Hungarian Rhapsody".

Also, in Junior High School I started learning to play the String Bass. I wanted to learn to play the trumpet, but the teacher would not let me, and the only instrument left was the string bass. I was never very good at playing the string bass but I continued to play it through High School, and also played in the San Antonio Junior Symphony Orchestra. I started to play the string bass with the band my first year at New Mexico State University, but I dropped out because they took week end trips and I did not want to miss my Saturday engineering classes.

Boy Scouts

Continuing, another big component of my early education came when I turned eleven years old. At this time I joined the Boy Scouts, and immediately became a leader. This was particularly interesting because I was a very small boy weighing only 87 pounds at age 14. I only earned a few merit badges, and did become a "First Class Scout". I participated in the Boy Scouts at the Episcopal Church in downtown San Antonio until I was about fifteen years old. I remember many camping trips where we would pitch tents, learned to build cooking fires and cook our meals. I also remember going on many hiking trips during our campouts and playing war games like "Steal the Flag". At Scout meetings sometimes we would skate in the church skating rink, and sometimes we would play dodge ball, and Red Rover, let "someone come over" and break the hands-held line. I also remember sometimes we were very cold at night and stayed by the fire to try to stay warm. I also remember when I was fourteen years old I used to drive boys to camping trips in my father's 1949 Chevrolet. My father taught me to drive when I was thirteen years old, and I got my driver's license when I was fourteen. A big event for us as Boy Scouts was to collect news papers and put them in my father's trailer and then when we had enough, my father would take us to sell the collected news papers for recycle money, and give it to the troop.

Another big Boy Scout event was our annual Boy Scout Jamboree at the San Antonio Colosseum. We, the Boy Scouts, would sell tickets to raise money for the troop, and then many of the Boy Scout troops would set up displays such as cooking and wood craft for visitors to see.

Boy Scout troops were usually run by church leader men, and we didn't have to worry about Gay, or women troop leaders. (Note: I see no problem with women troop leaders because that is today's culture) When my son Dion was a Boy Scout he asked me to go to a troop parents meeting at the home of one of the parents, and of course there were women there. As a consequence of my going to that meeting, Boy Scout Circle 10 executives proceeded to come to my work to investigate me. I gave these executives an audience, but have no idea why they were investigating me, or what the outcome of their investigation was. This was, of course, a lot different from when I was a Boy Scout in the 1950's.

Junior High School

Another big step in my education was at Hawthorn Junior High School, from the seventh grade to the ninth grade. I remember my eighth grade math teacher who told me I would not be able to take Algebra I because I got "C" in her math class. But, I took Algebra I anyway, and got an "A". It was much more interesting than my eighth grade math class. I also remember my eighth grade English teacher, who taught me eighth grade English, and how well he taught me English Grammar, and sentence structure. This English teacher's teaching empowered me for the rest of my life. Also of considerable significance to me in junior high school was the eighth grade business course I took where I learned typewriter and check writing and letter writing. This typing of course empowered me for the rest of my life, especially when I would start programming computers using a card punch machine in college, and then when I started programming computers with keyboards in the 1980's.

Another thing I remember about Junior High School was that we had the "board of education", i.e. the paddle. And we didn't whine about it. If we misbehaved we got the paddle, and we learned to behave because we didn't want the paddle. Also, if we had conflict between boys, we could put on gloves in the gym under supervision from the coach.

High School

The next big phase of my education was at Thomas Jefferson High School in San Antonio. At that time, this high school was a college preparatory school, and was in the center of an affluent Jewish community. A grade of "A" was from 93 to 100. A grade of "B" was from "85 to "92". A grade of "C" was from 78 to 85, and a grade of "D" was from 70 to 77. So, on a scale of 1 for "D" and 4 for "A" it was much harder than normal schools, even today to get a 4.0. Of considerable significance at Thomas Jefferson was the fact that city buses transported us to and from high school from all over the city, and we paid our own bus fare. There was no such thing as forced busing or school buses. There were also many Jewish students, many of whom helped me, even though I never participated in any society events. So, the cultural diversity at Thomas Jefferson was very rich, and helpful to me.

Also significant at high school was the fact that I took ROTC (Reserve Officer Training Corps) all three years I attended Thomas Jefferson. I also went to summer school to make up deficiencies, or to just get ahead. I had considerable difficulty with Alegbra II. I got a "D" for my first class, so I took the class over again, and got a "B". I also remember taking Honors History and Honors English. I never had homework because in both junior high and high school we had study hall, except for these honors courses. I remember having to write a term paper for Honors History, and going to the San Antonio Library at night for research. I also remember having to memorize part of Chaucer's Canterbury Tales for Honors English at home. And, I also remember sitting down at the typewriter my mother bought me when in the 12th grade to study physics. I would get home from work at 10:00pm and type every lesson until midnight. I got a "C" the first semester, and a "B" the second semester.

At high school we didn't have Calculus like today's high schools, or Math Models for students that can't master the regular math curriculum. After Algebra II we had Geometry, Solid Geometry, and Trigonometry. The only school work that was saved from my high school studies was a project in Solid Geometry. My mother saved this work for me for many decades until she died in 1986. Then she passed it on to me. Also, in high school, we of course didn't have desk top computers or internet, or calculators like students today do beginning in first grade. For computations we either used long hand arithmetic, or slide rules for multiplication, division and logarithms.

University Studies

I learned a long time ago that the best investment we can make is in ourselves, and so I did. I graduated from high school in 1960. In the summer of 1960 I took a college algebra course at San Antonio Junior College. This course, although I only made a "C" in the course, gave me significant impetus in starting my college career.

Having applied and being accepted to attend New Mexico State University (NMSU), my mother sold a small insurance policy on my father for $300.00, and borrowed $500.00, packed my trunk, put me on a Greyhound Bus, and off I went to college to study Mechanical Engineering. I went to university because I wanted to learn and study to become an engineer, and not for any other reason. Like today, I was and am happy studying and learning.

New Mexico State University

Arriving at NMSU, I took and passed entrance examinations, and when registering I was asked how I was going to pay. I told them what money I had, and they said I would need more help. I was assigned to the oldest dorm on campus built in early 1900's for $90.00 a semester. I was signed up for ROTC, and that paid my tuition. I was given, a job in the cafeteria for my meals.

My first semester at New Mexico State was fairly routine, except for my first calculus course, Calculus I. I struggled with that first calculus course, but with help from my professor passed the course with a grade of "C", and got a 2.75 GPA for my first semester. This GPA qualified me to be accepted to the cooperative student program with the Physical Science Lab (PSL). So for my second semester at NMSU I now had a paying job with PSL, started training for their coop program to do satellite tracking research around the world for Johns Hopkins University, and no longer had to stink from washing dishes.

My second semester at NMSU, after starting my coop training, I was captivated by electronics, and I switched my major from Mechanical Engineering (ME) to Electrical Engineering (EE). Nevertheless, I had to study Mechanical Engineering, Civil Engineering (CE), Math (my best subject), Physics, Chemistry, English Composition, Electrical Machinery, Electronics, Communication theory, and Semiconductor theory (my best

EE course, although I only got a "C"), History, Psychology, Philosophy, and Art. I enjoyed all of my courses, but my first year was my best because my life was peaceful, and I was not yet corrupted.

I tried going to the Baptist Church, and the Baptist Student Union, but soon lost interest. I tried to talk to the director of the Baptist Student Union about love, i.e. brotherly love, parent child love, husband wife romantic love, and my loneliness, but the director wasn't interested, so I left, and never returned.

After that, I attended the Mormon Church for a while where they promised to teach me to understand the Christian Bible. Although I was ordained a priest in the Aaronic Priesthood, I soon left the Mormon Church in 1961 because they only taught me about the Book of Mormon, and everything they taught me was already in the Christian Bible. While attending the Mormon Church they sent me to visit a student on campus, Jerry. I found out Jerry was also an Electrical Engineering student. Jerry offered me a beer and popcorn, and we started studying together. I never returned to church. I did not attend church again until my first daughter Denise was born in 1968, when my first wife and I attended a Methodist Church in Dallas, Texas.

The biggest progress for me in my first year (Fall, Spring, and Summer) was taking Intro to Calculus (B), Calculus I (C), Calculus II (A), and Intro to Applied Math (Differential equations—B). In the Fall of 1961 I took my last undergraduate math course, Vector Algebra (B). What really made my engineering studies was the Applied Math course, which normally is a Junior, 3rd year, level course. The reason is that most all of my engineering courses involved differential equations, so all of my engineering courses seemed a breeze to me, although I didn't make A's. The Vector Algebra course seemed strange to me, but I nevertheless got a grade of "B". I was not to use vector algebra again until I started graduate school at the University of Texas at Arlington (UTA) in 1967, where I obtained my Master of Science Degree in Electrical Engineering. At UTA I used vector analysis and Matrix Theory in my first course, Advance Engineering Analysis, involving Euclidean Space. I never used vector analysis again.

I attended university classes year round, except when I took time off for the cooperative student program to operate satellite tracking stations at different locations around the world. In 1964 I quit the cooperative student program and started working at White Sands Missile Range in the evenings, first running computers doing data processing for missile testing, and then doing missile data reduction. But, I still continued to attend classes year round until I completed my degree course requirements in August of 1965. Then, I just left without attending any graduation. My diploma from NMSU was mailed to my mother in San Antonio, Texas.

I then graduated from NMSU with my BSEE degree in the summer of 1965 with 142 credit hours and a very modest 2.408 GPA. This very modest GPA limited my opportunities to start my professional career but did not hold me back, as it soon became apparent that I knew electronics and electronic systems well. It took me an extra year to graduate from NMSU because I had to take 2 semesters off for my cooperative program work.

Graduate Studies

University of Texas at Arlington

I started my graduate studies in Electrical Engineering at the University of Texas at Arlington in the Fall of 1967 with the encouragement of my first wife whom I married in February, 1967. But, I stopped my studies in 1969 because I was discouraged with difficulties in my marriage. After my divorce in 1971 I decided to return to my graduate studies at UTA in the Fall of 1972. I then finished my graduate studies at UTA in 1975 earning a Master of Science in Electrical Engineering (MSEE) with a GPA of 3.0. Again, I did not attend a graduation ceremony, I just left. My diploma was mailed to my mother in Mesquite, Texas.

I started my graduate studies at UTA on probation because of my low GPA for my BSEE degree. Then, I was very discouraged as I got a grade of "D" in my very first graduate course, Advance Engineering Analysis. I got a grade of "D" because I focused on the extensive proofs the professor from Cal-Tech presented, rather than the application. I took the course over again in the Spring of 1969 and got a grade of "B", and never made that mistake again.

I was then removed from Academic Probation in the Spring of 1968 after getting a grade of "B" in Introduction to Complex Variables. I really liked this course. This course was fun. Then, in the Fall of 1968, I was admitted to UTA as an undergraduate after getting a grade of "B" in both Advanced Calculus, and Logic Circuits I. I then remained in undergraduate status until I finished my degree requirements and was conferred the Master of Science degree in Electrical Engineering (MSEE). But, before I could graduate, I had to take the Graduate Record Examination (GRE) as a formality. I did not study for the GRE and did not do very well because I just took it as a formality. I do not like the GRE.

The courses I took at UTA for my MSEE degree really enlightened me intellectually and enabled my considerable intellectual growth. At UTA I studied electronic circuits, logic and computer circuits, system simulation with GPSS (a Xerox business modeling language), and Digital Signal Processing, in addition to the mathematics courses. My thesis, involving system simulation, for the MSEE degree at UTA was done over a 2 semester period. I was really interested in system modeling, and I modeled the manufacturing environment where I worked at the time, using GPSS. My GPSS modeling thesis made my MSEE degree a hybrid degree, but did not limit my career. After resigning from my job in 1975, I was able to obtain a job as a Senior Quality Control Engineer. I was fortunate in pursuing my MSEE because the companies I worked for paid for all of my tuition at UTA.

I did not return to graduate studies until 1980, when I resigned from my technical sales job. I was doing very well as a Technical Sales Representative, but was asked to resign after I bought tires for my company car without permission, even though I had plenty of budget, or so I thought.

University of Texas at Dallas

In the Fall of 1980 I enrolled at the University of Texas at Dallas (UTD) as a graduate Computer Science Student. I decided I no longer wanted to be in sales or Electrical Engineering. At UTD I completed 12 graduate hours of study in Computer Science in the Spring of 1981 with a GPA of 3.25. I did not work in the Fall of 1980, but attended UTD fulltime. I used money I had saved and an $8000.00 loan to pay for my tuition, books, and living expenses during my second marriage. The courses I studied at UTD were interesting and empowering. These courses were Introduction to System Programming, Discrete Mathematics (graphs and trees), and Computer Science I and II (PL1 and assembly language). In January of 1981, I was able to find and get a job as a Software Engineer, with the assistance of my instructor at UTD for System Programming. I did not know it at the time, but the field of Software Engineering was just beginning. At the time, the company I went to work for was hiring teachers and psychologists and training them to be Software Engineers. I stayed with this company until my layoff in 2002 as a Senior Software Engineer.

As a Software Engineer I had numerous assignments in various areas using assembly language, Pascal, and C-language. About 1993 I studied the Unix Operating System at work, and bought my first PC for $1500.00. The Packard Bell PC had only 2MB of RAM (memory), and only a 150MB hard drive, but that was enough. I partitioned the hard drive to run Microsoft Windows 3.1 on one partition, and Mark Williams Company Coherent X-Windows, a Unix-like MIT X-Window port, on the other partition. Then came the opportunity for me to take the lead to convert the software in our group from the older HP computers to SunOS, a Unix operating system. After I did the original basic transport, the whole Software Engineering group began to transport HP C-language software to SunOS.

But in 1994, I realized that I was getting outdated in my programming technology, so I returned to studying until 2000. At first I registered at the University of Texas at Arlington in the Spring of 1994, to study Software Engineering. But, I soon realized that this study was too theoretical, and was not going to help me, besides which I already knew the material. The benefit of beginning this study was that I learned which direction not to go to update my technical expertise, and I was not laid off due to a required reduction in workforce. Instead, another senior software engineer was laid off, keeping only young software engineers and myself, the oldest.

Richland Community College

In the Fall of 1994 I studied C++, an object oriented programming language, at Richland Community College in Dallas and at work. As a consequence of studying C++, an opportunity presented about itself about 1996 when a young software engineer was fired for inappropriate use of internet access, and I was plugged into a critical C++ programming task, and completed it. This job extended my usefulness as a Senior Software Engineer until I was laid off in 2002.

At Richland College I completed 61 credit hours studying C++, Personal Computer maintenance, and Network Engineering for Novell and Microsoft, earning 3 certifications in Network Engineering in 1998 and 1999.

University of Texas at Austin and Carnegie Mellon

Continuing my studies, in 1995 I entered a study program at the University of Texas at Austin, sponsored by my work, to earn a Master's Equivalent Certification in Systems and Software Engineering in 1997 in conjunction with the Systems and Software Engineering Institute at Carnegie Mellon and the Society for Design and Process Science, no longer in existence. These studies focused on Process Science, Requirements and Design, Quality Assurance, Object-Oriented Techniques, and Project Management from Carnegie Mellon.

For whatever reason, I got the idea to share these studies with several Vice Presidents at work. It seemed to me that these studies would be far more useful to them than to me except to acquire new technology. To my surprise I got telephone calls from two (2) Vice Presidents thanking me for "going beyond the call of duty". One Vice President of Engineering actually started attending our presentations, and wanted to see all of my studies, and then he got a big promotion. This pleased me a whole lot, even though I remained in the Intellectual Dungeon of Industry.

Texas Tech University

Then, in 1999 I entered a study program at Texas Tech University sponsored by my work to earn a Master of Engineering degree in 2000. These studies focused on Numerical Analysis, Engineering Science, Problem Solving, Robust Design and Optimization, a Project Management group project, plus my Master's Report (thesis) entitled "Application of Meta-Fusion House of Quality". The UT Austin studies were rolled into the Texas Tech graduate program to fulfill the degree requirements.

Between 1994 and 2000 I completed 97 college and university credit hours with a GPA of 3.618 while working full time. This GPA consisted of 61 credit hours at Richland college with a GPA of 3.689, and 36 graduate credit hours at Texas Tech University with a GPA of 3.5.

Overall, my lifetime undergraduate work consisted of 203 credit hours with a GPA of 2.79. My lifetime graduate work consisted of 82 credit hours with a GPA of 3.256. And so ends my college and university education. My lifetime GPA then, ends up being 2.926. This GPA is certainly not stellar, but my performance showed that I knew how to use my education. My high I.Q. did not begin to be reflected in my studies until my graduate courses, and then just barely, but my high E.Q. (Emotional Intelligence) is reflected throughout my education, and both my high I.Q, and my high E.Q. are reflected throughout my forty plus years work career.

Brookhaven Community College

And so ends the account of my formal education. However, in 2003, I attended a continuing education course at Brookhaven College in Farmers Branch, Texas, to study Pedagogy, the art and science of teaching, and secondary math teaching skills. I did this study to better equip myself to work as a substitute teacher.

And what for? Certainly not for any glory, recognition, or appreciation. All of this was just to survive the intellectual dungeons of industry, accomplish and to prove myself. However, it is true that my salary continued to increase, ever so modestly, and I was able to earn a nice retirement when I was laid off in 2002, and a nice Social Security benefit.

What is your lifetime education, or if you are just beginning, are you preparing for the next technology to impact your career, or the next phase of your career, or are you going to get left behind.

CHAPTER 2

Career

I am very appreciative and indebted for the career opportunities provided me by all of the corporations I worked for, in spite of the difficulties I encountered. Every corporation I worked for was an opportunity to grow and learn in a manner that would not have been otherwise. At each corporation I worked on or with electronic systems, equipment, computer systems, and high quality people, I would not otherwise have had the opportunity to work with and learn and grow.

I particularly appreciate the many people that gave me opportunity for my career, in spite of many difficulties, for many decades.

Nothing in this account of my professional career is intended to defame, dishonor or denigrate anyone. In all situations I just use job titles in my account of what happened in my life and career. However, what was said and done is exactly what I am truthfully writing about as it impacted my life, as I remember, without betraying any confidence. "The Moving Finger writes; and, having writ, Moves on; nor all your Piety nor Wit Shall lure it back to cancel half a Line, Nor all your Tears wash out a Word of it." Rubaiyat of Omar Khayamm.

My professional career began with interviews at Mexico State University in a ritual familiar to many universities across the country. I only interviewed 3 companies that I remember.

Electrical Engineer

However, I did get an offer of $150.00 per week from my first company with offices in downtown Dallas, Texas. I arrived a day later than instructed to report in a 1965 Ford with only $10.00 in my pocket, and a Gulf gas credit card. After I completed my course requirement at New Mexico State University my sisters and I took a two week vacation to Mexico City and Acapulco, and that made me one day late to report to my new job. I took a room at the Downtown Dallas YMCA. The $150.00 per week became even less because I started sending half of my weekly check to assist my sisters in college. But, I survived by living very modestly.

At this company I started working at a drafting table along with 3 other young engineers, and regular draftsmen. The other 3 engineers were from Texas A&M, SMU and University of Mississippi. We were assigned to make cabling and wiring drawings for shipboard communications. We didn't have personal computers, or laptops or Computer Aided Design (CAD) like today. All cabling and wiring drawings had to be done by hand.

Well, it didn't take long for me to prove myself. I was taking work home to study, and also advised system engineers on how to connect wiring to electronic equipment with transistor interfaces. Soon after that, I was sent to Mobile, Alabama, to check out a shipboard communication equipment installation.

It was at my next job in New Orleans that I got my first opportunity to work with electronics and tuning high powered transmitters and I loved it. I learned to work with electronics watching a technician servicing electronic circuits. One engineer said of me "we trust in God and Dion (my boyhood name)". This engineer was a ham radio operator, and ham radio operators were the communication and electrical engineers of that time. A technician, said of me "Dino thrives on problems". Once, when I was not at work, a technician came to adjust some circuits on some electronic equipment. And when I returned our technician would not tell me what was done. So I figured out what was done, and adjusted the circuits myself. That impressed our technician.

Flight Test Intrumentation Engineer

In November, 1967, I finished checking out the shipboard communications systems at Avondale Shipyard in New Orleans and returned to Dallas with my wife, whom I met in Mobile, Alabama, and her 3 children from a previous marriage. From there I was asked to go to work at NASA in Houston, Texas, but my wife did not want to go, and I wanted to start my graduate engineering studies. So, I found a position as a Flight Test Instrumentation Engineer making installation drawings for instrumentation to check jet aircraft test flight parameters.

Things were going well for me at until I got a call from a Lead Engineer who wanted me to go work for him to work on a proposal. So, I left my nice job as a Flight Test Instrumentation Engineer and went to work on the proposal which did not materialize, so I found myself without a job.

However, I met another engineer, also an electrical engineer, on the proposal effort. This engineer got laid off first and went to work for a start up plant to manufacture electronic telephone switching systems. Then this engineer called me to ask me to go to work for him. I went to interview, and was hired. Then, I was offered another job to stay where I was at, but I turned that offer down because I was excited about working with electronics.

Final Test Engineer

So, in February, 1970 I went to work as a Final Test Engineer writing test procedures from design specifications and designing test set modifications and assisting technicians with problems during final test. After I started work as a final test engineer, I got a call from the company I had been at and I was told that there had been a misunderstanding for me to get laid off, and would I go to work in Huntsville. I of course turned down the offer.

As a final test engineer, I was responsible for the final test of one quarter of a million dollars of equipment shipped every week. I did this work until May of 1975 when I was told that I was subject to lay off. No one had ever told me that I was not doing a good job. On the contrary, I only remember praise for my service to. Even so, as I walked out on the spot, a very foolish move, I was asked by a shop supervisor if I would help solve one more problem, so I returned, fixed the problem and left, never to return.

I was very upset by the possibility of being laid off because I had worked very hard without any assistance from anyone. Sometimes I had to work late, because of unexpected problems in final test, missing important family events, like my daughter Denise's 3rd birthday celebration. Another time, there were so many problems with the final test of a new product that I worked around the clock changing technicians every 8 hours for 36 continuous hours without rest. I was so exhausted when I finished that I fell asleep for 3 days. Then, I was not allowed to return to work without a physical examination. A shop supervisor, said of me "Dion can find problems in places you don't even know exist". A department chief, said of me "don't ever give Dion a project you don't want him to complete". Another department chiefs said of me that I was the most intense young man he knew. I was not intense, just focused.

Senior Quality Control Engineer

After quitting my job as a final test engineer, I went to work as a Senior Quality Control Engineer. After I started working as a Senior Quality Control Engineer, I got a call from another group, where I had been a Final Test Engineer, asking me to go to work for them at the same salary I had before. I actually took a pay cut from $18,000.00 per year to $16,000.00 per year to go to work as a Senior Quality Control Engineer. But, I turned them down also because I had lost confidence in the lost confidence in the corporate mentality of that company. I worked as a Senior Quality Control Engineer from June, 1975 until January, 1977. As a Senior Quality Control Engineer, the electronic test supervisor said of me "Dino shakes a problem until he solves it".

As a Senior Quality Control Engineer I worked on outdated electronic spares projects that were not passing test specifications because the original electronic component specifications were too general, and the spare electronic boards were not passing original specific tests. So, we had to learn to screen electronic components that would meet the original test specifications.

International Marketing

In January, 1977, I was offered a job in international marketing at $22,000.00 per year to market communication products in South America because I spoke Spanish, and because I knew communication products. I accepted. However, this job only lasted until November, 1977, and I was out of a job again.

One of the first things I did for international marketing was to assist at a South American Military Conference in Santiago, Chile. The conference lasted 3 days and each day I would present military communications equipment in Spanish to military personnel. Then came the reward. The reward for the Rockwell International Marketing personnel was a banquet feast with beautiful Chilean Folkloric dancing entertainment.

Another big event that I coordinated for in international marketing was a demonstration of communications equipment and give banquet in Quito, Ecuador, again for military personnel from South America. I was given $6000.00 to pay for the banquet, and returned about $2000.00. Then came the reward. The reward for the international marketing personnel was a banquet feast with beautiful Ecuadorean Folkloric dancing entertainment at an equally beautiful mountain retreat.

In this South American Marketing effort I dealt with Venezuela, Ecuador, Columbia, Bolivia, Peru, Argentina and Chile, and I presented many expensive quotes and studies to these countries prepared by engineers. In the process I got one contract with Ecuador for $1 Million dollars.

After my job in International Marketing ended, I tried to go back to Quality Control Engineering, but was told by the Quality Control Engineering Supervisor that they didn't need a super engineer, So I had to go looking for another job.

Technical Sales and Marketing

Then, I went looking for another sales position, and I found a job through an employment agency marketing telecommunications test equipment to telecom and utilities that used microwave radio communications. Then I was transferred to market cable communications equipment until August of 1980, when I was asked to resign.

The first year I traveled the southwest demonstrating telecom test equipment, and of course processing orders. But there was not enough business to justify me, so I was transferred to market cable communications equipment, again marketing in the southwest. By this time my salary was $29,000.00 per year plus commissions on about $1Million dollar sales a month. I was doing well, but then difficulties began. In August of 1980 I was called to meet with the National Sales Manager where he curtly and summarily simply asked me to resign without giving me any reason, and I was out of a job again.

I briefly considered looking for another job in sales and marketing, but after a few telephone calls, I decided I no longer wanted to deal with the sales mentality, and returned to university at the University of Texas at Dallas (UTD) full time in the Fall of 1980. At UTD I studied Computer science subjects and completed 12 graduate credit hours. In the meantime I went to a company named Haldane and paid $2000.00 to learn how to market myself to look for a job using my combined experience and education. I made contact with a vice president in January of 1981. This vice president gave me an opportunity to go interview. So I was interviewed by an engineer who had been one of my professors at UTD, passed my physical examination, and was hired as a software engineer.

Software Engineer

I started work as a software engineer January 21 of 1981 at about $22,000.00 per year, and I was laid off February 22 of 2002, earning about $75,000.00 per year.

From January, 1981 until June of 1981, I took my final graduate Computer Science course at UTD in PL/1 programming, and took various software engineering training courses.

As a software engineer, I performed many technical computer tasks, and worked with many different people, young and old. In the process I received two Senior Software Engineer promotions.

My first major task as a software engineer was to work with a team of software engineers to design and implement a microprocessor emulator in assembly language and test and evaluate microprocessor code, generate test procedures, prepare discrepancy reports, and design review presentations.

Then, I got an assignment to do database interface in Pascal.

Then, I was assigned to work on a Digital Signal Modeling Task using Fast Fourier Transforms (FFT), which I completed.

Then I was assigned to design antenna factory calibration software in Pseudo-Design-Language (PDL). For this task I design 16000 lines of PDL with B-spline data compression, Fourier analysis, auto-correlation, numerical analysis, histo-gramming, analog-to-digital, and digital-to-analog conversions. For this task I also invented and designed convergence formulas to normalize errors.

After that, I implemented the code for the antenna factory calibration and provided consultation to two (2) Senior Software Engineers for the implementation of the antenna calibration, and updated the PDL design.

Then, I was transferred to another group where I supervised two (2) young Associate Software Engineers doing programming in Pascal type graphics, and Fortran communication simulation and development. For this task I designed a three-piece-wise linear interpolation so that the simulation would match mainframe computations.

Next, and finally, I was assigned to the last and most difficult group I was to work in, a large group of system engineers, hardware (electronics) engineers, software engineers, electronic and systems technicians. Many times I survived by extreme effort and depth of perception because I knew nothing about the technology, and neither did anyone else because the original engineers were gone. Exhausted, I got no rest. As soon as I finished one project I got assigned to another high priority project that no one else could or wanted to do. If I couldn't do the project, so what; the project was already dead, and I was out of a job, and that actually did happen in 2002. Alone, isolated, abandoned and grieving, I hung it up when I was given one too many broken down systems. My mind just suddenly shut down, and I did a few more clean up jobs before I accepted a layoff package in February of 2002. However, my health has skyrocketed since then.

In this last group, I transitioned through 4 Software Engineering managers, witnessed many layoffs, firings, and complete changes in Software Engineers. And in this last group I transitioned through several technologies from tape driven operating systems and HP computers to MSDOS and laptop and desktop PC's; from HP computer operating systems to SunOS UNIX to Solaris2/Labwindows, and to WindRiver OS and Radstone single board computers. I also transitioned from structured programming in C-Language to Object Oriented Programming in C++ Programming Language.

My main task in this group was to design and/or modify software to test electronic hardware. In the meantime, on the side I taught technicians to program the old HP computers in C-language so they could maintain electronic hardware testing software I had developed over a period of years. And, they did well, and their careers were extended and made more valuable. And, I returned to college and university to study C++ programming and to obtain three (3) Network Engineering certifications, one Master's Certification in Software and Systems Engineering, and one Master of

Engineering degree, for a total of 97 college and university college credit hours with a GPA of 3.6.

Then about August of 2000 I was asked to prepare a bid to transport proprietary test software from an older HP computer to PC/National Instruments Test Stand/C-language, which I did. But, when I was asked to perform the work, I refused because the National Instruments Test Stand software system was really for technicians and not for software engineers. This was the beginning of the end for me because my type of work was disappearing. So, another engineer was brought in to do the actual transporting of this older software to the National Instruments Test Stand.

The last real software engineering job I performed was to assist a young female engineer that had been assigned to check out an older computer controlled electronics box. But I could not salvage the job. Then, I was set up in a back room with an old computer and with no technician. I hooked up the computer system by myself and got computer communication addresses from a young experienced engineer. However, the test computer could not communicate with the outdated onboard computer, and I just reported to my SW Manager that this job exceeded my level of expertise. I could have figured out the computer communication problem, but for whatever reason my mind just suddenly shut down, and I was out of a job again.

Two more efforts are worth mentioning that I performed before I was laid off in Feb of 2002. The first effort was to inventory about 1 Million lines of software done over the last 15 years where all of the system, hardware and software engineers were gone. The new software engineering group would not have known about what had been done on various projects and applications on various development platforms.

I then developed a Microsoft Access database for my Software Engineering Manager, to maintain personnel information, and then I was gone.

And so ends my software engineering career, and my thirty seven (37) year engineering career, helping younger engineers, and older outdated engineers. But I fared better than many others (some taking early medical retirement) and I witnessed many engineers hired and fired. I have worked on ancient Tape Operating Systems and state-of-the art computer systems. I have programmed in Fortran, assembly language, Pascal language, C-language, C++ Object Oriented programming, and Rocky Mountain Basic, always serving honestly.

Computers

In my engineering career I have programmed many computers. I began in 1964 on an IBM 1401 with card punch programming in Fortran II at New Mexico State University to solve power system problems. I also programmed the IBM360 with card punch programming, and the IBM 3033. In 1981 the IBM 3033 was the first computer I worked on from a remote terminal, keyboard and command line. From 1984 to about 1995 I worked on my HP computers. In 1987 I was introduced to my first McIntosh Desktop Publishing computer with windows. I thought to myself "This is no computer. It has no command line", and I was very leery of it, but eventually I started using the MacIntosh. I have in fact worked on many more computers than I have mentioned, but this is sufficient for purposes of this book. However, I will just simply list here the computer expertises I mastered in my career.

Computer Languages experience/training:
Orbix/CORBA, Tcl/Tk, Java, C/C++, Motif, Unix-Internals, Fortran, Pascal, ADA, PL/1, GPSS, Basic, IBM ALC, IBM JCL, PDL, Microtec Metta Assembler

Computer Operating Systems:
WindRiver, WindowsNT, Novell, Windows2000/98/95/XP, SunSparC/Solaris 1.1F, SunOS5.1, Unix, HP/RTE-A, HP/RTE-6, VAX8200/VMS, MS-DOS, HP-UX, Grid-OS, Cyber/NOS2, IBM 3033-OS/MVS, VAX11/VMS

Computer Experience:
Radstone SBC, SunSparC-20, SunSparC-10, Force-5V, Force-2CE, HP1000 (A900, A600, A400, & M-series), IBM-PC, VAX/8200, HP9000, IBM 3033, VAX/780, Cyber180, GridCase, Grid Compass

Computer ApplicationsExperience:
Macintosh Desktop Publishing, MS Word2000, MS Access2000, MS Project2000, MS Excel2000, Internet, RAZOR software configuration management

Integrated Development Environments:
Semantic Cafe, Microsoft Visual C++, Turbo-C++, Turbo-C, Rational Rose/RequisitePro/ClearCase/ClearQuest, National Instruments LabWindows

Instrumentation: National Instruments GPIB, National Instruments DIO96(parallel interface)

Email and Internet

In 1994 I learned about email. I was clueless when I went to register at the University of Texas at Arlington and the secretary asked me if I had email—oops. So, I went to Richland Community College in Dallas to study Network Engineering, where in my first course I had to look very dumb and ask what WWW meant. I didn't understand what World Wide Webb meant. In 1996 I got my first PC at work connected to the internet. I had to ask the young female engineer in the cubicle next to me "how do I check my internet?". She told me to put **cnn.com** in the URL space, and I was on my way.

Home Computing

In 1984 I bought my first home computer, a Radio Shack Color Computer with a 5 ¼ inch floppy disk drive. All of my children learned to use the word processor on this 8-bit computer with a daisy wheel printer. My oldest daughter Denise produced very nice typed papers for her course of study at Richland College. We used this 8-bit computer until I bought my first Packard Bell PC in about 1990 with 2 Megabytes of memory, and 150 Megabytes of disk space, using Windows 3.1, and we could still use the daisy wheel printer.

Then I had to upgrade to Windows95 and a newer computer, but I couldn't understand why my daisy wheel printer would not work. I found out that I had to use a graphics inkjet type printer. Then when I had to add disk space I found out that that I had to upgrade to Windows98. Then I found out about viruses and spyware and I had to add spyware protection.

Then I bought a second used desktop PC and had to go to Windows 2000 when my computers crashed because of viruses. That is when I started using Norton Antivirus. Fortunately I was able to backup all of my data, and

I never lost any data. Now I am using a desktop PC with WindowsXP with 256 Megabytes of memory and a 40Gigabyte Hard Drive. However, I was beginning to use too much disk space for digital photography so I added a 250 gigabyte external hard drive. Today I am writing this manuscript on a Compaq laptop that I bought in 2001 for my daughter Elizabeth while she was in high school so she could study C++. This laptop has WindowsXP with 2 Gigabytes of memory, and a 40 Gigabyte Hard Drive, and a 1.79 GHZ clock. Elizabeth now has a newer Dell Computer.

And so ends the chapter on my rocky engineering career. What does your career look like, or what will your career look like if you are just starting.

CHAPTER 3

Health

As I see it, there are four (4) aspects of health: **mental**, **intellectual**, **physical**, and **spiritual**. That is what I will write about in this chapter.

However, what I write about here is about my experiences over a lifetime, and what I do, and what I believe in to protect my health. I take a strict regimen of vitamin, mineral and natural herb supplements. What is good for me may be good for you, but you should check with your personal physician, or homeopathic doctor before you take any vitamin, mineral or natural herb supplements.

Those of us that are born without birth defects are fortunate, but many take their health for granted until it is too late. My sisters and I were fortunate growing up in the 1940's and 1950's in that most of the time we walked everywhere, for example to school, and to church. In addition, our mother was very careful to give us non-fat well rounded meals. Unfortunately, today many of us depend on fast foods, with limited nutritional value, making it important for us to take vitamin and mineral supplements.

Mental Health:

Mental health has two (2) aspects: (1) does you brain function right?, psychiatry, and (2) thought processes and emotional balance, psychology. In his book, Change Your Brain, Change Your Life, Dr. Daniel Amen, neuroscientist, psychiatrist, and medical director of the Amen Clinic for Behavioral Medicine, writes "Do we make better decisions when our brains work right? Of course we do . . .". In this book, Dr Amen also states "our personality is intimately connected to brain function, but . . . brain function is also intimately connected to our thoughts and environment". [pp 299].

In his book, "Magnificent Mind at Any Age", Dr. Daniel Amen writes "The brain is the most complicated organ in the universe. It is estimated that the brain has one hundred billion nerve cells and more connections in it than there are stars in the universe." Dr. Amen continues "If you take a piece of brain tissue the size of a grain of sand, it contains a hundred thousand neurons and a billion connections all communicating with one another." But, Dr. Amen cautions, "If you are not thoughtful (learning), the brain loses an average of eighty-five thousand brain cells a day . . .". [pp 13]

In the introduction to his paperback edition, Change Your Brain, Change Your Life, Dr. Amen identifies brain disorders that impair our mental health: depression, anxiety problems, aggression, attention deficit disorder (ADD), bipolar disorder, and post-traumatic stress disorder. Dr. Amen also states that "Researchers consistently find that drug and alcohol can cause serious brain damage." [pp 224]

Using a nuclear medicine study called SPECT (single photon emission computed tomography), Dr Amen measures cerebral blood flow, and metabolic activity to show the physical evidence of brain function or dysfunction, as opposed to a purely psychological problem in thinking [pp 4]. If people do not have access to Dr. Amen's clinic for a SPECT analysis, Dr. Amen provides written tests that can be used to self diagnose brain function problems.

Dr. Amen further writes that "You cannot be who you really want to be unless your brain works right". Dr. amen continues that "Your brain patterns help you (or hurt you) with your marriage, parenting, work, and religious beliefs, along with your experiences of pleasure and pain" [pp 3]. Dr. Amen also writes that research can be used to show "the effects of drug abuse, head injuries, and negative thinking on the brain" [pp 4].

The amazing thing about Dr. Amen's practice is that through SPECT the part of the brain that isn't working can be identified, and treatment can be targeted to that area [pp 6].

So, not withstanding brain dysfunction, there are some simple things we can do to maintain brain health. I take a health supplement called "Brain Pep", a proprietary blend of Kola Nut, Ginkgo Biloba, Gotu Kola, Eleuthero root, Schizandra, Ginger root; and L-Glutamin. I used to take a product named "Ginkgo 1000" manufactured by Natrol, Inc, Chatsworth, California, but when that product was discontinued, I started taking "Brain Pep". So what is all of this stuff in "Brain Pep"?

Kola Nut: Kola nut, which contains high amounts of caffeine, helps combat fatigue and is most commonly used as a central nervous system stimulant that focuses on the cerebrospinal centers. It also contains theobromine, a stimulant found in chocolate as well as in green tea. Kola nut also contains tannins, phenolics, phlobaphens, kola red, betaine, protein, starch, fat, thiamine, riboflavin, and niacin. The Journal of the American Medical Association advocates the use of kola over other stimulants, because it is not addictive and does not lead to depression. Because kola nut is also a diuretic, its use has been suggested for those with renal diseases, cardiac or renal edema and rheumatic and rheumatoid conditions. Most people around the world are familiar with kola; many have tasted it and do not even know it. In the 1800s, a pharmacist in Georgia took extracts of kola, sugar and coca and mixed them with carbonated water. His accountant tasted it and called it "Coca Cola." Today, Coca-Cola still uses kola in its original recipe. [Katherine Kim, Rebecca J. Frey PhD, The Gale Group Inc]

Ginkgo Biloba: Today, people use ginkgo leaf extracts hoping to *improve memory*; to treat or help prevent Alzheimer's disease and other types of dementia; to decrease intermittent claudication (leg pain caused by narrowing arteries); and to treat sexual dysfunction, multiple sclerosis, tinnitus, and other health conditions. [National Center for Complementary & Alternative Medicine]

Gotu Kola: Gotu kola (Centella asiatica) has been used as a medicinal herb for thousands of years in India, China, and Indonesia. It was used to heal wounds, improve mental clarity **(blood circulation in the brain)**, and treat skin conditions such as leprosy and psoriasis. Historically, gotu kola has also been used to treat syphilis, hepatitis, stomach ulcers, mental fatigue, epilepsy, diarrhea, fever, and asthma. Today, American and European herbalists use gotu kola most often to treat chronic venous insufficiency (a condition where blood pools in the legs). It's also used in ointments to treat psoriasis and help heal minor wounds. [University of Maryland Medical Center]

Eleuthero root: [from EVtiamins.com] Eleuthero is an "adaptogen" (an agent that helps the body adapt to stress). It is thought to help support adrenal gland function when the body is challenged by stress. [Wagner H, Nörr H, Winterhoff H. Plant adaptogens. Phytomed 1994;1:63-76 [review]]

Also Eleuthero has been shown to enhance mental acuity and physical endurance without the letdown that comes with caffeinated products.[Economic and Medicinal Plant Research, vol 1, ed. Wagner H, Hikino HZ, Farnsworth NR. London: Academic Press, 1985, 155-215 [review].]

And, research has shown that eleuthero improves the use of oxygen by the exercising muscle. [Asano K, Takahashi T, Miyashita M, et al. Effect of Eleutherococcus senticosus extract on human working capacity. Planta Medica 1986;37:175-7.] This means that a person is able to maintain aerobic exercise longer and recover from workouts more quickly.

Schizandra: Schizandra is thought to be a mild sedative and sexual enhancer. Some believe that it preserves beauty and is a youth tonic for men and women. Other health Benefits of schizandra are: speeds recovery, increases stamina, strengthens immune system, increases eye acuity, improves adrenal health, protects against motion sickness, increases lung health, and protects the liver (aids in the regeneration of liver cells, especially after the mass consumption of alcohol which destroys liver cells), helps balance body functions. [hubpages.com]

Ginger root [from herbal-supplements-guide.com]: Some of the Health Benefits of Ginger Root are:

1. Aids in Digestion—Perhaps the best herb for digestion, ginger root prevents indigestion and abdominal cramping. Ginger also helps break down proteins, aiding the digestion process.

2. Alleviates High Blood Pressure—Ginger improves and stimulates circulation and relaxes the muscles surrounding blood vessels, facilitating the flow of blood throughout the body.

3. Treats Nausea and Morning Sickness—Ginger has been widely shown to prevent as well as treat motion sickness. Ginger root relaxes the stomach and relieves the feeling of nausea.

4. Lowers LDL Cholesterol—Ginger root extract can help reduce the levels of LDL (bad) cholesterol in the body, reducing the risk of developing heart disease.

L-Glutamin: L-Glutamine is the most prevalent amino acid in the body. The most important function of L-Glutamine is the support of cellular growth, energy, and repair. Deficiencies of L-Glutamine may be linked to gastrointestinal disorders such as Crohn's disease and colon inflammation. L-Glutamine may also reduce tumor growth. In addition, amino acids promote the production of various neurotransmitters and enzymes critically needed in *brain metabolism*. Amino acids allow smooth, balanced cognition and fluid transition from thought to disciplined action. Amino acids also aid in the reduction of stress, frustration and cognitive overload. [Nutrition Health Center; Chesterton, Indiana]

Sugar (wikipedia.org) :

Glucose is a primary source of energy for the brain, and hence its availability influences psychological processes. When glucose is low, psychological processes requiring mental effort (e.g., self-control, effortful decision-making) are impaired.

[Fairclough, Stephen H.; Houston, Kim (2004), "A metabolic measure of mental effort", Biol. Psychol. 66;.

Gailliot, Matthew T.; Baumeister, Roy F.; DeWall, C. Nathan; Plant, E. Ashby; Brewer, Lauren E.; Schmeichel, Brandon J.; Tice, Dianne M.; Maner,

Jon K. (2007), "Self-Control Relies on Glucose as a Limited Energy Source: Willpower is More than a Metaphor", J. Personal. Soc. Psychol. 92;

Gailliot, Matthew T.; Baumeister, Roy F. (2007), "The Physiology of Willpower: Linking Blood Glucose to Self-Control", Personal. Soc. Psychol. Rev. 11 ;

Masicampo, E. J.; Baumeister, Roy F. (2008), "Toward a Physiology of Dual-Process Reasoning and Judgment: Lemonade, Willpower, and Expensive Rule-Based Analysis", Psychol. Sci. 19]

Intellectual Health:

I have a saying, actually I have many sayings, but I have one in particular about the brain, and that is "I'm stupid, but my brain is smart". Now why would I say such a stupid thing? Well, because most of us, including me, dwell in a sensory world with our conscious mind. We have been told that we only use about ten percent (10%) of our brain. Well, that only applies to the conscious mind. Our subconscious mind is working around the clock, even when we are sleeping, figuring out things from whatever experiences we have had each day, having dreams and nightmares.

It has happened to me, and I have heard of the same thing happening to others, and that is that sometimes we figure out solutions to problems in our sleep that we could not figure out during the stress of the day. And sometimes we have nightmares about our memories, and sometimes we have pleasant dreams.

The fact of the matter is that in our subconscious brains resides the memory of everything we have ever thought, saw, heard, or experienced since before birth. So now here is the kicker. What are we, you, me, putting into our brains? We have heard the saying "garbage in, garbage out". Well, that applies to our brains too. Although we are born with survival, mating, parenting, nesting and hunting and foraging instincts, instinctive emotions, we are not born with specific knowledge which is gained by learning. So, whatever we are learning is what our brains have to work with to help us survive, and navigate life and society. No, I am not a psychologist. I have learned these things by observation and experience.

So now, what in the world is intellectual health, and why should we care about it? Well, basically, intellectual health can be the pursuit of academic knowledge and understanding not only about ourselves, but also our environment, and our universe.

Or, intellectual health can be self taught general knowledge, creativity, and common sense. For example, can you figure things out when things go wrong. Intellectual health is important because it can lead to quality of life, or lack thereof.

Intellectual health is not just about IQ (Intelligence Quotient). Intellectual health also involves Emotional Intelligence, Daniel Goleman, 1995, and involves delayed gratification, perseverance, and controlling our emotions and natural instincts. While IQ is basically fixed for life, emotional intelligence has to be developed, and is more important for success than IQ because of self determination and tenacity.

Intellectual health involves making good choices such as good friends, good diet, good habits, exercise, mental and physical respite, avoiding illegal drugs, judicious use of alcoholic beverages, and pursuing a good education, such as high school, trade school, and/or college or university studies.

For example, do you associate with good people, or bad people, that is people that do not respect life, property or the laws of our nation? Do you associate with people that you can respect, admire and learn from, or do you associate with people that use and abuse you to satisfy their only selfish needs?

Intellectual health also involves pursuing, acquiring, believing in and practicing good morals. What are good morals? Well good morals can be as simple as being good and doing good. Good morals can be as simple as respecting, cooperating with, caring about, and appreciating our neighbors, our fellow employees, and/or customers, and being fair in our business dealings. Remember the legendary saying—"what goes around comes around".

Intellectual health also involves making good financial decisions, such as living within our means, budgeting and saving.

Now, back to the knowledge base stored in our subconscious brains. How do we get to it? How do we access and benefit from all of the knowledge and data stored in our brains? Well, actually, most of the time we don't have to worry about that because of something we call memory. Memory works for our conscious minds warning us and guiding us in our every day decision making. In this memory is our knowledge; our likes and dislikes; beliefs, and our emotions. Not only this, without our emotions, we can't make good decisions (Dr. Daniel Goleman, Emotional Intelligence).

However, sometimes we have to make really tough decisions, like taking tests, or what course to pursue in life, or who to marry and why. What do we do then? Well, then we do something called thinking, and sometimes we have to think really hard. As Joseph Smith supposedly told Brigham Young in a dream—"listen to the small voice within you".

To solve really hard problems, and to make really hard decisions in life, sometimes we have to shut out the sensory world we live in with all of the desires for sensory pleasure, and retreat into our inner minds by not only thinking but by a process called meditation, and "listen to the small voice within us". Then, we will have the answers we seek.

And finally, intellectual health involves constant learning. If you are not learning, your brain is dying (Dr. Daniel Amen).

Physical Health:

As a boy I rode a bicycle and delivered news papers. My younger sister, Ada, ran track in Junior High School. Ada continued running most of her life until she became ill in her early 60's. Even so, today Ada enjoys very good health, inspite of her illness, because of her lifetime of running. Today many schools require physical education which offers an opportunity for good physical exercise, beginning in elementary school. Of course, many students today are involved in sports, which is an excellent investment in their health. If you don't protect your health when you are young, you may have serious health problems when you get older, 40+ years.

Today, at 69 years of age, I am running/walking 20 to 30 minutes a day and working out on my weights another 20 to 30 minutes a day. These workouts can take care of many ills. In my 20's, weighing about 140# to 150#, I ran a 5 to 6 minute mile. In my 30's, 40's and 50's, weighing about 175#, I was running a 10 minute mile. Now in my 60's, weighing about 210#, I run a 14-16 minute mile. This past summer I developed hip joint pain and could not complete a mile run because I had to limp back home. Then I added Magnesium, Calcium and Vitamin D which are recommended for joint pain, to my GNC multivitamin. After several weeks of my upgraded vitamin and mineral supplement I was able to complete my morning run again without hip or knee pain. Also, I was able to work on my weights without any pain in my shoulder.

Today, my 30 minute morning weight exercise after my morning run includes:

1. leg curls—30 lbs X 30
2. reverse leg curls (hamstring)—30 lbs 12
3. bench press—60 lbs X 30
4. lats (back muscles)—30 lbs X 30
5. pectorials (chest muscles)—30 lbs X 30
6. bicep curls (2 hand)—30 lbs X 30
7. French curls (tricep, 2 hand)—30 lbs X 30
8. military press—60 lbs X 12

At bedtime I do one hand 30 lb curls X6, and French curls X12.

In my late teens when I first went to college, I started building up by using a chest spring pull with up to 5 springs. I am still benefiting from this. This type of equipment is no longer available, that I can see. When I was in my 30's, I used to lift 30,000 and 40,000 lbs in one three to four hour afternoon with a clean and press using a 135 lb bar. I was also doing 150 lb squats on my squat stand. I am still benefiting from all of this.

Physical health of course requires good cardiovascular and muscular exercise and good balanced nutrition. You don't have to be an Olympic athlete to have good health. Doctors tell us that the difference between good health and bad health is just 15 minutes exercise per day. Doctors tell us that to have good health you should elevate your heart rate at least 10 or 15 points for 5 or 10 minutes a day, health limitations not withstanding.

Good exercise habits can be such simple things as in place running or jumping jacks, or both; walking or jogging, or both; swimming. Swimming is the best cardiovascular and muscular exercise because it puts less stress on your body, and yet gives you the cardiovascular and muscular exercise you need.

Sugar (glucose) (wikipedia.org) :

From wikipedia.org we read that glucose is directly utilized as an energy source by brain cells, intestinal cells and red blood cells, while the rest reaches the liver, adipose tissue and muscle cells, where it is absorbed and stored as glycogen (under the influence of insulin).

From wikipedia.org we also read that glycogen is the body's 'glucose energy storage' mechanism because it is much more 'space efficient' and less reactive than glucose itself.

So it appears to me that the human body needs glucose for energy. However, it also appears to me that if glucose energy is not burned due to lack of exercise, then the glucose level in the blood gets too high.

Aspirin and Garlic:

I take a 375mg aspirin and a 500mg garlic tab daily, Monday through Friday. Why? An aspirin a day is excellent for cardiovascular health because it is an anticoagulant, although most doctors recommend a baby aspirin or less per day because there can be hazards in taking an aspirin a day. In addition, I use garlic salt for all of my food seasoning, instead of regular table salt.

Mayoclinic.com tells us that clotting can happen within the blood vessels that supply your heart and brain with blood. If your blood vessels are already narrowed from atherosclerosis — the buildup of fatty deposits in your arteries — a fatty deposit in your vessel can burst. Then, a blood clot can quickly form and block the artery. This prevents blood flow to the heart or brain and causes a heart attack or stroke. Aspirin therapy reduces the clumping action of platelets — possibly preventing heart attack and stroke.

Homeremedies.com tells us that garlic (Allium Sativum) is a plant with a very strong and bitter flavor which has been used for both culinary and medical purposes for hundreds of years. The key medicinal ingredient in garlic is allicin, which is known to have wonderful anti-bacterial, anti-viral, anti-fungal and anti-oxidant properties. I have also read that you can rub raw garlic on facial warts and that will make them go away. I can't say because I don't have facial warts.

Homeremedies.com further tells us that garlic can be used to treat high cholesterol, parasites, respiratory problems, poor digestion, and low energy. Studies suggest that regularly eating garlic helps lower blood pressure, controls blood sugar and blood cholesterol, and boosts the immune system. Garlic has also been found to reduce the risk of esophageal, stomach, and colon cancer.

Fountains of Youth:

There are two (2) fountains of youth. One is a **colon cleanser**, and the other is **pH balance**.

Colon Cleanser:

Very simply, if your colon is not clean, as in clogged up, you cannot process food, vitamins and minerals, and your body slowly dies. Colon cleanser can be such a simple thing as an apple a day; eating roughage like lettuce daily; eating bran or fiber cereals. Or, you can do what I do, and that is to take a colon cleanser, like Nature's Bounty Colon Cleanser that captures all of the advantages of bulk-producing fiber. Nature's Bounty Colon Cleanser contains Psyllium seed husk, Citrus Pectin, Goldenseal root, Cascara Sagrada bark, wheat grass juice, Aloe Vera leaf, Buckthorn bark, Gentian root, and Lactobacillus Acidophilus. I take two (2) capsules daily, Monday through Friday.

pH Balance and Health

Today, we are not as fortunate as in the past to receive good nutritional value from our food. LE Magazine March, 2001, reports that since the early 1960's the levels of vitamins and minerals in our produce and meats has dropped significantly. So this means that it is important to take vitamin and mineral supplements. In addition, Wikipedia reports that our bodies, also need microminerals, also known as trace minerals, for good overall health. F.H.Nielsen, United States Department of Agriculture, The FASEB Journal, Vol. 5, Pages 2661-2667, September 1991, reports that trace minerals are usually found at very small levels in our bodies, in the parts per million range, but that they play a vital role in our health. Dr. Michael Cutler, truehealth.com, tells us that trace minerals are important in balancing the pH, potential of Hydrogen, in our bodies and is essential for our health. Dr. Cutler also tells us that a healthy person with perfectly balanced pH has a reading of about 7.4 in their blood, slightly alkaline. The pH in our bodies can be balanced with mineral supplements such as are in most multivitamins.

Dr. Cutler further tells us that if our pH balance is too acidic, our body works hard to neutralize acid, and bring us into balance. To do that, Dr. Cutler tells us, your body needs certain trace minerals that are known to neutralize acid. According to Dr. Cutler, many of us get far too few of these essential minerals—and so your body has no choice but to "borrow" them from organs and tissues where they're needed. Essential minerals are stolen away from our heart, our brain, our bones and joints, our muscles and skin, and our lungs, liver and every other organ in your body. And as our organs begin starving for the minerals they need to function properly, they begin to weaken, function less effectively, and fail.

Dr. Cutler further tells us that each of the 100 trillion cells in your body absorb nutrients and excrete acid waste. Quoting Dr. Stefan Kuprowsky, Boucher Institute of Naturopathic Medicine, New Westminster, Canada, "Acid wastes build up in the body in the form of cholesterol, gallstones, kidney stones, arterial plaque, urates, phosphates and sulfates. These acidic waste products are the direct cause of premature aging and the onset of chronic disease."

Quoting Dr. Charles Northen, stomach disorders & nutritional disorders, "In the absence of minerals, vitamins have no function. Lacking vitamins, the system can make use of the minerals, but lacking minerals vitamins are useless."

Vitamins, Minerals and Natural Herbs:

I have been on a strict vitamin, mineral and natural herb regimen for many years, and believe that I owe my general good health to this regimen as evidenced by my latest Annual Physical Exam Lab Report on 7 June, 2010. Today, because of my vitamin, mineral and natural herb regimen I have no typical health issues such as blood sugar, high blood pressure, high cholesterol, high PSA, and high triglycerides. All of these medical issues I have been able to keep under control, with vitamins, minerals and natural herbs, and exercise. To wit, my PSA (prostate specific antigen) has decreased from 4.7 to 4.1 in the last year.

However, *there is a hazard* when you take as many health supplements as I take. For several years, my annual physical lab tests showed an elevated liver-ALT metric. An elevated ALT indicates liver damage. Then it occurred to me that I might be taking too many supplements at one time. So, I started taking my supplements over a period of several hours. This worked. In subsequent annual physical lab tests, my ALT metric has been in range. No, my doctor never said a word about my elevated ALT.

Following is a comparative analysis of my latest Annual Physical Exam Lab Report, 18 June, 2010:

	Metric	compare—7/20/2009	Range	
1.	Glucose = 101	(up from 98)	70-105	(increase magnesium & exercise)
2.	Triglycerides = 131	(up from 124)	<150	(increase Omega-3)
3.	CHOL = 179	(dwn fm 183)	<200	**(IMPROVED)**

4.	HDL = 36	(up from 35)	> 39	(need to exercise)
5.	CHOL/HDL = 4.97	(dwn fm 5.23)	<5.0	(IMPROVED)
6.	LDL (calculated) = 117	(dwn from 123)	<100	(IMPROVED)
7.	MCH = 33	(dwn fm 34)	27-33	(IMPROVED)
8.	MPV = 7.6	(up from 7.2)	7.54-11.24	(barely in range)
9.	C-Reactive Protein=3.23	(none)	0.0-3.00	(NEW—HIGH RISK Heart attack)

(Note: probably result of past damage due to much chest pain over many years—NOT CONCERNED)

10.	PSA = 4.1	(dwn fm 4.7)	<3.0	(ALERT!!!—chg fm <4.0)

(Note: I am not concerned. **This new metric Range is absurd**)

11.	FERRITIN = 68	(none)	18-464	(NEW—in range—OK)
12.	ESR = 6	(none)	0-20	(NEW—in range—OK)
13.	TSH W/REFLEX to FT4 = 3.04 (none)		.465-4.68	NEW—in range—OK)
14.	VIT B12 = 718	(none)	239-931	(NEW—in range—OK)
15.	VIT D, 25-Hydroxy = 12 (none)		30-100	(NEW—WARNING—Very Low)

(Note—increase Vit D supplement—200iu/day to 800 iu in new GNC Multivitamin); Also started Bone & Joint Supplements—coral calcium 350mg; Magnesium 400mg; Already in multivitamin for Bone & Joint Supplements—Calcium 100mg; Magnesium 50mg; Zinc 12.5mg)

Then, after my 17 Jan,2011 follow up blood lab tests, I found that my adjustments in vitamins, minerals, Omega3 and exercise resulted in very significant improvements.

1. Glucose	88	(dwn fm 101)	(Much improved)
2. Calcium	9.3	(up fm 8.8)	(improved)
3. Bilirubin	.9	(up fm .7)	(improved)
4. Alkaline Phosphatase,S	74	(up fm 67)	(improved)
5. AST (SGOT)	32	(dwn fm 39)	(improved)
6. ALT (SGOT)	49	(dwn fm 56)	(improved)
7. Cholesterol, total	165	(dwn fm 179)	(Much improved)
8. Triglycerides	87	(dwn fm 131)	(extreme improved)
9. HDL Cholesterol	48	(up fm 36)	(extreme improved)
10. LDL Cholesterol	100	(dwn fm 117)	(Much improved)
11. Vitamin D, 25 Hydroxy	17.7	(up fm 12)	(improved—add 400 i.u. Vit D)

(Note: Jan, 2011—Doctor prescribed increase to 1200 i.u./day)

Vitamin, mineral and natural herb supplements (taken daily):
Men's Premium Multivitamin w/mineral & Herbs—GNC formula
Garlic—500mg
Aspirin—325mg

Omega 3 & 6 (EPA—Eicosapentaenoic Acid; DHA—Decosahexaenoic Acid) 1000mg

Calcium 450mg ; Magnesium 400mg; Vitamin D 1200i.u.

Colon Cleanser: psyllium seed husk, citrus pectin, Goldenseal, cascara sagrada, wheat grass,

Aloe Vera, buckthorn, Gentian root, Lactobacillus Acidophilus

Omega 3 & 6 (EPA—Eicosapentaenoic Acid; DHA—Decosahexaenoic Acid) 1000mg

Echinacea & Goldenseal (Echinacea, Goldenseal, Burdock root, Gentian root, Cayene pepper,

Wood Betony) 450mg

Brain Pep—proprietary blend = 874mg (Kola Nut, Ginko Biloba, Gotu Kola, Eleuthero root,

Schizandra, Ginger root; L-Glutamin—260mg)

CoQ10-50mg plus Vitamin E 5IU pHion Balance—Neutralizes Excess Body Acid with Mineral buffers to rid body waste; plus Cellular hydration (I currently indicate saliva pH of 7.25 with litmus strip; urine pH is usually 1.0 lower)

Coenzyme Q10 (CoQ10):

According to DrWeil.com, CoQ10 is a potent antioxidant that has been linked to normal cardiac functioning and many cardiologists recommend supplemental CoQ10 to those taking statin drugs (which can effectively lower cholesterol, but reduce the production of CoQ10). It also has shown potential benefits for anyone with risk factors for heart disease.

Echinacea & Goldenseal:

According to Nature's Bounty, Inc, Echinacea & Goldenseal work together to support the immune system. I have heard of studies that conclude that Echinacea does not cure colds. That conclusion may very well be true, but Echinacea is not advertised to cure colds. Echinacea is just advertised to support the immune system, so the immune system can do what it is supposed to do.

From Bing.com/health we read that the immune system is the body's defense against infectious organisms and other invaders, and is made up of a network of white blood cells, tissues, and organs that work together to protect the body. The immune system attacks organisms and substances that invade body systems and cause disease.

Omega-3 & 6:

According to Nature's Bounty, Inc, O mega-3&6 fatty acids help support and maintain the cardiovascular system. Omega-3&6 are considered good fats important for cellular, heart, and metabolic health, and help maintain triglycerides within a normal range (note: it worked for me when my triglycerides were elevated)

Prostate Health:

Up to 1995, when I was 53 years old, I had never had a physical exam, except for employment. But, because of my age I decided to start annual physical exams. Then I got a prostate infection and was put on medication but my PSA (prostate specific antigen) became elevated from 4.0 to 24. I was referred to a urologist who in May of 1996 performed a "cytoscopy and prostate massage". The result was that my PSA went from 25 to 5.9. Let me tell you that when the anesthesia wore off I was in a lot of pain.

Subsequent to that I started taking saw palmetto, and then upgraded to saw palmetto complex, which includes zinc. I took this saw palmetto complex for several years and did very well to control my PSA, which is now 4.1. I stopped taking saw palmetto complex when I started taking GNC Men's Multivitamin, the best available, because it has saw palmetto, as well as Zinc and many other vitamins and minerals, and my PSA remains under control.

Onion Health Benefits [hubpages.com]:

Onion is Beneficial in the following conditions: Asthma, Influenza, Colds, Tuberculosis, Insomnia, Pneumonia, Antiallergy, Obesity, Reduce inflammation, Slightly laxative, High Blood Pressure, Lowers cholesterol, Prolong longevity, Helps destroy worms and other parasites, Bronchitis, Neuritis (inflammation of the nerves), Vertigo (inflammation of nerves), Diuretic (increases the secretion of urine), Diabetes mellitus—lowers blood sugar, Valuable for the hair, nails of the fingers and toes, and for the eyes, Sinus conditions—helps to drain mucus from the cavities and loosen phlegm, fresh or cooked onions have antiplatelet, adhesiveness, thus preventing thrombosis.

Chili pepper Health [whfoods.com]:

Chili peppers contain a substance called capsaicin, which gives peppers their characteristic pungence, producing mild to intense spice when eaten. Capsaicin is a potent inhibitor of substance P, a neuropeptide associated with inflammatory processes. The hotter the chili pepper, the more capsaicin it contains. The hottest varieties include habañero and Scotch bonnet peppers. Jalapeños are next in their heat and capsaicin content, followed by the milder varieties, including Spanish pimentos, and Anaheim and Hungarian cherry peppers.

Health benefits of Chili pepper are: fight arthritis inflammation, osteoarthritis pain, reduce blood cholesterol, triglyceride levels, and platelet aggregation, clear sinus congestion, helps fight infection of mucous membranes, Help Stop the Spread of Prostate Cancer, help prevent stomach ulcers, helps lower risk of Type 2 Diabetes.

Sweat for health [sweatforhealth.com] :

Sweating accomplishes three (3) important things: 1) rids the body of wastes, 2) regulates the critical temperature of the body at 37 degrees C (98.6 degrees F), and 3) helps keep the skin clean and pliant.

In addition, dry saunas have been shown to lower blood pressure over time.

Iodine Health [Newsmax.com—Dr. David Brownstein]:

1. necessary for thyroid hormone production
2. necessary for balancing hormonal or endocrine system
3. necessary for your immune system to function properly
4. proven effective for treating fatigue, headaches, high blood pressure, liver disease, fibrocystic breasts and ovarian cysts.
5. Iodine also contains potent antibacterial, antiparasitic, antiviral, and even anticancer properties.

Every Day foods Health [source unknown—circulating the internet]:

1. carrots greatly enhance blood flow to and function of the eyes
2. tomatoes are loaded with lycopine and are pure heart and blood food
3. grapes are heart and blood vitalizing food.

4. walnuts help develop more than three (3) dozen neuron-transmitters for brain function
5. Kidney Beans heal and help maintain kidney function
6. Celery, Bok Choy, Rhubarb and many more look just like bones. These foods specifically target bone strength. Bones are 23% sodium and these foods are 23% sodium. If you don't have enough sodium in your diet, the body pulls it from the bones, thus making them weak. These foods replenish the skeletal needs of the body.
7. Avocadoes, Eggplant and Pears target the health and function of the womb and cervix of the female—they look just like these organs. Today's research shows that when a woman eats one avocado a week, it balances hormones, sheds unwanted birth weight, and prevents c ervical cancers.
8. Figs increase the mobility of male sperm and increase the numbers of Sperm as well to overcome male sterility.

Depression [my experience]:

From what I can tell, everyone experiences depression. In his book "The Road Less Traveled", Dr M. Scott Peck, psychiatrist, writes "Depression is a normal and basically healthy phenomenon". Dr. Peck essentially tells us that "depression becomes abnormal when depression is prolonged and cannot be resolved". [pp 70].

In my experience, depression can be crippling. I have seen people take medication for depression just to be able to function in every day life, without making any attempt or progress to resolve whatever is happening in their lives to cause them to be depressed. Also in my experience, if people do not resolve whatever is happening in their lives to cause them to be depressed, then they become dependent on the medication, which can lead to worse problems.

I sometimes become depressed, sometimes to the point of not being able to carry on with my daily responsibilities. In this case, for mild depression, with a mild headache, I take Kava-Kava, 400mg, and Ibuprofen, 200mg. For more serious depression, with a crippling headache, I double the Kava-Kava and Ibuprofen. I have done this for a good many years, and the way I distinguish between a depression headache and a regular headache, is that for me a depression headache is accompanied by very drowsy sleepiness because something went wrong. For a crippling depression, I actually have to lay down and sleep it off. So, my crippling depressions usually don't last very long because I deal with whatever is bothering me through positive thinking, prayer and meditation with whatever has gone wrong in my life. I either accept what has gone wrong, and move on, or remove whatever or whoever is disturbing me, or fix whatever has gone wrong, even though sometimes it may take a long time to remedy whatever has gone wrong. Sometimes, the sadness remains, but the depression is not crippling, and I just live with it until it eventually goes away.

Another way that I deal with depression, aside from the Kava-Kava and Ibuprofen, and sleeping it off, is to do something interesting and distracting so as not to focus on my depression. I heard of a story where friends of a man who had been seriously depressed and dysfunctional for years asked a psychologist what they could do to help their depressed friend. So the story goes, the psychologist told the man's friends to tell their depressed friend to shower and shave and to put on clean clothes. Well, so the story goes, the friends did as the psychologist recommended, and it worked to break their friend's depression.

Now, having shared my thoughts about depression, what works for me may not work for you. I see occasional depression as normal in everyone's life, but if you suffer prolonged crippling depression, you should seek professional help from a licensed counselor. Also, Kava-Kava can be harmful to people with liver problems, and excessive consumption may impair ability to drive or operate heavy equipment [herbalremedies.com].

High Cholesterol (LDL); High Blood Sugar; High Triglycerides:

For high cholesterol I took 400 i.u. of Vitamin-E for about six (6) months to lower my LDL to an acceptable level. Then, I just relied on my Men's super multivitamin (GNC formula) vitamin-E content (50i.u. or 166% of minimum daily requirement). However, my sister has high cholesterol, and she was taking 1000i.u. of vitamin-E, and her LDL cholesterol did not go down.

For high blood sugar I just increased my multivitamin to a daily intake of one (1) tablet per day, from only three (3) times weekly in order to increase my magnesium intake (50mg or 12.5% of MDR). And my blood sugar went down from 119 on March 7, 2005 to 85 on 20 April, 2005.

For high Triglycerides I did quite a few things. I started using Smart Balance butter spread with Omega-3 and vitamin-D; I started using cooking oil with only 1 gram of saturated fat; I started drinking Braum's 2% milk. And, my Triglycerides went from 324 on 7 March, 2005, to 142 on 02 May, 2005.

Now, there might have been some difference between the labs that performed my blood analysis, but I don't think so because my blood sugar and triglycerides have remained normal ever since. My lab analysis on 7 March, 2005, were done by LabCorp of Dallas, Texas, and my lab analysis on 02 May, 2005, were done by Quest Diagnostics of Irving, Texas. I went to a different doctor on 02 May because my doctor at the time would not retest me so soon after my 7 March, 2005 lab analysis. The reason my doctor gave me for not retesting me was that he maintained that my lab analysis results could not change so soon. But my lab analysis results did change.

Therapeutic Massage:

I have found that therapeutic massage is extremely healthy. Specifically, foot massage, hand massage, head massage, spinal massage, and muscle massage, and heart massage can be very healthy. I will not elaborate much on these here, but I will provide some information.

The only heart massage I have ever heard of is "rhythmic compression of the heart during a heart attack to restore blood and oxygen circulation". However, I have successfully used self-heart massage to relieve debilitating heart pain due to extensive grief or stress. I have also taught one of my daughters to self-heart massage over the telephone during times of great stress. I accomplish self-heart massage by placing both of my hands over the middle of my chest and slowly compressing my chest to relieve the stress pain in my heart muscle. Of course, heart massage is only an emergency procedure and you should always seek medical attention for chest pains. In DrWeil.com, Dr. Weil writes that "The healing touch of massage can reduce heart rate, blood pressure and stress hormone levels". Dr. Weil also writes that "Those with eating disorders, anxiety or depression can take advantage of the effects massage has on the mind".

Spinal Massage:

One last word on massage is that I find that spinal massage is extremely important for health. What is spinal massage? Spinal massage is a massage of the spine to relax connecting vertebrae to insure relief and protection for the very important spinal cord. The spinal cord has nerves that control the function of every single organ and most muscles in the human body. From Amanda Dickerson, licensed massage therapist and writer for **ehow.com**, we read that the spinal cord is a bundle of nerves that passes through the vertebrae, and it sends sensations to the brain from the body, and returns motor commands to the various parts of the body.

In addition, Dickerson writes, the spinal cord is also responsible for most reflexes. Visceral reflexes control heart muscle, glands and organs. Somatic reflexes control involuntary movement of the skeletal muscles

Dickerson also writes that the spinal cord is responsible for the **sympathetic** and **parasympathetic** nervous system. The sympathetic nervous system draws blood from the digestive system and sends it to the muscles, causes the heart to beat harder and the pupils to dilate. The parasympathetic nervous system, Dickerson continues, has the opposite function, and it slows the heart rate, moves the blood to the digestive system and is also involved in producing erections in males.

Needless to say, spinal massage should only be done by a licensed massage therapist, and then only under the direction of a licensed chiropractor. Therapeutic massage can have considerable health benefits, possibly avoiding prescription medications, or even surgeries.

Spiritual Health:

Wow, "now what", you say? If you have gotten this far, we are experiencing a miracle. You say—"you have written about mental, intellectual and physical health, and now you want me to read about "spiritual health". Well, yes because spiritual health is what holds everything else in place in our lives.

But, you say, "I go to synagogue", or "I go to church", or "I go to temple". The priests, the preachers, the rabbi's or the monks, why they study their bible, preach and teach us, so we can be saved and go to heaven, or they teach us how to meditate so we can have good spiritual health and experience Nirvana, or they teach us about reincarnation so we can be good and have good Karma after our cosmic journey. So, why do I need to read about your spiritual health. Well, of course you don't have to read anything I write, unless you want to learn why I write about spiritual health, and how it applies to all of us. Every one has the same basic spiritual needs, regardless of religious beliefs, without theological or cultural boundaries.

Or, you might say—"I am very wealthy", or "I am very important". Why do I have to read about your spiritual health", or anything you write. Well again, you don't have to read anything I write, unless you want to learn why I write about spiritual health, and how it applies to all of us. Every one has the same basic spiritual needs, regardless of our socio-economic status, without theological or cultural boundaries.

All humans, regardless of theological inclinations or cultural heritage, have the same spiritual needs, and these are our **Human Needs**, and the **Needs of the Soul**. Regardless of your theological practices, or cultural heritage, we all have the same basic human needs, and the same needs of the soul, and these are very closely related to the third (3rd), fourth (4th) and fifth (5th) level in Maslow's Hierarchy of needs (Abraham Maslow in his 1943 paper "A Theory of Human Motivation"), the five (5) levels being:

1. Physiological (Biological needs)—food, clothing, shelter
2. Safety
3. Love/Belonging
4. Status (Esteem)
5. Actualization/spiritual (highest)

Our basic human needs are:

A. Human Connection—need to belong and to have a place in life. Without this belonging we have situations like the 1999 Columbine massacre/suicide (13 killed), and the 2007 Virginia Tech massacre/ suicide (30 killed). Without this belonging we have suicides at all socio-economic levels, genders, or ages.
B. Caring—we all have a need to care for and about others, and be cared for and about by others.
C. Mating—most normal people have a need to mate and procreate.
D. Faith—we all have a need to have faith. Faith in what? Well, faith in our beliefs; faith in ourselves—our knowledge and abilities; faith in our mate; faith in our fellow man; faith in our way of life; faith in the future.

The Human Soul:

Emotions—sadness, happiness, anger, fear, disgust, and surprise. compassion, boredom, embarrassment, love, hate
Beliefs—God, heaven, hell, religious practices, marriage, family, children, work, education, after life, sexual behavior, honesty, fairness, gambling

Self Image—good, bad, lethargic, pretty, ugly, handsome, superiority, inferiority, capable, incapable, competent, incompetent

Thoughts—all of our thoughts reside in and emanate from the human brain, and consequently is part of the Human Soul.

Knowledge—everything we have ever read, seen, heard, or smelled is knowledge that resides in the human brain, and consequently is part of the Human Soul."

Note that I have listed two emotions together, love and hate. However, these are not natural emotions that we are born with, and they are mutually exclusive. To love, or hate, not only must we be taught the one or the other, they cannot both reside in us at the same time. But, if you love your fellow man, you cannot long hate your fellow man.

While happiness is a component of our emotions and spiritual health, I have included a separate chapter (4) on happiness because happiness has recently become a very important separate focus of psychology with the purpose to study about what it takes to go beyond balance.

Now, for spiritual health and happiness, all of our human needs and our soul must be consciously held in **balance** for the purpose of enjoying life, living and being alive by being good and doing good toward the purpose of achieving a **balance** and **peace** with life, nature, and the creator of the universe and life on earth. These are my thoughts, beliefs and conclusion after a lifetime of study, prayer and service to God, and Country and Family. Believe them or not; respect them or not, that is your choice.

Confession & Forgiveness:

Confession, regardless of theology, with a contrite heart (sincere) purges the Soul, and forgiveness frees the Soul. To forgive means to not harbor hatred, or anger toward those that harm us because to harbor hatred or anger separates us from balance and destroys us to ruin whatever hope we have for happiness. So forgive those who harm you and leave your pain.

CHAPTER 4

On HAPPINESS, FUN & MEDITATION

Happiness, fun and meditation are extremely important for quality of life. We saw from Maslow's Hierarchy of needs (Abraham Maslow in his 1943 paper "A Theory of Human Motivation"), the five (5) levels being:

1. Physiological (Biological needs)—food, clothing, shelter
2. Safety
3. Love/Belonging
4. Status (Esteem)
5. Actualization/spiritual (highest level)

In this hierarchy of human existence, each level must be satisfied before the next level can be experienced and satisfied. So, what happens next. Well, next we can aim for happiness, fun, and meditation.

MEDITATION:

Let's start with meditation. My definition for meditation is to shut out the conscious sensory world, and tune in to the world of our inner mind. In my section for intellectual health I identified meditation as a means to solve problems. This is certainly true. But, another benefit of meditation can be just to rest the mind from the rat race of survival. The mind needs rest, just as the body does. If our mind is not troubled, it might be possible to rest the mind during sleep, but the mind has other duties to perform when we are asleep.

So my experience is to perform a conscious meditation with incense. Now why incense. Incense reaches the deepest centers of our brain because, as I understand it, the olfactory sense, that being smelling, is the most primitive (oldest center) of the brain. In the quietness of meditation our brains can relax and rest.

There are many theories on meditation, such as transcendental meditation, and the YOGA Lotus Position, but I will leave those for your curiosity to research. For now my thoughts are sufficient for the purposes of this book.

HAPPINESS:

In 1998 University of Pennsylvania psychologist Martin Seligman, president of the American Psychological Association (A.P.A.), decided on a new goal for psychology. Seligman proposed "We needed to ask, What are the enabling conditions that make human beings flourish?"

In an article in Time Magazine, "The New Science of Happiness", Jan. 09, 2005, Claudia Wallis presents considerable discourse on this subject.

Seligman wanted the psychology community "to look at what actively made people feel fulfilled, engaged and meaningfully happy. Mental health, he reasoned, should be more than the absence of mental illness. It should be something akin to a vibrant and muscular fitness of the human mind and spirit."

So, this is a good tie in to the purpose of this chapter on health, the four (4) aspects of health: **mental**, **intellectual**, **physical**, and **spiritual**. Seligman's research, over a period of decades, had focused on optimism, "a trait shown to be associated with good physical health, less depression and mental illness, longer life and, yes, greater happiness". And, I find Optimism (aka faith) to be a good positive trait for happiness.

RELIGION—YES:
Wallis reports that "On the positive side, religious faith seems to genuinely lift the spirit, though it's tough to tell whether it's the God part or the community aspect that does the heavy lifting."

FRIENDS—YES:
Friends?A giant yes writes Wallis. "A 2002 study conducted at the University of Illinois by Diener and Seligman found that the

most salient characteristics shared by the 10% of students with the highest levels of happiness and the fewest signs of depression were their strong ties to friends and family and commitment to spending time with them."

PLEASURE—NO; RELATIONS—YES; PURPOSE—YES:
Wallis further reports that "Seligman finds three components of happiness: **pleasure** (sensual gratification), **engagement** (the depth of involvement with one's family, work, romance and hobbies) and **meaning** (using personal strengths to serve some larger end). Of those three roads to a happy, satisfied life, *pleasure is the least consequential.*" Wallis further reports that Seligman insists: "This is newsworthy because so many Americans build their lives around pursuing pleasure. It turns out that **engagement and meaning are much more important**."

COUNT your BLESSINGS—YES:
Gratitude exercises: Wallis reports that Sonja Lyubomirsky, University of California at Riverside psychologist, found that "taking the time to conscientiously count their blessings once a week significantly increased subjects' overall satisfaction with life"

Wallis also reports that psychologist Robert Emmons, University of California at Davis, found that gratitude exercises "improve physical health, raise energy levels and, for patients with neuromuscular disease, relieve pain and fatigue. Quoting Emmons, "The ones who benefited most tended to elaborate more and have a wider span of things they're grateful for," he notes.

ACTS of KINDNESS—YES:
"Another happiness booster", writes Wallis, "say positive psychologists, is performing acts of altruism or kindness—visiting a nursing home, helping a friend's child with homework, mowing a neighbor's lawn, writing a letter to a grandparent. Doing five kind acts a week, especially all in a single day, gave a measurable boost to Lyubomirsky's subjects".

GIVING—YES:
Wallis further writes that Christopher Peterson, University of Michigan, says that "Giving makes you feel good about yourself."

FUN:

Nowhere have I been able to find a psychology of fun, even though it might exist somewhere. However, my youngest daughter, who graduated Summa Cum Laude with a Bachelor of Science degree in Electrical Engineering, so aptly reminded me recently, you have to write about fun.

I agree because I could see in her life, even though I know very little about fun, that having fun was very important for her delicate nature as she poured herself into her studies, achievement, success and accomplishment. She could not have achieved her success if her life had not been punctuated by moments of happiness, fun and laughter.

What activities does my daughter enjoy for having fun? My daughter enjoys playing table games and video games, like Guitar Hero, with friends and family. My daughter also enjoys Creative Memories scrap booking and dancing, cruises, and theme parks. My daughter also enjoys television programs like Smallville, America's Got Talent, and American Idol. All of these things are fun things for my daughter. This is not very intellectual, but is very important for my daughter's mental and intellectual health.

For other's fun activities are such things as sports. The point being that fun involves happiness and laughter and appears to me to be good for mental and intellectual health as long as fun does not become obsessive, and doesn't consume our lives to the point that we ignore work, responsibilities and family. My daughter says that fun is a reward for hard work.

For myself, I know very little about fun, except for physical exercise, running and riding my motorcycle, relaxing, studying, watching documentaries on public television. Otherwise, my whole life being a life of work, study, torment and struggle for survival, punctuated by moments of happiness in my brief marriages, the birth success and happiness of my children and the happiness of my sisters and their children and grandchildren. And yet, I enjoy considerable peace of mind and soul for having achieved my lifetime goals.

CHAPTER 5

On Religion

My Walk of Faith—January, 1997

God has impressed on me for many years to write some things on salvation. These things didn't come out of thin air, for you see I received my salvation and was baptized at age 9, in 1951, by Dr. Perry F. Webb at the first Baptist Church in San Antonio, Texas. Missionaries took my sisters and me to that church and I still remember their names: Mrs. Brent and Mrs. Anderson.

My sisters and I were raised by the first Baptist Church of San Antonio, Texas. Until I left at age 18, in 1960, the church was our whole life and we accepted our salvation and the Bible by faith. But, when I left the church and home to make my way in the world, I found that the world didn't follow the same rules as the church, and that the church was only teaching me denomination and society, and I wanted to find God.

I looked desperately for someone to teach me about God, but no one even cared about my quest, much less to teach me about God or answer my questions about God. Then, I found some Mormons who said they would teach me about God, but they were only interested in teaching me about Joseph Smith and his tablets and the Mormon Tabernacle in Salt Lake City, Utah, and I was only interested in God, the Bible and God's heavenly tabernacle. Even though I was baptized into the Aronic priesthood, I left the church and the Mormons to their denomination and their society to find God on my own.

From time to time I attended different churches during 3 different marriages. I attended a Methodist church, a Presbyterian church, an Episcopal church, and finally in 1989, I returned to the Baptist church, with my 2 little children, ages 4 and 6, so that my children could learn the plan of salvation like I did. However, I still keep my distance.

In the mean time, in 1963, at age 21, I set out on a quest to find universally applicable truth. In the process I conquered the world, became an intellectual, found God, found love, and found respect. This didn't happen overnight, and I had to prove myself many times over. It took me over 25 years to accomplish this, at which time I realized that universally applicable truth was in the Bible where I had started in faith almost 40 years earlier, but now I understood it.

And, finding universally applicable truth wasn't easy. It took much studying, many campaigns, many victories and many failures. It took much pain and suffering through life.

One would ask what I meant by conquering the world, and it simply means that I determined to take everything the world dished out and never strike back, although sometimes I slipped.

And then one might ask what I mean by universally applicable truth, and it simply means truth that is applicable to all men, past, present and future. And, I found universally applicable truth by studying many cultures, anthropology, and many religions from the east to the west, and in the faces and hearts of many peoples I encountered in my travels around the world. So then, what is universally applicable truth? Well, here it is. It is what Rabbi Bemperod referred to as "the human connection" on his radio talks, while he was at Temple Emmanuel in Dallas, Texas in the early 1980's. It is the love that Jesus taught us, and that is that no human functions very well without love. In fact, without love, most humans function very badly in society and life.

And how you ask did I learn about love. Well I learned about love through marriage and in caring about and for my children. It isn't that I hadn't been loved, like by my mother, but that I hadn't really loved in return, and it wasn't until I learned to return love that I found God. And it wasn't until I was in a state of God's love that I really returned my mother's love. I had been too busy all of my life proving myself and conquering the world. And it isn't that God didn't care about me or for me, so much as that I wasn't aware of God's love. So, it wasn't until I was in this state of love that I began to experience God's presence, and began to be receptive to God's quiet, beautiful voice and guidance and wisdom, even though I had had these all along.

Then come the matters of finding respect and becoming an intellectual. It was not until I was in this state of love that my academic studies and professional work were rewarded with respect and I became the intellectual I wanted to be. It was not until I was in this state of love that I realized the power of Jesus' teachings to number one, love God with all our might, and number two, to love my neighbor (fellow man) as myself.

However, the happiness I found in God and God's love also brought me great sadness, because then I became acutely aware that the most common form of love I saw around me, even in churches, was self love, as if each individual becomes a demigod. And, I became acutely aware that the most common form of worship I saw around me, even in churches, was not worship of God, but self worship, especially when people go to church dressed to kill, instead of to honor God. I also became acutely aware that Jesus never taught us to love him, rather he taught us that if we loved him, then we would keep his commandments to love one another. I also became acutely aware that Jesus taught to call him Master, but not Good Master. **"you call me Master and Lord, and so I am"—John 13:13 "Why call me good Master. There is none good, but God"—Matt 19:17)**

Now we come to the subject of heaven, which is the subject of most religions, and the goal of most sane mortals, i.e. we all want to go to some perfect heaven when we die. Now I realize what Jesus meant when he told Peter, "I give you the keys to the kingdom of heaven", and that is "whatever you bind on earth, your bind in heaven, and whatever you loose on earth, you loose in heaven". We find this in 2 places in the New Testament.

Now I realize that the nature of heaven is spiritual, and was ushered in to this earth at Pentecost, 50 days after Jesus' death, when Jesus gave us the Holy Spirit to guide us after Jesus departure. And, while this realization brought me great happiness, that we can enter the kingdom of heaven without a physical death, but only with a spiritual birth, it also brought me great sadness. This realization brings me great sadness because I realize that many people wait for a physical death to enter the kingdom of heaven, and in doing so, they miss the boat.

So then you ask, "how do we catch this boat to heaven?" Well, the answer to this comes from John the Baptist, who told us to repent of our sins and prepare for a spiritual baptizer, Jesus. I now realize that this means to die to our physical, earthly existence, seeking only gratification of self and our senses and to be born into the "state of love" where we love only God and our fellow man. So, it is here that we apply the keys to the kingdom of heaven. If we bind the love of God on earth, we bind the love of God in heaven. If we loose our fleshly desires on earth, we loose our fleshly desires in heaven. Herein is the nature and the definition of our salvation.

So, it is in this manner that I have been teaching my children that we can enter spiritual heaven now, but that when we die we will enter a perfect heaven because we will no longer be subject to earthly temptation and pain to distract us from our love of God.

Now we may ask, "well, what are these sins that John the Baptist talked about?", and didn't Jesus die for our sins. Well, sin is anything we say, do or think that separates us from God, and yes, Jesus did die for our sins, but that doesn't redeem us. Only experiencing God's love redeems us.

Well, we ask, "doesn't Jesus forgive our sins?" Yes, Jesus does forgive our sins, but only if we repent of our sins and ask for forgiveness, so that we can have a spiritual birth into God's spiritual heaven. Jesus taught us that "if you have seen me, you have seen my Father in heaven", so they are one and the same that forgive our sins. That is, we must abandon our self serving nature, through repentance, into a loving relation with God. We must sincerely enter a "state of love" with God in order to enter God's spiritual heaven.

Now we might ask, "what good did it do for Jesus to die for our sins, if we still have to repent?" To understand this, we must realize that the New Testament tells us that Jesus came first to save the nation of Israel, which until Jesus' arrival was offering blood sacrifice for the forgiveness of sin, and that at that time, the world was in total darkness, without knowledge of Godly love. Jesus' death on the cross was the last perfect blood sacrifice offered for us by the perfect lamb of God, so that we no longer need to offer blood sacrifice for the forgiveness of sin, but we now simply have to ask for forgiveness from our precious Lord and Savior, Jesus Christ, who taught us God's love.

Then we ask, "how do we understand this sin that we must ask forgiveness for and why is it so important to us?" Well, again, sin is anything that we say or do, or even think, that separates us from God. You see, now I realize that because of our human nature we are either in a "state of sin", or a "state of love", and that these two concepts are mutually exclusive and cannot coexist in an individual human form. So you ask "what happens if I sin? Will God send a bolt of lightning to strike me if I sin? Will God judge me if I sin?" Not necessarily. Now I realize that our punishment for our sin is to live without God's love, guidance and protection, outside of God's spiritual heaven, and this is the nature of hell where Satan and evil reign.

So now we ask, "what is evil"? Now I realize that evil is anything done, said or thought of a fleshly, worldly nature to cause us to sin. Examples of sin are given to us by Paul in the New Testament and the Ten Commandments, and these are uncontrolled anger, vice, avarice, greed, lust, stealing, murder, and hatred.

Now we come to a typical erroneous attitude toward salvation. We might say that we're not perfect and that we might as well go on living an earthly life of lustful self serving gratification. Well, I realize that this is just not true, because if we truly repent of our sinful nature, and if we truly trust in Jesus and our salvation, even as little children trust their father, then the Holy Spirit will strike our conscience as we err and we will remember to ask God for forgiveness, and God will forgive us.(This is the concept of once saved always saved). Every day we live for Christ we will err and lust less and less until we err and lust no more (sin), and we reach a perfect existence in Gods spiritual heaven.

One might say, "why can't I go on enjoying the pleasures of life until I die, and then ask for forgiveness, and enter heaven?" Well you can try that but it won't work because your repentance won't be sincere. You will only be asking for forgiveness because you're afraid of going to hell, but it will be too late because you will already be in hell for your eternal damnation. In other words, salvation from Hell cannot be negotiated.

Now, we may ask about going to church. One might ask "won't I go to heaven if I go to church every Sunday?" Well, not necessarily. About eleven years ago I was studying with the Church of Christ, but I stopped because I couldn't agree with them that they were the only church that was going to heaven and they gave several reasons, the two most significant being that they were the only ones that obeyed the Bible by number one, serving the Lords supper (communion) every Sunday, and number two, that they didn't play musical instruments in church. Now, I see nothing wrong with serving the Lords supper every Sunday, for Jesus taught us that "as often as you eat this bread and drink this cup you remember me until I return". And, I see nothing wrong with singing in church without musical instruments. Actually, I prefer singing without the often loud, distracting instruments. But, what I do see wrong is the message about going to heaven if we go to that church only.

So, we continue, and ask "what good does it do then for me to go to church if it won't get me to heaven?" Well, now I realize that it will do a lot of good, and it might get you to heaven. The reason is that Jesus taught us that "wherever two or more gather in his name, there will I be also". That's one. Number two is that the church building itself is a sanctuary, consecrated for the purpose of providing refuge from the problems, challenges and responsibilities and evils of the world where we can shut out the world and hear an inspiring choir and an inspiring sermon and prayer from an angel of God, in an inspiring environment. Then, within this sanctuary and with this inspiration, and with the caring of the community of Saints we might get to a point sufficiently in love with God to be receptive to God working in our lives through the Holy Spirit, and therein is our salvation.

Then, we can ask about this thing called prayer. "What is this prayer?" Well, now I realize that prayer is that time that we set aside whether in church, or anywhere else, to commune with God. Not that God needs to hear us articulate our needs, for he already knows our hearts, but that we need to be receptive to God's will in our lives. God wants us to embrace him gently, and tenderly, and caringly through prayer, even as he gently and tenderly and caringly reaches for us. Prayer is for our benefit, not Gods, for it is in taking our cares and our needs to God in prayer, in total faith, as a child trusts his/her father, that God can work in our lives to provide for us, and so it has happened to me more times than I can count.

Now this brings us to another issue in our pursuit of a spiritual heaven, and that is, what about reading the Bible? How does this fit into our salvation? We might say that the Bible is too complicated for us to understand. One might also say that we are not theologians, and don't have a PhD degree in divinity, and so how then can we be expected to understand the Bible, and we might ask how reading the Bible will help us. The answer is simply this. Reading the bible can help us because it is the divinely inspired word of God and the Holy Spirit helps us understand the scripture we read. If we trust in God through prayer and Bible study, God will provide us the wisdom as we need it to live life in Gods service.

Then, finally one might ask, "well what about after salvation, prayer, Bible study, and going to church?" We might ask "what is there for me after salvation?" Well, there is growth as Paul tells us in the New Testament—"I press for the high calling of Jesus Christ". And, we do this by service, Bible study, prayer, and worship. Then, we might ask, "what kind of service do I do?" In the new testament Jesus tells us that "inasmuch as you do it unto the least of these, you do it unto me" (I prefer the King James version here). That is, helping the poor, the widowed, the lonely and those in prison. The New Testament also tells us that Jesus taught that we will be cast into hell if we don't serve him.

And now God moves me to speak to one more issue and that is that many people say that the phrase "God helps him who helps himself" is not in scripture, so that they don't have to help themselves. This is wrong. New Testament scripture tells us this in the parable of the talents. In this parable

Jesus tells us that he who invests his talents receives more, and he who does not use his talents looses them and is cast into eternal damnation.

And, so I close, with one final thought, and that is that I pray my every action, thought and word be a prayer.

Amen.

CHAPTER 6

Principles of Enlightened Christianity

After reading an email on 16 July, 2006, from Dr James Denison, Senior Pastor at Park Cities Baptist Church, Dallas, Texas, I was inspired to write this commentary on the greatest of Christian Principles, which I now call "Enlightened Christianity". I spent many hours that day, and since, researching these scriptures, and it seems prophetic that I was doing this when I received a call from my sister that my niece's husband, Tom Knoff, has just been called to pastor a larger church than the church he was pastoring, and that members of the 2 churches are combining. So I offer this to you for this special day. Enlightened Christianity focuses on the spiritual nature of God and Heaven. Each one of these principles is a sermon in itself, and the references are from either the King James version, or the Revised English version.

Dino Commentary: Thanking God for everything, good or bad, is one of the greatest principles in Christianity—1Thessalonians 5;18. The greatest principles in Christianity are of course:

1. "The kingdom of God is within you"—Luke 17:21
2. "God is a Spirit; and they that worship him must worship him in spirit and the truth"—John 4: 24
3. "Blasphemy against the Holy spirit cannot be forgiven"—Matt 12: 31
4. "believe in the Lord Jesus Christ and you and your house will be saved"—Acts 16:31
5. "And he(Jesus) is the propitiation (sacrifice) for our sins: and not for our's only, but also for the whole world.—1John 2:2

6.   "whoever believes in him (Jesus) will not perish, but have eternal life. For God so loved the world that he gave his only begotten son that whoever Believes in him will not perish, but have everlasting life"—John 3: 15-16

7.   "He that sees me sees the Father"—John 14:9

8.   For the Son of Man did not come to be served, but to serve"—Matt 20:28; Mark 10:45

9.   Jesus said "if you love me keep my commandments";—John 14: 15

10. the greatest commandment being "Love God and your neighbor. On these two commandments hang all the law and the prophets"—Matt 22: 37-40

10a. Truly I tell you, whatever you did for one of the least of these brothers and sisters of mine, you did for me. -Matthew 25:40

11. and the great commission—"Go and teach all nations, baptizing them in the name of the Father, the son, and the Holy Ghost."—Matt 28:19

12. "In my Father's House are many mansions (rooms). I go to prepare a place for you I will come again and take you to myself"—John 14:2,3

13. "Think not I am come to destroy the law, or the prophets. I am not come to destroy, but to fulfill."—Matt 5:17

14. "you call me Master and Lord, and so I am"—John 13:13

15. "Why call me good Master. There is none good, but God"—Matt 19:17

16. "No man can come to me, except the Father which has sent me draw him, and I will raise him up at the last day"—John 6:44

17. "My sheep hear my voice, and I know them & they follow me"—John 10:27

18. "This is covenant that I will make with the house of Israel . . . ; I will put my laws into their mind, and write them in their hearts."—Hebrews 8:10

19. "It is not the healthy who need a physician, but the sick."—Matt 9:12

20. "I require mercy, not sacrifice. I did not come to call the virtuous, but sinners."—Matt 9:13

21. "Let the children come to me; do not try to stop them; for the kingdom of God belongs to such as these"—Mark 10:14

22. "He that is greatest among you shall be your servant"—Matt 20:26; Mat 23: 11

23. "Whoever will be chief among you let him be your servant"—Matt 20:27

24. "except man be born of water and of the spirit, he cannot enter into the Kingdom of Heaven"—John 3: 5

25. "whoever humbles himself as a child shall be great in Heaven";—Matt 18 : 4

26. "Lay not up for yourselves treasures upon earth, where moth and rust corrupt, and where thieves break through and steal. But lay up for yourselves treasures in heaven, where neither moth nor rust corrupt . . ." Matt: 6: 19-20

27. "seek first the kingdom of Heaven, and all will be provided for you."—Matt 6:33

28. "If you have faith of a grain of mustard seed, you can move mountains"—Matt 17:20

29. "For where 2 or 3 are gathered together in my name, there am I in the midst of them"—Matt 18:20

30. "Whatever you ask in prayer, believing, you shall receive"—Matt 21: 22

30a. Therefore I tell you, do not worry about your life, what you will eat or drink; or about your body, what you will wear. But seek first God's kingdom and his righteousness, and all these things will be provided to you. - Matthew 6:25,33

31. "If you forgive others the wrongs they have done, your heavenly Father will also forgive you" (this does not mean to excuse or pardon wrong doing, just do not harbor hatred, anger, or resentment, for these will alienate you from God)—Matt 6: 14

32. "That your alms may be made in secret, and you Father who sees in secret himself shall reward you openly"—Matt 6:4

33. "When you pray, enter into your closet and pray to your Father in secret and your Father who sees in secret shall reward you openly"—Matt 6:6

34. "For as you judge others, so you will yourselves be judged"—Matt 7: 2

35. "You hypocrite! First take the plank out of your own eye, and then you will see clearly to take the speck out of your brother's eye."—Matt 7:5

36. "Do not give dogs what is holy; do not throw your pearls to the pigs: they will only trample on them, and turn and tear you to pieces."—Matt 7:6

37. Golden Rule: " . . . whatsoever you would that men should do to you, do even so to them: for this is the law and the prophets."—Matt 7:12

38. "Have you never read that in the beginning the Creator made them male and female (not male and male) . . . That is why a man leaves his father and mother, and is united to his wife (not man), and the two become one flesh. Therefore what God has joined together, man must not separate."—Matt 19: 4-6.

39. "A bishop then must be blameless, the husband of one wife (not one man), vigilant, sober, of good behavior, given to hospitality, apt to teach "—1 Timothy 3: 2

40. " . . . through the grace of the Lord Jesus Christ we shall be saved . . ."—Acts 15:11

41. " . . . there is a remnant, chosen(saved) by the grace of God. But if it is by grace, then it does not rest on deeds (works)."—Romans 11: 5-6

42. "Faith is the substance of things of things hoped for, the evidence of things not seen."—Hebrews 11:1.

43. " . . . faith, if it has not works, is dead, being alone."—James 2:17

44. "For the Son of man shall come in the glory of his Father with his angels; and then he shall reward every man according to his works."—Matt 16: 27

45. "And though I bestow all my goods to feed the poor, and though I give my body to be burned, and have not charity (love), it profits me nothing (in heaven)."—1 Corinthians 13: 3

46. "For we know that the law is spiritual; but I am carnal, sold under sin."—Romans 7: 14

47. "For as many as are led by the Spirit of God (good), they are the sons (children) of God—Romans 8:14

48. "And if children, then heirs; heirs of God, and joint heirs with Christ;"—Romans 8:17

49. David's prayer: "The sacrifices of God are a broken spirit: a broken and contrite heart, O God, you will not despise."—Psalm 51:17

50. The 10 Commandments—Exodus 20: 1-17

51. God guides, protects, and keeps us—Psalm 23.

52. The perfect prayer—The Lord's Prayer—Matt 6: 9-13.

53. Jesus' promise to the oppressed—The Beatitudes—Matt 5: 3-12.

54. Every person must submit to the authorities in power (Government), for all authority comes from God . . . for they are God's agents. . . . That is also why you pay taxes. The authorities are in God's service.—Romans 13: 1-7

55. (for protection from my enemies) Psalm 59,138, 143

CHAPTER 7

Love and Marriage

Here I present the 7 measures of Love between a man and a woman as I define them. As far as I know, no one else has ever identified these measures. The 5 languages of love are well known, as defined by Dr. Gary Chapman in his book "5 Languages of Love" first published in 1992.

Eyes for You:

Here are the things you need to remember about love. The most important thing to be aware of in love is compatibility. There is an old Indian saying, "she has eyes for you". That's where it starts. She looks at you if she likes what she sees, how you look, how you talk, how you dress, how you act. Then, you the boy/man return the look if you like what you see in her at first glance. If your eyes connect, and hold and you smile at each other, then you are off and running. Some people try to start a romantic relation when they don't have eyes for each other. Good luck. That is a hard road to hold.

Flirting:

Flirting is extremely important at all stages of a romantic relation, but especially at the beginning of a romantic relation. Well, if you have eyes for each other, then flirting can begin. What is flirting? Flirting is small talk, a smile, a wink. Flirting is a way of saying "I like you" without actually saying the words, with a "hello, what's your name?". The tone of the response, if there is one, tells you that you can continue your small talk, like "Where are you from"? "What is your career, education"? "What are your interests"? "Where do you work"?

The Invitation:

If the first conversation continues, you, the gentleman that you are, could get to the point of inviting your new possible romantic acquaintance to do something interesting like, a movie, theater, museum, lunch, dinner, coffee. If your new acquaintance accepts, then you have the start of a romantic relation.

But, what ladies, if he is shy, but you like him and he seems to have potential, and he doesn't invite you to meet again. Then what? Well, then, being the smart lady that you are, you can invite him with something like, "Why don't you call me sometime"? Ladies, if you are not willing to assume some responsibility when your new shy gentleman acquaintance misses a queue, then you may miss out on an excellent romantic relation.

Continuing:

So now what? You meet; you like; you flirt; you have your first invite. Well then you start to get to know each other and decide if you want to continue with a follow up invitation. If you have a follow up invitation, then you have to start asking yourself some serious questions. "Is this the right person for me, and should we continue"? If the answer is yes, then you need to seriously consider the seven (7) measures of love that I define here.

If you love someone with an intimate, caring bonding and they love you then you both do the following:

1. you respect each other, and your ideas and ideals
2. you admire each other.
3. you like each other, and spending time together.
4. you care about each other and your happiness.
5. you help each other with your responsibilities and goals.
6. you inspire each other to be more of who and what you are.
7. you are intellectually, spiritually and socially compatible, i.e— you understand each other, and you have compatible beliefs.

Then, if you are in love by the 7 measures, then love needs to be nurtured by the 5 languages of love:

1. you both regularly speak words of love and compliment to each other (not just one of you)
2. you both regularly give each other small gifts, like flowers
3. you both do things of service for each other, like help with chores, or back, hand or foot rubs/massage.
4. you both spend quality time with each other, just enjoying each other's company.
5. you lovingly touch each other, like small kisses, holding hands.

Never Get Mad at Each Other:

Finally—Never, never get mad at each other, or say anything ugly, or unkind, or critical to each other. Every time you do, a part of your love dies, and each time it is harder to return to Love, until you can't return to Love. Respectful critique and suggestions is OK if you meet the 7 measures of love and you have the 5 languages of love.

Counseling and Marriage:

Then, if you have the 7 requirements for love, and the 5 languages of love, you might want to consider getting counseling and evaluated if you want to be committed long term to each other, and possibly marry. Of course, if you have total confidence in each other, you can probably skip counseling and evaluation, but I highly recommend counseling and evaluation before marriage for high quality marriages. If both of you don't want marriage, then you can just stay good friends.

CHAPTER 8

Intellectual and Spiritual Enlightenment

Intellectual and Spiritual Enlightenment is about looking at the human existence objectively without theological or cultural boundaries. This whole book is about intellectual and spiritual enlightenment and my journey through life, and what I have learned. It seems to me that it is possible that my story could be the untold story of many, and that my observations could find common sympathy in many as they might read this book and compare their own lives.

All of the chapters I have written are revealing for the purpose of intellectual and spiritual enlightenment: Education, Career, Health, Happiness, Fun, and Meditation, Religious Experiences, Principles of Enlightened Christianity, Intellectual and Spiritual Enlightenment, America, A Christian Nation, Intelligent Design, Quotations to Live By.

However, there is far more to intellectual and spiritual enlightenment, and that is what this chapter is about. Today we have far more knowledge about human nature than we did even twenty (20) years ago. Not only have I consummated my own intellect in technical achievements, academic studies, and the scholarly professors I have studied with, I have studied on my own from many scientists, medical doctors, psychologists and theologians to sort my way through the maze of religions and cultures in our America today for my own mental, intellectual, physical and spiritual health.

Remembering America:

I fervently wish that our America of fifty (50) years ago could be returned to us. With the advent of civil rights, many cultures have taken over America to use American and mold the country into their own culture and religion, or lack thereof. I remember when we could pray in school without fear of being accused of violating the First Amendment to the Constitution of the United States of America, which referred only to the establishment of religion by the Congress of the United States. In the United States, schools were originally established to learn to read the Christian Bible.

From the book Christian Life and Character of the Civil Institutions of the United States, requested by United States Senator Charles Sumner from Massachusetts, and written in 1864 by B.F. Morris, John Quincy Adams is quoted as saying, "The highest glory of the American Revolution was this: it connected in one indissoluble bond the principles of civil government with the principles of Christianity". [Title sheet, B.F. Morris, 1864]

And, from George Washington, "I am sure that there never was a people who had more reason to acknowledge a divine interposition in their affairs than those of the United States; and I should be pained to believe they have forgotten that agency which was so often manifested in the Revolution, or that they failed to consider the omnipotence of that God who is alone able to protect them. He must be worst than an infidel that lacks faith, and more than wicked that has not gratitude enough to acknowledge his obligations". [Christian Life and Character of the Civil Institutions of the United States, pp33-34, B.F. Morris, 1864]

In chapter 8 I provide history from that very same book, Christian Life and Character of the Civil Institutions of the United States, about the men and the State Constitutions from the states that sent their representatives to the Convention of Commissioners to write the Federal Constitution (Constitution of the United States) in 1787.

Constitution of the United States:

According to B.F. Morris, "the framers of the Constitution of the United States profoundly felt the magnitude and solemnity of their work". Morris continues, "the Articles of the old Confederation had proven too weak for the ends of a strong government, and fears pervaded the minds of public men and the people that the objects for which they had labored would be lost". [pp246, B.F. Morris, 1864]

The Convention of Commissioners from all the States met in Philadelphia on May 14, 1787, and formed the Federal Constitution, which was sent to the States for ratification. [pp246, B.F. Morris, 1864]

This Constitution states Morris contains no recognition of the Christian religion, nor even an acknowledgement of the providence of God in national affairs. When reminded of this in 1789, President George Washington states "I am persuaded you will permit me to observe that the path of true piety is so plain as to require but little political direction". And Washington continues, "To the guidance of the ministers of the gospel this important object is, perhaps more properly committed". [pp248, B.F. Morris, 1864]

Nevertheless, B.F. Morris reminds us that the "The various States who had sent these good and great men to the convention to form a Constitution had, in all their civil charters, expressed, as States and as a people, their faith in God, and the Christian religion". And Morris continues, "These statesmen, met to form a Constitution for a free and growing republic, were at times baffled in reaching desirable and harmonious results". [pp249, B.F. Morris, 1864]

Inauguration of George Washington:

Washington was inaugurated and took the oath of office on the 30th of April, 1789, administered by Chancellor Livingston, laying his hand on the open Bible, said audibly "I swear, so help me god", and the Chancellor said, "It is done!". Then, the whole assembly went to St. Paul's Church, where prayers suited to the occasion were read by Dr. Provost, Bishop of the Protestant Episcopal Church in New York, who had been appointed one of the chaplains of Congress. [pp 270-271, B.F. Morris, 1864]

War on Poverty: From wikipedi.org we find that the "War on Poverty" was begun by President Lyndon B. Johnson in 1964 in an attempt to reduce the poverty level in America, which was at that time around 19%. The poverty level is defined as the level of income below which families or individuals are considered to lack the income to meet basic needs, such as food, shelter and clothing. While the "War on Poverty" has had some success, by and large, poverty has become a way of life for many dependent on the "War on Poverty" programs, and typically remains around 11% to 15%. Quoting Kent B. Germany, faculty.virginia.edu, "With the War on Poverty, American liberalism's insistent optimism and deep faith in expertise met head-on a domestic crisis of race, social order, and political economy comparable in scope only to the Civil War and the Great Depression". Also, according to Kent Germany, a massive tax cut, in 1964, designed to stimulate the economy and passed Congress in February, and organizing a task force to shape the War on Poverty contributed to an extraordinary economic expansion.

Originally, the War on Poverty programs included such programs as Volunteer in Service to America (VISTA), Job Corps, Head Start, Legal Services and the Community Action Program, and was administered by the Office of Economic Opportunity (OEO). The OEO administered the federal funds to benefit the poor, but was replaced in 1973 by President Nixon, by the "Community Services Administration".

Also, from Kent B. Germany, "the administration of President Ronald W. Reagan, replaced the Community Services Administration with the Community Services Block Grant system, redesigned job training, cut back the Food Stamp program, and initiated what some scholars have called a War on Welfare". Germany also reports that "President Reagan and others on the political right convinced many that the War on Poverty represented a failure of big government. **Instead of helping to alleviate poverty, the programs supposedly encouraged sloth, dependency, crime, single parenthood, and unproductive citizenship.** Conservative critics, led by Charles Murray in his book *Losing Ground*, charged that most of the programs were misguided, mismanaged, mangled attempts at social engineering in which liberal overspending stifled market-based solutions and covered up for the faults of individuals.

Primarily because of increased criticism of the "welfare state", President Bill Clinton ended the welfare programs, but continued as "Head Start", VISTA, and "Job Corps". Head Start is of particular significance and continues today to help preschool children from low-income families with a program to meet emotional, social, health, nutritional, and psychological needs. The Job Corps helps 70,000 youths annually.

From faculty.virginia.edu, Kent B. Germany, "other important measures with antipoverty functions included an $11 billion tax cut (Revenue Act of 1964), the Civil Rights Act (1964), the Food Stamp Act (1964), the Elementary and Secondary Education Act (1965), the Higher Education Act (1965), the Social Security amendments creating Medicare/Medicaid (1965), the creation of the Department of Housing and Urban Development (1965), the Voting Rights Act (1965), the Model Cities Act (1966), the Fair Housing Act (1968), several job-training programs, and various Urban Renewal-related projects".

Also, according to Kent Germany, while the Office of Economic Opportunity received an initial appropriation of slightly less than $1 billion and experienced only marginal increases after that, other programs probably had more impact on American lives. Quoting Germany, "The Food Stamp program, for instance, fed hungry Americans and eventually reached almost ten percent of the population and 60 percent of the poor. Medicare subsidized health care for the elderly (with almost 40 million enrollees in 2000 according to the Centers for Medicare and Medicaid Services), while Medicaid applied to qualified poor residents. The Elementary and Secondary Education Act provided money to local school districts who were supposed to use the funds to help their poor students. The Higher Education Act eased the financial burdens of millions of college students. The Civil Rights Act opened up new spaces in the American marketplace, while the Voting Rights Act did the same for the political marketplace. The Fair Housing Act established an important base of law to combat housing discrimination.

Ultimately, reports Germany, "the War on Poverty did not end poverty". Instead, Germany reports, that "Many scholars also argue that War on Poverty programs assisted middle class Americans as much or more than poor Americans", such as doctors, lawyers, farmers, grocers, hospital administrators, medical professionals, social welfare professionals, and politicos who built homes, businesses, and careers.

Affirmative Action: According to "legal-dictionary.thefreedictionary. com/Affirmative%20action" affirmative action in the United States of America refers to employment programs required by federal laws and court orders to prevent employment discrimination based on race, color, sex, creed, and age. These affirmative action laws were based on the Civil Rights guarantees within the "Equal Protection Clause" of the Fourteenth Amendment to the Constitution of the United States. During the 1960's and 1970's, minorities and women sought increased equality in education and employment. However, affirmative action programs suffered setbacks when quotas were used to seek minority applications over more qualified applicants—Regents of the University of California v. Bakke, 1978.

In general, the issue for affirmative action is "whether the Equal Protection Clause of the Fourteenth Amendment can be employed to advance the welfare of one class of individuals for compelling social reasons even when that advancement may infringe in some way upon the life or liberty of another". So far, according to legal-dictionary.thefreedictionary. com/Afirmative%20action, "The continuing existence of affirmative action laws and programs suggests that so far, the Supreme Court's answer has been yes".

According to legal-dictionary.thefreedictionary.com/Afirmative%20action, "affirmative action plans are required by law to qualify for federal contracts. Plans required to qualify for federal contracts are enforced by the Office of Federal Contract Compliance Programs (OFCCP), an agency of the U.S. Labor Department". What this means is simply that qualified minority applicants for employment, like myself, must be sought for employment in order to qualify for federal contracts. According to "legal-dictionary", "affirmation action plans are subject to mandatory compliance procedures, which may include monitoring by review, conciliation of disputes, exclusion from federal contract work, or even suit by the Justice Department".

In my case, I got no special consideration for employment. I had to compete for employment through out my professional career, and many times I got only the worst of opportunities where no other qualified professional was available to do the work. But, at least I got opportunities for employment as long as I could perform difficult engineering tasks, and my employers with government contracts got credit for affirmative action.

However, affirmative action can go too far. In 2009, the Supreme Court of the United States ruled in favor of the twenty mostly white firefighters in New Haven, Connecticut where the city threw out test results for promotion when only one "Latino", and no African-Americans qualified for promotion. According to CNN.COM (29 June, 2009), the issue here was "whether there was a continued need for special treatment for minorities, or whether enough progress has been made to make existing laws obsolete, especially in a political atmosphere where an African-American (Barack Hussein Obama) occupies the White House".

In 2003, according to legal-dictionary.thefreedictionary.com, the U.S Supreme Court agreed to hear appeals of each decision in the "reverse discrimination law suit by white students against the University of Michigan's undergraduate school, and its law school. Here, "The administration of George W. Bush filed a brief opposing these programs. 'The method used by the University of Michigan to achieve this important goal is fundamentally flawed,' said the statement from President Bush". According to legal-dictionary.thefreedictionary.com "On June 23, 2003, the Court ruled 6-3 against the under graduate policy because it made each candidate's race the 'deciding' factor but up held 5-4 the law school's process because a compelling state interest exists for universities to create racially diverse campuses".

Social Security and Out Sourcing:

Not only that, Congress has taken money from Social Security in the trillions of dollars that will never be repaid, and now Social Security is jeopardized. And, because of the demands of labor unions, and the general public, the cost of doing business in America has gotten so high that Corporate America has had to out source manufacturing to countries with less expensive labor, as well as intellectual work, like legal work and customer service. This out sourcing has not only jeopardized jobs in America, it has also jeopardized inputs to Social Security. Why, because Americans' expensive life styles, that often as not require a two (2) income family to sustain, cost Corporate America too much, to say nothing about the fact that now there are not enough jobs to go around with unemployment nationwide somewhere in the ten (10) % range. It is estimated that now there are more women in the work force in America than there are men.

Illegal Immigration:

Yes, I remember when America belonged to America and America lived within our financial means. And, I remember when illegal immigrants did not have such a tremendous political and economic stronghold on America that they can hold America hostage with such political power that the President of the United States can order the U.S. Justice Department to file a Federal Law suit against the new Arizona Illegal Immigrant law to prevent Arizona from protecting itself from illegal immigrants.

National Debt and China:

Not only that, "Made in China" has empowered China so much, that China is practically the only country that can afford to buy U.S. Treasury Bonds with a national debt now over $13 Trillion dollars, and debt service in 2010 of over $200 Billion dollars, and a balance of trade in 2010 of about $49 billion dollars more imports than exports from America. "Made in China" has so empowered the economy of China that China has surpassed Japan as the number 2 economy in the world, the United States being the number 1 economy in the world, but is expected to surpass the United States by 2030 or 2040.

Middle East Oil and Terrorists:

Not only that, because of America's thirst for Middle East oil for the last fifty years, billions of U.S. dollars have poured into the Middle East and now terrorists can kill at will at just about any where in the world they choose. Might there be a coincidence.

Obama Health Care Reform:

Not only that, our current Democratic Congress and President Barack Hussein Obama have virtually decimated American health insurance financed by working America imposing requirements that health insurance was never intended to do. American health insurance was never intended to cover people that are unemployable and uninsurable, and was never intended to cover preexisting health conditions, or children to age of 26 years of age. And how does Congress plan to pay for this extravagant health care plan? Why, with astounding deficit spending. CNN.com reported on 25 September, 2009 that the Congressional Budget Office estimated that the House bill costs $1.1 trillion over 10 years, and that is only the beginning as more and more uninsurable people are poured into the National Health Care Plan. Yes, I remember when America belonged to America.

And now at least twenty (20) states have filed lawsuits in federal court in Florida to present their challenge to President Barack Hussein Obama's health care overhaul because they face harm from its requirements. And guess what, the Justice Department asked a federal judge to dismiss their lawsuit, but the twenty states, the National Federation of Independent Business and several individual taxpayers filed their response Friday in Pensacola federal court on Friday, 6 August, 2010.

And, recently Missouri voters cast 71 percent of their ballots in favor of a state measure to bar the government from requiring people to carry health insurance, and penalizing those who don't. This vote is not binding, but meaningfully represents America's pain and suffering caused by the Obama health care reform law.

And, there is a glimmer of hope for America to get relief from the destructive Obama administration's health care reform. Virginia Attorney General Ken Cuccinelli claimed in a federal lawsuit that "Congress doesn't have the authority to require citizens to buy health insurance or pay a penalty". On 2 August, 2010, Federal Judge Henry Hudson ruled in a 32-page decision that the law raises a host of complex constitutional issues, and denied the Justice Department's attempt to have the lawsuit dismissed. A hearing was set for 18 October, 2010.

But there is hope to declare the Obama health care reform law unconstitutional. As of 13 Dec, 2010, U.S. Federal Judge Henry E. Hudson ruled in favor of Virginia Attorney General Ken Cuccinelli that "requiring most people to get insurance or pay a fine, as the law mandates starting in 2014, is an unprecedented expansion of federal power and cannot be justified under Congress's authority to regulate interstate commerce", and as such is unconstitutional. [washingtonpost.com—14 Dec, 2010]

Further, on 31 January, 2011, Federal Judge Roger Vinson, in Pensacola, Fla., ruled in favor of now 26 states, that "as a result of the unconstitutionality of the 'individual mandate' that requires people to buy insurance, the entire law must be declared void". [foxnews.com—31 Jan, 2011]

As far as I can remember, there has never been such overwhelming states opposition to Federal law. The reason for the overwhelming states opposition to the Obama Health Care Reform Law is that the law is largely a Democratic initiative, with little or no Republican support. No law of such great destructive significance should ever be passed without bipartisan support. Even so, the Obama administration is still bent on trampling on state's rights, and individual rights. According to FoxNews. com, 31 Jan, 2011, "Department of Justice spokeswoman Tracy Schmaler said the department plans to appeal Vinson's ruling to the 11th Circuit Court of Appeals". And, according to Kate Pickert, Time Magazine 17 January, 2011, " . . . in the hands of a Supreme Court that tilts to the right, it's conceivable the individual mandate could fall". Not only that, according to Pickert, the fallout of a Supreme Court striking the individual mandate would be that "new insurance regulations requiring insurers to cover everyone, even those with pre-existing conditions, at the same prices would be jeopardized without the individual mandate". In other words, Obamacare would be a bust.

In the meantime, according to vindy.com/news, a Republican majority U.S. House of Representatives voted 19 January, 2011, to repeal the Obama Health Care Reform Law. In the meantime, also according to vindy.com/news, "congressional committees will propose changes to the existing legislation, calling for elimination of a requirement for individuals to purchase coverage, for example, and recommending curbs on medical malpractice lawsuits".

While the initiative to repeal the Obama health-care reform law failed in the U.S. Senate on Wednesday, 2 February, 2011, according to csmonitor.com/USA/Politics, this initiative is a significant start. While "the vast majority of spending in the (health care) law is mandatory", like "funds to expand coverage through Medicaid", according to Kate Pickert, Time Magazine, 17 January, 2011, the U.S. House of Representatives has the option to cut financing to Obamacare if only indirectly. According to Pickert, possible funding cuts in March, 2011, are funding "directly, or indirectly related to the Affordable Care Act, such as outlays for HHS (Health and Human Services) and the Internal Revenue Service".

Further, since the Democratic controlled U.S. Senate refused to consider the repeal of Obamacare, there will most assuredly be a backlash in the 2012 elections equal to the 2010 elections backlash that voted out Democratic representatives and voted in a Republican majority in the U.S. House of Representatives.

It is also possible that Obama will not be re-elected President of the United States of America in 2012, and Working America can reclaim our country and our health care insurance. Not only is Barack Hussein Obama's popularity down significantly (Gallup poll reveal conducted Feb. 2-5, 2011), some states, like Arizona, are considering passing legislation requiring Obama to present his birth certificate in order to get on the ballot in that state. However, according to FactCheck.org, "FactCheck.org staffers have now seen, touched, examined and photographed the original birth certificate, and concluded that it meets all of the requirements from the State Department for proving U.S. citizenship".

American Real Estate:

Not only that, I remember when American Real Estate belonged to America. From nreionline.com we read that in 2004, foreign investors plowed $13 billion into U.S. real estate, an increase of more than 60% over 2003, reports Real Capital Analytics. From nreionline.com we also read that German investors poured nearly $5 billion into U.S. commercial real estate in 2004, by far the largest source of foreign capital, and that Australians ranked No. 2 with $3.4 billion invested. German investors are looking for new ways to invest in American commercial real estate, and Australian commercial real estate investment is predominately in the office and retail. Further, according to Real Capital Analytics, Middle East invested nearly US$1.2 billion into U.S. real estate in 2004, up from just over $1 billion in 2003.

And, according to real estate services provider Jones Lang LaSalle foreign investors poured $163 billion into U.S. commercial real estate in the first half of 2007, a 37% increase over the first half of 2006. German and other European investors reportedly are largely acquired only stable downtown office buildings in only a handful markets such as New York, Washington, D.C., and Boston.

According to wsj.com, in 2010 China is in talks with Harvard University's endowment to buy its stakes in half a dozen U.S.-focused real-estate funds for about $500 million, and has commitments to invest $1 billion in Toronto and New York, and $1 billion in Hartford, Connecticut.

American Schools:

Not only that, I remember when American public schools were not held hostage by disruptive students that care very little about education, and students went to school to learn and respected each other and their teachers. Yes, I remember how America was fifty (50) years ago, and yes, I remember when America belonged to America, and we didn't have forced school busing.

In 2007 the Supreme Court of the United States tossed school diversity Race base Choice plans. Justice Clarence Thomas wrote "Simply putting students together under the same roof does not necessarily mean that the students will learn together or even interact," Justice Clarence Thomas further wrote. "Furthermore, it is unclear whether increased interracial contact improves racial attitudes and relations." The court struck down public school choice plans in Seattle, Washington, and Louisville, Kentucky, concluding they relied on an unconstitutional use of racial criteria, with the 5-4 vote reflecting the deep legal and social divide over the issue of race and education.

Intellectual and Spiritual Enlightenment:

For me intellectual and spiritual enlightenment includes findings of doctors, psychologists, scholars and theologians as found in a few publications I have acquired, studied and learned from. Here then is a list of those publications and a brief description of what they offer.

In teaching "Intellectual And Spiritual Enlightenment", I draw from a lifetime of personal experience, success, and study, as well as books that have opened the doors to success for me. These books include:

"Hidden Persuaders", Vance Packard;—1957,
(What makes us buy, believe and vote the way we do—Symbol Manipulation) published by David McKay Co, Inc—New York

"The Road Less Traveled", M. Scott Peck, M.D.—1978
(A new Psychology of Love, Traditional Values and Spiritual Growth) published by Simon & Schuster, New York

"Emotional Intelligence", Daniel Goleman, Ph. D. Psychology—1995
(The mechanics of emotion. Self-control, zeal, persistence and motivation are more important for success than IQ) published by Science Journalist; Bantam Books, New York

"The Measure of a Man", Dr. Gene A. Getz, psychologist—2004
(20 qualities of maturity Paul outlined in letters to Timothy & Titus in Christian Bible) published by Regal Books, Ventura California

"The Measure of a Woman" Dr. Gene A. Getz, psychologist, and Elaine A. Getz;—2004 (Paul's character profile for women outlined in letters to Titus in Christian Bible) published by Regal Books, Ventura California

"The Language of God", Francis S. Collins, head of the "Human Genome Project" studying DNA—the code of life—2006
(Faith in God and Faith in Science can be harmonious—science does not conflict with the Bible) published by Free Press, New York

"Divine Proportion—(Golden Ratio)", Priya Hemenway—2005
Divine Proportion reveals a number of simple patterns that are found throughout art, nature, and science, and has been as aesthetic guide in art and architecture for thousands of years published by Sterling Publishing Co, Inc—New York

"Change your Brain, Change you Life" Daniel G. Amen, M.D.; Amen Clinic for Behavioral Medicine—1998
(Brain imaging with SPECT technology to analyze mental illness— Single Photon Emission Computed Tomography) published by Three Rivers Press—New York

"The Brain in Love", Daniel G. Amen, M.D.—2007
(Your brain decides who is attractive to you and what to do with the feelings that develop. When the brain is dysfunctional, it causes you

to be impulsive, distracted, addicted, unfaithful, and hateful, ruining your chances for intimacy and love) published by Three Rivers Press—New York

"Magnificent Mind At Any Age" Daniel G. Amen, M.D.—2008
(When the brain is out of balance, you feel frustrated, or worse, depressed. By optimizing our brain function, we can develop qualities like increased memory and concentration, satisfying relationships, and goal oriented perseverance. This can be achieved though proper diet, natural supplements and vitamins, exercise, positive thinking and if needed, medication) published by Harmony Books—New York

"Gilgamesh" by John Gardner & John Maier—1984
(The story of Gilgamesh is one of the oldest recorded legends known to man, dating back to the invention of writing about 3000BC, discovered in Mesopotamia [modern Iraq]—an epic poem written on clay tablets in complex cuneiform alphabet) published by Alfred A. Knopf, Inc—New York

"Magnificent Mind at Any Age"—Dr. Daniel Amen—2008
This is a most revealing book by Dr. Daniel Amen about how our brain functions, and how to maximize our brain's potential. Dr Amen is a clinical neuroscientist, psychiatrist and brain imaging expert and he writes from 20 years experience treating patients at Amen Clinics across America using SPECT brain imaging to analyze his patients brain function. SPECT is Single Photon Emission Computed Tomography brain scan which measures blood flow and activity patterns. Dr. Amen also explains the benefits for our brains of proper diet, natural supplements, vitamins, exercise, thinking habits and medication. In this book, Dr Amen discusses how to deal with memory problems, anxiety, depression, ADD, and insomnia. published by Harmony Books—New York.

"Signature in the Cell", Dr Stephen Meyer, director of the Center for Science and Culture at the Discovery Institute in Seattle—2009
This book is a superb revelation of the intelligence of the human cell, and is a must read book for anyone that cares to be informed about the intelligent design of the human cell compared to the theories of Creationism and Darwinism. This book is not just theory, but is based on actual scientific studies based upon DNA. This book reveals the mystery of the digital code

in DNA, makes the case that Darwin did not refute Intelligent Design, and presents a new scientific view of the origin of life. Discovery Institute includes biologists, biochemists, chemists, physicists, philosophers and historians of science, and public policy and legal experts. Published by Harper Collins

CHAPTER 9

America, a Christian Nation

In chapter 8, I quoted B.F. Morris, writer of the book Christian Life and Character of the Civil Institutions of the United States, requested by United States Senator Charles Sumner from Massachusetts, and written in 1864, where he states that the Constitution of the United States of America contains no recognition of the Christian religion, nor even an acknowledgement of the providence of God in national affairs. When reminded of this in 1789, President George Washington states "I am persuaded you will permit me to observe that the path of true piety is so plain as to require but little political direction". And Washington continues, "To the guidance of the ministers of the gospel this important object is, perhaps more properly committed". [Christian Life and Character of the Civil Institutions of the United States, pp248, B.F. Morris, 1864]

Also in chapter 8, I wrote that B.F. Morris reminds us that "The various States who had sent these good and great men to the convention to form a Constitution had, in all their civil charters, expressed, as States and as a people, their faith in God, and the Christian religion". And Morris continues, "These statesmen, met to form a Constitution for a free and growing republic, were at times baffled in reaching desirable and harmonious results". [pp249, B.F. Morris, 1864]

In this chapter I provide history from that very same book, Christian Life and Character of the Civil Institutions of the United States, about the men and the State Constitutions from the states that sent their representatives to the Convention of Commissioners to write the Federal Constitution (Constitution of the United States) in 1787.

From John Hancock, first signer of the Declaration of Independence, "I have the most animating confidence that the present noble struggle for liberty will terminate gloriously for America. And let us play the men for our God, and for the cities of our God: while we are using the means in our power, let us humbly commit our righteous cause to the great Lord of the Universe, who loveth righteousness and hateth iniquity. [Christian Life and Character of the Civil Institutions of the United States, pp117, B.F. Morris, 1864]

And, from John Adams, the second President of the United States, "The Christian religion, as I understand it, is the brightness of the glory and the express portrait of the character of the eternal, self-existent, independent, benevolent, all-powerful, and all-merciful Creator, Preserver and Father of the universe, the first good, the first perfect, and the first fair". [pp117-118, B.F. Morris, 1864]

John Adams further says that "Religion and virtue are the only foundations, not only of the republicanism and of all free governments, but of social felicity under all governments and in all the combinations of human society". [pp 118, B.F. Morris, 1864]

And after the signing of the Declaration of Independence, Adams wrote, "The fourth day of July, 1776, will be a memorable epoch in the history of America. I am apt to believe that it will be celebrated by succeeding generations as the great anniversary festival. It ought to be commemorated as the day of deliverance, by solemn acts of devotion to Almighty God". [pp118, B.F. Morris, 1864]

From Benjamin Franklin, signer of the Declaration of Independence, "I believe in one God, the Creator of the universe. That he governs it by his Providence. That he ought to be worshipped. That the most acceptable service we render him is in doing good to his other children. That the soul of man is immortal, and will be treated with justice in another life respecting its conduct in this. There I take to be the fundamental points in all sound religion. As to Jesus of Nazareth, my opinion of whom you particularly desire, I think the system of morals, and his religion, as he left them to us, is the best the world ever saw, or is likely to see. [pp128, B.F. Morris, 1864]

Now, from Thomas Jefferson, writer of the Declaration of Independence, "I shall need the favor of that Being in whose hands we are, who led our fathers, as Israel of old, from their native land, and planted them in a country flowing with all the necessaries and comforts of life; who has covered our infancy with his providence, and our riper years with his wisdom and power; and to whose goodness I ask you to join with me in supplications that he will so enlighten the minds of your servants, guide their counsels, and prosper their measures, that whatsoever they do shall result in your good and shall secure to you the friendship and approbation of all nations." [pp134-135, B.F. Morris, 1864]

Jefferson continues, "Can the liberties of a nation be thought secure, when we have removed their only firm basis, a conviction in the minds of the people that these liberties are the gifts of God?—that they are not to be violated except with his wrath? Indeed, I tremble for my country when I reflect that God is just, and that his justice cannot sleep forever." [pp135, B.F. Morris, 1864]

And, now from Dr. Benjamin Rush, eminent physician and philanthropist, who signed the Declaration of Independence. John Adams said of Benjamin Rush that he "was as eminent as a Christian as he was distinguished for his influence in the councils of the country". John Adams further states of Rush, "He was an earnest advocate of introducing and reading the Bible daily, as a common-school book, in all public schools and in every seminary of learning". [pp140-141, B.F. Morris, 1864]

Dr. Benjamin Rush wrote, "My arguments in favor of the use of the Bible as a school book are founded, first, in the constitution of the human mind. The memory is the first faculty which opens in the minds of children". Rush continues, "My second argument in favor of the use of the Bible in schools, is founded upon an implied command of God, and upon the practice of several of the wisest nations of the world. In the sixth chapter of Deuteronomy we find the following words, which are directly to my purpose:—'And thou shalt love the Lord thy God with all thine heart, and with all thy soul, and with all thy might. And these words which I command thee this day shall be in thine heart: and thou shalt teach them diligently unto the children . . . ' ". [pp141, B.F. Morris, 1864]

And now we have Fisher Ames, distinguished lawyer and member of Congress from Massachusetts during the eight years of Washington's administration. Ames wrote, "Why, then should not the Bible regain the place it once held as a school-book? Its morals are pure, its examples captivating and noble. The reverence for the sacred book, that is thus early impressed, lasts long, and probably, if not impressed in infancy, never takes firm hold of the mind". [pp144, B.F. Morris, 1864]

In September, 1777, John Jay, Chief Justice of the Supreme court of New York, delivered a charge to the Grand Jury of Ulster county, "The

Constitution, however, has wisely declared that the 'liberty of conscience, thereby granted, shall not be so construed as to excuse acts of licentiousness or justify practices inconsistent with the peace or safety of the state.' In a word, the convention by whom that Constitution was formed were of opinion that the gospel of Christ, like the ark of God, would not fall . . . ". [pp149-151, B.F. Morris, 1864]

Is it possible President Barack Hussein Obama has not read the words of Justice John Jay when he ordered a Federal Law Suit against the State of Arizona Law protecting Arizona from illegal immigrants; the President who addresses an Islamic meeting about their religious rights in the United States of America, but refuses to hold a public ceremony in the East Room to recognize the National Day of Prayer as have previous Presidents Ronald Reagan and George H.W. Bush. It seems very appropriate to recognize the National Day of Prayer respecting the Christian origins of the United States of America, the faith of our founding fathers, and the many Christian faiths in America, established since the founding of the original thirteen colonies, and has nothing to do with any church clergy running the government of the United States of America.

And now we have James Madison, statesman, civilian of the Revolution, and Father of the Constitution, educated at Princeton College, under Dr. John Witherspoon, eminent Christian scholar, and patriot. James Madison wrote, "Recollecting always that, for every advantage which may contribute to distinguish our lot from that to which others are doomed by the unhappy spirit of the times, we are indebted to that Divine Providence whose goodness has been so remarkably extended to this rising nation, it becomes us to cherish a devout gratitude, and to implore from the same omnipotent source a blessing on the consultations and measure about to be undertaken for the welfare of our beloved country". [pp155-156, B.F. Morris, 1864]

And now James Monroe, active patriot and statesman of the Revolution and twice elected President, "I enter on the trust with my fervent prayers to the almighty, that he will be graciously please to continue to us that protection which he has already so conspicuously displayed in our favor". Monroe continues, "With a firm reliance on the protection of almighty God, I shall forthwith commence the duties of the high trust to which you have called me". [pp156-157, B.F. Morris, 1864]

Now, from William Livingston, Christian lawyer of New York, Christian statesman and Governor of New Jersey, "May the foundation of our infant state be laid in virtue and the fear of God, and the superstructure will rise gloriously and endure for ages. Then we may humbly expect the blessing of the Most High, who divides to nations their inheritance and separates the sons of Adam". [pp161, B.F. Morris, 1864]

And from George Washington, a devout Christian, who led the armies of the Revolution, who presided in the council that formed the old articles of Confederation, who was president of the convention that formed the Constitution, and who was the first President, "It is impossible to govern the universe without the aid of a Supreme Being. Let us, therefore, unite in imploring the supreme Ruler of nations to spread his holy protection over these United States". [pp166, B.F. Morris, 1864]

We continue with John Quincy Adams, eminent statesman and politician, and President of the United States, "In taking a survey of the concerns of our beloved country with reference to subject interesting to the common welfare, the first sentiment which impresses itself upon the mind is of gratitude to the Omnipotent Dispenser of all good, for the continuance of the signal blessings of his providence, and especially for that health which to an unusual extent has prevailed within our borders". Then, in letters to his son, between 1811 and 1813, Adams wrote, "So great is my veneration for the Bible, and so strong my belief that, when duly read and meditated upon, it is of all books in the world that which contributes to make men good, wise, and happy". [pp181-182, B.F. Morris, 1864]

Then we have Andrew Jackson, military hero and popular President, and a believer in the Christian religion and its evangelical doctrines. B.F. Morris writes that "In his public life at Washington, as President, he bore unvarying testimony to the divinity of the Bible, as a book essential to civil government and to the salvation of the soul". Jackson said in his second inaugural address, "It is my fervent prayer to that Almighty Being before whom I now stand, and who has kept us in his hands from the infancy of our republic to the present day, that he will so over-rule all my intentions and actions and inspire the hearts of my fellow-citizens, that we may be preserved from dangers of all kinds, and continue forever a united and happy people". B.F. Morris writes that in 1839 at the Hermitage church, Jackson made a public profession of his faith in Christ, and as tears trickled freely down his furrowed cheeks, all were overcome with emotion. On his death bed on 8 June, 1845, Jackson said to his family "My dear children and friends and servants, I hope and trust to meet you in heaven, both white and black". Jackson's final words, "Oh, do not cry, be good children and we will all meet in heaven". [pp 186,187190,191, B.F. Morris, 1864]

First Continental Congress:

From Daniel Webster, "No doubt the assembly of the first Continental Congress may be regarded as the era at which the Union of these States commenced. This even took place in Philadelphia, the city distinguished by the great civil events of our early history, on the 5th of September, 1774, on which day the first Continental Congress assembled. Delegates were present from New Hampshire, Massachusetts, Rhode Island, Connecticut, New York, New Jersey, Pennsylvania, Delaware, Maryland, Virginia, North Carolina, South Carolina, and Georgia". Webster continues, "At that day, probably, there could have been convened on no part of the globe an equal number of men possessing greater talents and ability, or animated by a higher and more patriotic motive". And Webster adds, "In such a constellation it would be invidious to point out the bright particular stars. Let me only say—what none can consider injustice to others—that George Washington was one of the number". [pp209-210, B.F. Morris, 1864]

John Adams writes, "The proceedings of the Assembly were introduced by religious observances and devout supplications to the throne of grace, for the inspiration of wisdom and the spirit of good counsels". John Adams further writes, "He was a stranger in Philadelphia, but had heard that Mr. Duche, an Episcopalian clergy-man, might be desired to read prayers to the Congress to-morrow morning". And, Adams continues, "Accordingly, next morning he appeared, with his clerk and in his pontificals, and read the collect for the seventh day of September, which was the thirty-first Psalm". And Adams further concludes, "After this, Mr. Duche, unexpectedly to everybody, struck out into an extemporaneous prayer, which filled the bosom of every man present". [pp211-213, B.F. Morris, 1864]

And, from Thatcher's Military Biography, an excerpt from Mr. Duche's prayer, "Be thou present, O God of wisdom, and direct the councils of this honorable assembly". And, "All this we ask in the name and through the merits of Jesus Christ, thy Son, our Saviour. Amen". [pp213, B.F. Morris, 1864]

Then reports Goodrich, "a minister, bound to forms, finding extemporaneous words to suit the occasion, and the Quaker, the Presbyterian, the Episcopalian, and the Rationalist,—some kneeling, some standing, but all praying, and looking to Heaven for wisdom and counsel in this hour of doubt, anxiety, and responsibility. Adams and Sherman, the Puritans, standing erect,—Thomson, the Quaker, with Washington, Henry, and other Episcopalians, kneeling, according to their creed, and all invoking wisdom from above, would make a touching and instructive picture". [pp213-214, B.F. Morris, 1864]

About the Sabbath, The Provincial Congress of Massachusetts, on the 15th of June, 1775, adopted the following, "And as among the prevailing sins of this day, which threaten the destruction of this land, we have reason to lament the frequent profanations of the Lord's day, or Christian Sabbath; many spending their time in idleness or sloth, other in diversions, and others in journeying, or business which is not necessary on that day; and as we earnestly desire that a stop may be put to this great and prevailing evil, it is therefore, 'Resolved, That it be recommended by this Congress to the people of all ranks and denominations throughout this colony, that they not only pay a religious regard to that day, and to the public worship of God thereon, but that they also use their influence to discountenance and suppress any profanation thereof in others. And it is further Resolved, That it be recommended to the ministers of the gospel to read this resolve to their several congregations, accompanied with such exhortations as they shall think proper." [pp224, B.F. Morris, 1864]

So then B.F. Morris writes, "This shows the religious sentiments and make us acquainted with the religious feelings of the members of the Continental Congress. That body of statesmen paid respect to religion by system, on principle, and in their official acts". [pp225, B.F. Morris, 1864]

Mr. Giddings said in Congress, "Thus our republic was founded on religious truth, and it was thus far emphatically a religious government. It has ever been sustained by the religious sentiment of the nation, and **it will only fail when this element shall be discarded by the people**. The Philadelphia Convention (continental Congress) will be remembered in coming time as the first, in the history of political parties of our nation to make religious truths the basis of its political action, and first to proclaim the rights of mankind as universal, to be enjoyed equally by princes and people, by rulers and the most humble. **It was the first to proclaim the fatherhood of god and the brotherhood of man**". [pp225, B.F. Morris, 1864]

Now regarding the Constitution of the United States and Religion, writes, Mr. Webster in the Convention of Massachusetts, in 1820, "**I am clearly of opinion that we should not strike out of the Constitution all recognition of the Christian religion. I am desirous, in so solemn a transaction as the establishment of a Constitution, that we should keep**

in it an expression of our respect and attachment to Christianity,—not indeed, to any of its peculiar forms, but to its general principles". [pp229, B.F. Morris, 1864]

State Constitutions and Christianity:

In 1778, the Constitution of **South Carolina** declared Christianity to be the fundamental law of the State, "That all persons and religious societies who acknowledge that there is one god, and a future state of rewards and punishments, and that god is to be publicly worshipped. The Christian Protestant religion shall be deemed, and is hereby constituted and declared to be, the established religion of the State. That all denominations of Christian Protestants in the State, demeaning themselves peaceably and faithfully, shall enjoy equal religious and civil privileges". [pp230, B.F. Morris, 1864]

The Constitution of **Pennsylvania**, adopted in 1776, that the Legislature shall consist of "persons most noted for wisdom and virtue," and that every member should subscribe the following declaration, "I do believe in one god, the Creator and Governor of the universe, the Rewarder of the good, and the Punisher of the wicked; and I acknowledge the Scriptures of the Old and New Testaments to be given by inspiration". [pp233, B.F. Morris, 1864]

The Constitution of **North Carolina** declares in 1776 "That no person who should deny the being of god, or the truth of the Protestant religion, or the divine authority of either the Old or New Testaments, or who should hold religious principles incompatible with the freedom and safety of the State, should be capable of holding any office or place of trust in the civil government of this State". [pp233, B.F. Morris, 1864]

In the first Constitution of **Delaware**, the following declaration is made, "That every citizen who should be chosen a member of either house of the Legislature, or appointed to any other office, should be required should be required to subscribe to the following declaration:—'I do profess faith in God the Father, and in the Lord Jesus Christ his only Son, and in the Holy Ghost, one God and blessed for evermore; and I do acknowledge the Holy Scriptures of the Old and New Testaments to be given by divine inspiration' ". [pp233, B.F. Morris, 1864]

Maryland formed a State Constitution in 1776, and the Declaration of Rights (Article 35) says, "That no other qualification ought to be required on admission to any office of trust or profit than such oath of support and fidelity to this State, and such oath of office, as shall be directed by this Constitution or the Legislature of this State, and a declaration of belief in the Christian religion". [pp234, B.F. Morris, 1864]

Now, from the Legislature of **New Jersey** to its delegates in Congress in 1777, "We hope you will habitually bear in mind that the success of the great cause in which the United States are engaged depends upon the favor and blessing of Almighty God; and therefore you will neglect nothing which is comopetent to the Assembly of the States for promoting *piety* and *good morals* among the people at large". [pp234, B.F. Morris, 1864]

And the State Constitution on **New Hampshire**, formed in 1776, declares "That morality and piety, rightly grounded on evangelical principles, would give the best and greatest security to government, and would lay in the hearts of men the strongest obligation to due subjection; and that the knowledge of these was most likely to be propagated by the institution of the public worship of the Deity and instruction in morality and religion". [pp235, B.F. Morris, 1864]

And, the Constitution of Georgia, adopted in 1777, declares that "all the members of the Legislature shall be of the Protestant religion". [pp235, B.F. Morris, 1864]

Then, the Constitution of **Vermont** declares that "Every sect or denomination of Christians ought to observe the Sabbath or Lord's Day, and keep up some sort of religious worship, which to them shall seem most agreeable to the revealed will of God". [pp235, B.F. Morris, 1864]

Then, the Constitution of the state of Connecticut, Part 7, sec.1, declares "It being the duty of all men to worship the Supreme Being, the great Creator and Preserver of the Universe, and their right to render that worship in the mode most consistent with the dictates of their consciences, no person shall, by law, be compelled to join or support, nor be classed with or associated to, any congregation, church, or religious association". [pp236, B.F. Morris, 1864]

Continue we then with the Charter of **Rhode Island**, granted by Charles II in 1682, which Constitution continued until 1843, and says "The object of the colonist is to pursue with peace and loyal minds, their sober, serious, and religious intentions of godly edifying themselves and one another in the holy Christian faith and worship . . .". [pp236, B.F. Morris, 1864]

The Constitution of the state of **New York** is not specific about an allegiance to Christianity. [pp236, B.F. Morris, 1864]

Current Constitutions of various States:

However, B.F. Morris concludes that "An examination of the present Constitutions of the various States, now existing, will show that the Christian religion and its institutions are recognized as the religion of the Government and the nation". Morris continues, "In perusing the thirty-four Constitutions of the United States, we find all of them recognizing Christianity as the well known and well established religion of the communities whose legal, civil, and political foundations they are". [pp237, B.F. Morris, 1864]

Appointing a Chaplain to General Convention:

And, in response to a plea by Dr. Franklin, "I will suggest, Mr. President, the propriety of nominating and appointing, before we separate, a chaplain to this convention, whose duty it shall be uniformly to assemble with us, and introduce the business of each day by an address to the Creator of the universe and the Governor of all nations, beseeching him to preside in our council, enlighten our minds with a portion of heavenly wisdom, influence our hearts with a love of truth and justice, and crown our labors with complete and abundant success". Morris states that, "The motion for appointing a chaplain was instantly put, and carried, with a solitary negative". [pp252, B.F. Morris, 1864]

Conclusion to General Convention:

To conclude, Washington writes on July 20, 1788, "We may with a kind of pious and grateful exultation trace the finger of Providence through those dark and mysterious events which first induced the States to appoint a general convention, and then led them one after another, by such steps as were best calculated to effect the object, into an adoption of the system recommended by the general convention, thereby, in all human probability, laying a lasting foundation for tranquility and happiness, when we had too much reason to fear that confusion and misery were coming upon us". [pp255, B.F. Morris, 1864]

Arriving in Philadelphia, in addressing the people, Washington spoke the following—"When I contemplate the interposition of Providence, as it has been visibly manifested in guiding us through the Revolution, in preparing us for the General Government, and in conciliating the good will of the people of America towards one another in its adoption, I feel myself oppressed and overwhelmed with a sense of the Divine munificence". [pp256, B.F. Morris, 1864]

In summary, Senator Frelinghuysen said in congress, in 1830, "That Christianity is the religion of this country, and as such is recognized in the whole structure of its government, and lies at the foundation of all our civil and political institutions,—in other words, that Christianity, as really as republicanism, is part and parcel of our laws,—is evident from the following:—'Such was the relation of Christianity to civil government in the several States as they existed prior to the formation of the present Federal Constitution and there is no evidence that in acceding to said Constitution they surrendered such relation either to the general or to their own particular governments'" [pp265-266, B.F. Morris, 1864]

CHAPTER 10

Intelligent Design

My 1977 Living Webster Encyclopedic Dictionary of the English Language contains no reference to Intelligent Design. From mariam-webster.com we read that intelligent design is "the theory that matter, the various forms of life, and the world were created by a designing intelligence".

From britanica.com we read that intelligent design is an "argument intended to demonstrate that **living organisms were created in more or less their present forms by an 'intelligent designer'** ". Also from britanica. com we read that "Intelligent design was formulated in the 1990s, primarily in the United States, as an explicit refutation of the theory of biological evolution advanced by Charles Darwin (1809-82), and builds "on a version of the argument from design for the existence of God advanced by the Anglican clergyman William Paley (1743-1805).

Wikipedia.org offers an extensive discussion on Intelligent Design with 247 references from which this chapter draws many quotes.

From "Top Questions-1.What is the theory of intelligent design?". Discovery Institute, 2007, and "Primer: Intelligent Design Theory in a Nutshell" (PDF), Intelligent Design and Evolution Awareness Center, 2004, wikipedia offers the following—**Intelligent design is the proposition that 'certain features of the universe and of living things are best explained by an intelligent cause, not an undirected process such as natural selection'** ". This, I believe, is the true and accurate description of Intelligent Design.

Then, wikipedia offers the following from Kitzmiller v. Dover Area School District, 04 cv 2688 (December 20, 2005)., Ruling p. 26 and Devon Williams (December 14, 2007). "CitizenLink: Friday Five: William

A. Dembski". Focus on the Family—"**Intelligent Design's leading proponents**—all of whom are associated with the Discovery Institute, a politically conservative think tank [Barbara Forrest, 2005, testifying in the Kitzmiller v. Dover, and American Association for the Advancement of Science, 2007]—**believe the designer to be the God of Christianity**". This statement is totally irrelevant because Intelligent Design is based solely on verifiable scientific facts, regardless of any pontification, or any religious, philosophical or theological inference based on these facts. In fact, there no such thing as "the God of Christianity". Yes, the proponents of Intelligent Design associated with the Discovery Institute are primarily Christian, and yes, Christians do believe in a Triune God, but many religious faiths, and even many people that do not subscribe to any organized religion believe in God. From my point of view, there is only one God, creator of the universe, our galaxy, solar system, our earth, and life on earth, which God was believed in long before organized religion (Geoffrey Parrinder, Professor emeritus of the comparative Study, of Religions at the University of London, "World Religions", 1971).

And then the following is offered in wikipedia, "**Advocates of intelligent design seek to fundamentally redefine science to accept supernatural explanations,** [Stephen C. Meyer and Paul A. Nelson (May 1, 1996). "CSC—Getting Rid of the Unfair Rules, A book review, Origins & Design] **arguing that intelligent design is a scientific theory under this new definition of science**".[Top Questions about intelligent design". Discovery Institute. http://www.discovery.org/csc/topQuestions. php. 2007] [comment—science is and has been and should not and cannot be redefined because science is a well established procedure of studying, documenting and explaining]

But, then wikipedia offers this opposing statement—"**The U.S. National Academy of Sciences has stated that "creationism, intelligent design, and other claims of supernatural intervention in the origin of life or of species are not science because they are not testable by the methods of science.**"[Science and Creationism: A View from the National Academy of Sciences, National Academy of Sciences. 1999.] [**WRONG—The problem that scientists have with the concept of Intelligent Design is not so much that human existence and the supporting earth/atmosphere/ moon/sun ecological systems is intelligent and extremely complex, but that Intelligent Design assumes/implies an intelligent designer, such as God, or an external supernatural intervention [Intelligent Design and Evolution Awareness Center. 2004; Numbers, Ronald L. (2006)].** Yes, this supernatural intervention is certainly not testable, but the genetic code, albeit the blueprint of life on earth is testable by such scientific processes as genetic engineering and genetic medicine that can alter the human genome, the genetic code and blueprint for human existence. Also, the ecology of the earth/atmosphere/moon/sun are essential to human existence, and can be and are being tested and altered as can be understood and observed scientifically. Further, no scientist could possibly create the *3 billion letters long DNA* that exists in each human cell, much of which is not understood, much less create life of any kind. And, if that is not enough, where did the Big Bang come from at the creation of our universe some 13.5 billion years ago? Was the Big Bang a random process also, or a supernatural event? I suggest that the Big Bang was a supernatural event.—Dionysius the Divine]

Wikipedia further offers that In Kitzmiller v. Dover Area School District U.S. District Judge John E. Jones III ruled that "**intelligent design is not science, that it 'cannot uncouple itself from its creationist, and thus religious, antecedents', and that the school district's promotion of it therefore violated the Establishment Clause of the First Amendment to the U.S. Constitution**".[Kitzmiller v. Dover Area School District, 04 cv 2688 (December 20, 2005)., Conclusion of Ruling] [Right, Intelligent Design is not a science, but a conclusion inferred from the scientific observation. However, it is ***ABSOLUTELY WRONG*** that *intelligent design 'cannot uncouple itself from its creationist, and thus religious, antecedents'.* Intelligent Design begins with observable scientific evidence of genetic engineering and genetic medicine that can alter the human genome, the genetic code and blueprint for human existence, the irreducible complexity of the human anatomy, and the ecological systems of the earth/atmosphere/moon/sun are essential to human existence.—Dionysius the Divine] [*Creationism typically starts with a religious text and tries to see how the findings of science can be reconciled to it*—Discovery Institute — Center for Science and Culture, 24 Oct, 2009] [I agree with this statement of Creationism. Creationism is the religious belief [Eugenie C. Scott (with forward by Niles Eldredge) (2004). Evolution vs. Creationism: An Introduction. Berkley & Los Angeles, California: University of California Press. p. 114.] that humanity, life, the Earth, and the universe are the creation of a supernatural agency. However the term is more commonly used to refer to religiously motivated rejection of certain biological processes, in particular evolution, as an explanation

**accounting for the history, diversity, and complexity of life on earth
(the creation-evolution controversy).[NCSE : National Center for
Science Education—Defending the Teaching of Evolution in Public
Schools.". Creationism. 2008]**

So where and when did the concept of "intelligent design" come
from? Again, from widipedia.org, well, from Plato, Aristotle, 4th century
BC, Cicero, 45BC, Thomas Aquinas, 13th century, and William Paley,
19th century. Sir Thomas Browne, 17th century, wrote "one of the earliest
examples of 'proof' of the wisdom of God and gives examples of intelligent
design in botany". But, still from wikipedia.org, most notably, Paley
wrote in his "Natural Theology" in 1802 with arguments that led to the
development of what was called **"natural theology" as the "study of
nature as a means to understand "the mind of God".**

Still from wikipedia.org, **"Similar postulating a divine designer is
embraced today by many believers in theistic evolution, who consider
modern science and the theory of evolution to be fully compatible with
the concept of a supernatural designer".**

Well, is this thinking strictly theological? Dr. Wernher Von Braun, who
is clearly a scientist, and not a theologian, believed in intelligent design
in the universe long before it became controversial topic propounded by
Steven Meyer and the Discovery Institute in the 1990's. Quoting from
the freerepublic.com, "For me, the idea of a creation is not conceivable
without invoking the necessity of design" Von Braun wrote in a letter
to the California State board of Education in 1972. Von Braun added
in his letter, "It is in scientific honesty that I endorse the presentation
of alternative theories for the origin of the universe, life and man in the
science classroom. It would be an error to overlook the possibility that the
universe was planned rather than happening by chance".

From adherents.com, Dr. Von Braun is quoted as saying, "It is so
obvious that we live in a world in which a fantastic amount of logic, of
rational lawfulness, is at work. We are aware of a large number of laws of
physics and chemistry and biology which, by their mutual interdependence,
make nature work as if it were following a grandiose plan from its earliest
beginnings to the farthest reaches of its future destiny. To me, it would be
incomprehensible that there should be such a gigantic master plan without
a master planner behind it. This master planner is He whom we call the
Creator of the Universe . . . One cannot be exposed to the law and order of
the universe without concluding that there must be a Divine intent behind
it all."

And, Dr. Von Braun continues with a fantastic statement, also from adherents.com, "Theologians are trying to describe the Creator; scientists are trying to describe His creation. Science and religion are not antagonists; on the contrary, they are sisters . . . While, through science, man tries to harness the forces of nature around him, through religion he tries to harness the forces of nature within him . . ."

What? That is not good enough for you! Do you think you are a superior scientist to Dr. Von Braun. Well, what about Dr. Francis Collins, head of the Human Genome Project, and one of the world's leading scientist. Dr. Collins worked with the study of DNA, the code of life, and Dr. Collins has personally discovered some of the scientific evidence for the common descent of all living creatures, even though he repudiates the materialist, atheistic worldview argued by many prominent Darwinists [The Language of God, Francis S. Collins, 2006]. What is Darwinism? From wikipedia. com, "Darwinism is a set of movements and concepts related to ideas of transmutation of species or evolution, including ideas with no connection to the work of Charles Darwin. [John Wilkins (1998). "How to be Anti-Darwinian"]".

In his book, the Language of God, the great scientist Dr. Collins writes of his discovery, "The **human genome consists of all the DNA** of our species, the hereditary code of life. This newly revealed text was *3 billion letters long, and written in a strange and cryptographic four-letter code. Such is the amazing complexity of the information carried within each cell of the human body, that a live reading of the code at a rate of one letter per second would take thirty-one years, . . . day and night*. Printing these letters out in regular font size on normal bond paper and binding them all together would result in a tower the height of the Washington Monument". At the White House with President Clinton, Dr. Collins stated, "**It's a happy day for the world. It is humbling for me, and awe-inspiring, to realize that we have caught the first glimpse of our own instruction book, previously known only to God**". So, while Dr. Collins rejects young-earth creationism and intelligent design, this is Intelligent Design at its most basic meaning, and Dr. Collins maintains that "Faith in God and faith in science can be harmonious—combined into one worldview".

Now, again from wikipedia.org, "**Intelligent design in the late 20th and early 21st century is a development of natural theology that seeks to change the basis of science and undermine evolutionary theory.** [William Paley, 1803; David Steinmetz, 2005; William Dembski, 2001]

As evolutionary theory has expanded to explain more phenomena, the examples that are held up as evidence of design have changed, though the essential argument remains the same: *complex systems imply a designer.* Past examples have included the eye (the ear) and the feathered wing; current examples are typically biochemical: protein functions, blood clotting, and bacterial flagella". [

Now, consider Rene Descartes, French mathematician, philosopher and physicist, a great scientist who philosophized—"I think, therefore I am; I am therefore I think". Knowing what we know about human physiology, the earth and our universe, can we not now **infer**, "I think of God, therefore God exists; God exists, therefore I think of God". Inference is merely a logical conclusion drawn from observable evidence.

Now, let's regress a little back to Dr. Daniel Amens, great neuroscientist and psychiatrist. In his book, "Magnificent Mind at Any Age", Dr. Daniel Amen writes "The brain is the most complicated organ in the universe. It is estimated that the brain has one hundred billion nerve cells and more connections in it than there are stars in the universe." Dr. Amen continues "If you take a piece of brain tissue the size of a grain of sand, it contains a hundred thousand neurons and a billion connections all communicating with one another." [pp 13]. More evidence to consider about intelligent design, even if it originated by evolution from the primordial soup on earth 4.1 billion years or so ago.

Now, let's pontificate a little. We could say that God, or the creator of the universe, and earth and life on earth, cooked the primordial soup through many stages, from the beginning of the earth about 4.5 billion years ago, whether by random process, natural selection, adaptation, or mutation, until:

1. the ***development of single cell prokaryotes, which lack a cell nucleus, about 3.5 billion years ago*** [Wilde SA, Valley JW, Peck WH, Graham CM (January 2001); Schopf JW, Kudryavtsev AB, Agresti DG, Wdowiak TJ, Czaja AD (March 2002)],
2. to the appearance of molecular biomarkers that indicate photosynthesis, and demonstrate that ***life on Earth was widespread by 2.4 billion years ago*** [Cavalier-Smith, Thomas; Brasier, Martin; Embley, T. Martin (2006); Summons, Roger E.; et al. (2006)],
3. to the ***development of complex cells called eukaryotes, about 1.6-2.1 billion years ago*** [Berkner, L. V.; Marshall, L. C. (1965). "On the Origin and Rise of Oxygen Concentration in the Earth's

Atmosphere". Journal of Atmospheric Sciences 22 (3): 225-261.],
to

4. the *Cambrian explosion,* 530 million years ago, *when multicellular life forms began to proliferate.*[Kirschvink, J. L. (1992). Schopf, J.W.; Klein, C. and Des Maris, D. ed. Late Proterozoic low-latitude global glaciation: the Snowball Earth. The Proterozoic Biosphere: A Multidisciplinary Study. Cambridge University Press. pp. 51-52], to

5. the **Permian Extinction, Earth's largest extinction 251 million years ago that wiped out over two-thirds of land-dwelling vertebrates and 95 percent of ocean-dwelling species,** [Bob Strauss, **dinosaurs.about.com**] **to**

6. the *Triassic Period,* 250-208 Million Years Ago, when the following appeared: the **therapsids** (mammal-like reptiles), **archosaurs,** from which the first **dinosaurs like Herrerasaurus and Eoraptor evolved**, and the first **prehistoric crocodiles and pterosaurs,** and **primitive reptiles called pelycosaurs** (like Dimetrodon)., and when mammal-like reptiles evolved into the *first mammals* late in he Triassic period [Bob Strauss, **dinosaurs.about.com**] to

7. The **Jurassic Period,** 208 to 144 Million Years Ago, following the **Triassic-Jurassic Extinction about 205 Million years ago**, [Bob Strauss, **dinosaurs.about.com**] when gigantic dinosaurs appeared, such as

   A. **sauropods** like the *Vulcanodon*, about 20 feet long and 4 tons, and the *Barapasaurus*, about 60 feet long and 20 tons and

   B. **Brachiosaurus,** About 85 feet long and 50 tons, and

   C. **Diplodocus,** About 150 feet long and 25-50 tons.

   D. theropod dinosaurs like *Allosaurus*, about 40 feet long and 3 tons, and **Megalosaurus**, About 30 feet long and 2 tons,

   E. and the stegosaurs, typified by *Stegosaurus*, About 20 feet long and 2 tons, and

   F. The *first, mouse-sized early mammals.*

8. The **Cretaceous Period,** 144-65 Million Years go, ended by the **Cretaceous-Tertiary Extinction), [Bob Strauss, dinosaurs. about.com]** when dinosaurs appeared, such as **raptors** (small—to

medium-sized, bipedal, *carnivorous* dinosaurs and **tyrannosaurs,** such as **Tyrannosaurus Rex,** about 40 feet long and weighed 7 or 8 tons,. other varieties of **theropods**, including the fleet-footed ornithomimids ("bird mimics"), the strange, feathered **therizinosaurs,** and small, feathered dinosaurs, including the uncommonly intelligent **Troodon**. the lightly armored **titanosaurs,**.

A. The **Ceratopsians** (horned, frilled dinosaurs) like Styracosaurus, about 17 feet long and 3 tons, and **Triceratops**, about 30 feet long and 5 tons

B. **Hadrosaurs**, duck-billed dinosaurs, roaming the plains of North America and Eurasia in vast herds. the last dinosaurs left standing by the time of the **Cretaceous-Tertiary Extinction**, about 65 to 70 million years ago, were the plant-eating **ankylosaurs**, notably **Ankylosaurus**, about 30 feet long and 5 tons, and **Euoplocephalus**, about 20 feet long and 2 tons, and the **pachycephalosaurs** thick-headed lizards. *early mammals* would only emerge from the shadows after the dinosaurs had gone extinct.

C. The *first, mouse-sized early mammals*.

9. The earliest hominid's (human like creatures), **Sahelanthropus tchadensis,** with a small brain size of about 350cc, appearing on earth 6 to 7 million years ago, considered the time of the split between humans and living apes [Lewin 1987]. The following sequence of hominids is not considered by **talkorigins.org** to represent an evolutionary sequence:

A. **Orrorin tugenensis**—about 6 million years old; bipedal and tree climbing, limb bones are about 1.5 times larger than those of Lucy (about 3.2 million years ago; bipedal, about 107 cm, 3'6", tall and about 28 kg, 62 lbs, in weight)

B. **Ardipithecus ramidus**—about 4.4 million years; about 120 cm (3'11") tall and weighed about 50 kg (110 lbs), brain was small, about the size of a chimpanzee. Ardipithecus ramidus, nicknamed "Ardi," is a hominid species that lived 4.4 million years ago in what is now Aramis, Ethiopia.

C. **Australopithecus anamensis**—between 4.2 and 3.9 million years ago in Kenya; primitive features in the skull, and advanced features in the body.

D. **Australopithecus afarensis**—between 3.9 and 3.0 million years ago (**Lucy—bipedal, about 107 cm (3'6")** **tall (small for her species) and about 28 kg (62 lbs) in** **weight.**); an apelike face with a low forehead, a bony ridge over the eyes, a flat nose, and no chin; had protruding jaws with large back teeth; **skull is similar to that of a** *chimpanzee* **;** cranial capacity varied from about 375 to 550 cc; pelvis and leg bones far more closely resemble those of modern man, and leave no doubt that they were bipedal ; height varied between about 107 cm (3'6") and 152 cm (5'0").

E. **Kenyanthropus platyops**—about 3.5 million years ago in Kenya; size of the skull is similar to A. afarensis and A. africanus, and has a large, flat face and small teeth;

F. **Australopithecus africanus**—between 3 and 2 million years ago, all the australopithecines are found only in Africa; similar to afarensis but slightly bigger; Brain size between 420 and 500; teeth and jaws much larger than those of humans, but far more similar to human teeth than to those of apes (Johanson and Edey 1981); shape of the jaw is now fully parabolic, like that of humans, and the size of the canine teeth is further reduced compared to afarensis.

G. **Australopithecus garhi**—(no date avail); known from a partial skull; extremely large size teeth, especially the rear ones, and a primitive skull.

H. **Australopithecus aethiopicus**—between 2.6 and 2.3 million years ago; mixture of primitive and advanced traits. The brain size is very small, at 410 cc, and parts of the skull, particularly the hind portions, are very primitive, most resembling afarensis; brain size is very small, at 410 cc, and parts of the skull, particularly the hind portions, are very primitive, most resembling afarensis.

I. **Australopithecus sediba**—between 1.78 and 1.95 million years ago; possible candidate for the ancestor of Homo (Berger et al. 2010, Balter 2010) ; bipedal with long arms suitable for climbing, with a number of humanlike traits in the skull, teeth and pelvis.; boy's skull has a volume of 420 cc, about 130 cm (4'3"); may be an ancestor of robustus and boisei.

J. **Australopithecus robustus**—between 2 and 1.5 million years ago; body similar to africanus, but a larger skull and teeth; relatively small front teeth, but massive grinding teeth in a large lower jaw; average brain size is about 530 cc; skull more heavily built, has never been a serious candidate for being a direct human ancestor.

K. **Australopithecus boisei**—between 2.1 and 1.1 million years ago; similar to robustus, but the face and cheek teeth were even more massive, some molars being up to 2 cm across similar to robustus, but the face and cheek teeth were even more massive, some molars being up to 2 cm across; brain size is very similar to robustus, about 530 cc; boisei and robustus possibly variants of the same species; skull more heavily built, has never been a serious candidate for being a direct human ancestor.

L. **Homo habilis**—between 2.4 and 1.5 million years ago, very similar to australopithecines; habilis and all the australopithecines are found only in Africa; face is still primitive, but it projects less than in africanus; back teeth are smaller, but still considerably larger than in modern humans; average brain size, at 650 cc; brain shape is more humanlike; possibly capable of rudimentary speech; about 127 cm (5'0") tall, and about 45 kg (100 lb) in weight.

M. **Homo rudolfensis (sub specie of habilis)**—suggested species which is accepted by many scientists because habilis specimens have too wide a range of variation for a single species.

N. **Homo georgicus**—about 1.8 million years old in Dmanisi, Georgia; fossils seem intermediate between habilis and erectus; brain sizes of the skulls vary from 600 to 780 cc; height, estimated from a foot bone, about 1.5 m (4'11").

O. **Homo erectus**—between 1.8 million and 300,000 years ago; like habilis, the face has protruding jaws with large molars, no chin, thick brow ridges, and a long low skull, with a brain size varying between 750 and 1225 cc;

skeleton implies greater strength than modern humans; erectus was wide-ranging, and has been found in Africa, Asia, and Europe; evidence is that erectus probably used fire, and their stone tools are more sophisticated than those of habilis.

P. **Homo ergaster**—between 1.8 million and 300,000 years ago; some scientists classify some African erectus specimens as belonging to a separate species, Homo ergaster; erectus would have a larger brain size.

Q. **Homo antecessor**—about 780,000 years ago in spain, making them the oldest confirmed European hominids; many scientists are doubtful about the validity of antecessor

R. **Homo sapiens**—about 500,000 years ago; skulls have features of both Homo erectus and modern humans; brain size is larger than erectus and smaller than most modern humans, averaging about 1200 cc; many fossils between 500,000 and 200,000 years ago are difficult to classify as erectus or archaic sapiens.

S. **Homo sapiens neanderthalensis (Neanderthal Man)**—between 230,000 and 30,000 years ago, throughout Europe and the Middle East; average brain size is slightly larger than that of modern humans, about 1450 cc; brain case is longer and lower than that of modern humans, with a marked bulge at the back of the skull. Like erectus, they had a protruding jaw and receding forehead; midfacial area also protrudes, a feature that is not found in erectus or sapiens. Neanderthals mostly lived in cold climates, and their body proportions are similar to those of modern cold-adapted peoples: short and solid, with short limbs; men averaged about 168 cm (5'6") in height, and their bones are thick and heavy, and show signs of powerful muscle attachments; were formidable hunters, and are the first people known to have buried their dead.

T. **Homo floresiensis**—Indonesian island of Flores, possibly a dwarf form of Homo erectus; fully bipedal, used stone tools and fire, and hunted dwarf elephants.

U. **Homo sapiens** (modern humans)—about 195,000 years ago; brain size of about 1350 cc. The forehead rises sharply, eyebrow ridges are very small or more usually absent, the chin is prominent, and the skeleton is very slender.

(1) **Cro-Magnon**—about 40,000 years ago, usually just refers to Europeans— culture, tool kits started becoming more sophisticated, using a wider variety of raw materials such as bone and antler, and containing new implements for making clothing, engraving and sculpting. Fine artwork, in the form of decorated tools, beads, ivory carvings of humans and animals, clay figurines, musical instruments, and spectacular cave paintings appeared over the next 20,000 years (Leakey 1994). Some scientist believe that Cro-Magnon exterminated Neanderthal man

(2) **Paleolithic humans**—about 30,000 years ago; about 20 to 30% more robust than the modern condition in Europe and Asia. These are considered *modern humans*, although they are sometimes termed primitive.

(3) **Mesolithic humans**—about 10,000 years ago; about 20 to 30% more robust than the modern humans in Europe and Asia.

Returning to our pontification, do you see where the great minds of the world converge on "Intelligent Design"? The thinking of great scientists, philosophers, theologians all point to the reality of "Intelligent Design".

Now, continuing with the discussions for and against Intelligent Design the issue of complexity is argued pro and con. Basically, William Dembski, mathematician, philosopher, and theologian, **states that "when something exhibits specified complexity (i.e., is both complex and "specified", simultaneously), one can infer that it was produced by an intelligent cause rather than being the result of natural processes", and further defines** *complex specified information* **(CSI) as anything with a less than 1 in 10150 chance of occurring by (natural) chance.**

Opposing Dembski on the issue of complexity are John Wilkins and Wesley Elsberry who characterize Dembski's "explanatory filter" as eliminative, because it eliminates explanations sequentially: first regularity, then chance, finally defaulting to design. They argue that this procedure is flawed as a model for scientific inference because the

asymmetric way it treats the different possible explanations renders it prone to making false conclusions. [John S. Wilkins, Wesley R. Elsberry (2001). "The Advantages of Theft over Toil: The Design Inference and Arguing from Ignorance". Biology and Philosophy 16: 711-724.]

I will not comment on these differences on the issue of complexity because I do not see this type of argument as meaningful. The complexity that I see is more an issue of "irreducible complexity" which I will present shortly in considering the **complexity of human anatomy and the ecological systems of the earth/atmosphere/moon/sun that are essential to human existence.**

The next controversy of pros and cons for Intelligent Design is that of "universal constants". Center for Science and Culture fellow, Guillermo Gonzalez, states essentially that **"universal constants make matter and life possible** and are argued not to be solely attributable to chance". These **constants** include the **values of fundamental physical constants, the relative strength of nuclear forces, electromagnetism, and gravity between fundamental particles, as well as the ratios of masses of such particles.** Gonzalez further argues that "if any of these values were even slightly different, the universe would be dramatically different, making it impossible for many chemical elements and features of the Universe, such as galaxies, to form". [Guillermo Gonzalez (2004). The Privileged Planet: How Our Place in the Cosmos is Designed for Discovery. Washington, DC: Regnery Publ . . .]

Scientists have generally responded that this argument cannot be tested and is therefore not science but metaphysics. Some scientists argue that even when taken as mere speculation, these arguments are poorly supported by existing evidence. [The Panda's Thumb. review of The Privileged Planet]

The problem that I see here is that universal constants don't prove Intelligent Design, but rather are a measure or indication of Intelligent Design. What are such constants? Well, to name a few:

1. **Lets start with a simple constant, The Golden Ratio, Phi, (aka Divine Proportion) defined by Euclid, who lived approximately 325 to 265 BC, in his book, Elements, to be the ratio of the sum of 2 line sements (a+b) to the largest segment "b", to be the same as the ratio of the greater segment, "b", to the smaller segment, "a", and is equal to the irrational number, Phi, 1.6180339 . . .**

Phi is important because it appears in nature, such as the center of an apple, the shape of many shells, and the horns of some animals [Priya Hemenway, Divine Proportion, 2005]. According to Priya, the Golden Ratio also appears in clay tablets from ancient Babylon (1900 to 1600 BC), the pyramid at Giza and the Parthenon in Athens, art, architecture and music.

2. Atomic weights and electronic configuration of the elements
3. speed of light in a vacuum = 299792.458km/sec
4. velocity of sound in air at 20o C = 344 m/sec
5. acceleration of gravity on earth = 9.8 m/sec/sec
6. Planck constant = 6.6261×10^{-34} Js
7. electron charge = 1.6022×10^{-19} C
8. electron mass = 9.1094×10^{-31} kg
9. proton mass = 1.6726×10^{-27} kg
10. Boltzman constant = 1.3807×10^{-23} J/K
11. Human body (Dr. James Denison) consists of:

A. 206 bones wrapped with 650 muscles and seven miles of nerve fibers
B. 100 million receptors in the human eyes
C. 24,000 fibers in the human ear
D. 36 million heart beats every year
E. 60,000 miles of veins and arteries
F. 13 trillion nerve cells in the human brain

The next controversy of pros and cons for Intelligent Design is that of "the concept of God". Very simply, the problem here is that opponents of the concept of Intelligent Design have a problem with the fact that by-and-large the proponents of Intelligent Design believe in God, and further that these proponents of Intelligent Design believe that the Intelligent Designer is the Christian God, to the exclusion of all other religions. [Kitzmiller v. Dover Area School District, 04 cv 2688 (December 20, 2005), Ruling p. 26; William A. Dembski, Devon Williams (December 14, 2007). "CitizenLink: Friday Five"; Dembski, "Touchstone Magazine. Volume 12, Issue4: July/August, 1999] Well, what difference does that make? While the belief that the Christian God excludes the God of all other religions is a preposterous suggestion/ belief, it has no impact on Intelligent Design because Intelligent Design does not depend on any religious belief. Intelligent Design depends solely on scientific evidence. The human existence of diverse cultures and their attendant religious beliefs is the same complexity of human anatomy and the same ecological systems of the earth/atmosphere/moon/sun essential to human existence. All humans on this earth benefit from the same earth, the same oxygen in our atmosphere, and the same rain, and the same sun and moon, regardless of our culture or religious beliefs. Intelligent Design applies to all races, cultures and religious beliefs.

And the arguments against Intelligent Design gets even more ridiculous. Jerry Coyne states that "in light of the evidence, 'either life resulted not from intelligent design, but from evolution; or the intelligent designer is a cosmic prankster who designed everything to make it look as though it had evolved' ".[August 22-29, 2005, "The Case Against Intelligent Design". The New Republic 233 (8/9): 21-33] Again, while the mechanism/process for the creation of the earth and life on earth and existence of Intelligent Design is of interest in scientific theory, such as random process, natural selection, mutation, or adaptation, the speculative intentions of an Intelligent Designer is and should not even be an issue. It is preposterous to interject such arguments against Intelligent Design. Intelligent Design is just intelligent, period.

Asserting the need for a designer of complexity also raises the question "What designed the designer?"[Donald E. Simanek. "Intelligent Design: The Glass is Empty"] Once again, it matters not what designed the designer of Intelligent Design. Donald Simanek can ponder that question all he wants. Intelligent Design is just intelligent by virtue of irreducible complexity and the undeniable order of life on earth, the complexity of human anatomy and the ecological systems of the earth/atmosphere/moon/sun essential to human existence. Intelligent Design depends only on scientific evidence, including the human genome, the DNA blueprint of human existence, which no scientist can create. The benefit of scientific evidence is that the more scientific evidence of life on earth we have, the more we have to adjust the boundaries of religious faith and beliefs, except of course for the most basic of religious beliefs such as heaven, hell, life after death, God, reincarnation, Devine intervention, etc.

In general the major proponent of Intelligent Design, the Discovery Institute, has provoked opposition with it stated agenda the defeat the theory of evolution in favor a science consonant with Christian and theistic conviction:

> The overall goal of the movement is to "defeat [the] materialist world view" represented by the theory of evolution in favor of "a science consonant with Christian and theistic convictions". [Wedge Document, Discovery Institute, 1999]
>
> Phillip E. Johnson stated that the goal of intelligent design is to cast creationism as a scientific concept. [Johnson 2004. Christianity.ca. Let's Be Intelligent About Darwin; Johnson 1999. Reclaiming America for Christ Conference. How the Evolution Debate Can Be Won]

Where has the opposition come from. Well, for one, the Discovery Institutes agenda has provoked naturalist Barbara Forrest. From wikipedia, we read that "*Barbara Forrest*, who has written extensively on the movement, and describes this as "being due to the Discovery Institute's obfuscating its agenda as a matter of policy. She has written that the movement's 'activities betray an aggressive, systematic agenda for promoting not only intelligent design creationism, but the religious world-view that undergirds it'.["The Wedge at Work: Intelligent Design Creationism and Its Critics".—Barbara Forrest (infidels. org—Naturalism, 2001).]"

Also from wikipedia, "Both Johnson and Dembski cite the Bible's Gospel of John as the foundation of intelligent design.[Dembski: "Intelligent design is just the Logos theology of John's Gospel restated in the idiom of information theory," Touchstone Magazine. Volume 12, Issue4: July/August, 1999; Johnson 1999. Reclaiming America for Christ Conference. How the Evolution Debate Can Be Won]"

From wikipedia we read that "Barbara Forrest contends such statements reveal that leading *proponents see intelligent design as essentially religious in nature*, not merely a scientific concept that has implications with which their personal religious beliefs happen to coincide. [Barbara Forrest. Expert Testimony. Kitzmiller v. Dover (2005)—does involve a supernatural creator, and that is my objection]"

Well now, how interesting that Barbara Forrest (Ph.D. in philosophy from Tulane University, Humanist and professor of philosophy at Southeastern Louisiana University in Hammond, Louisiana) should so strongly oppose the concept of Intelligent Design as science because the proponents of Intelligent Design, i.e. Dembski, believe that Intelligent Design infers an intelligent designer, i.e. a supernatural creator. Barbara Forrest has successfully characterized Intelligent Design as *intelligent design creationism*, which it is not. Repeating, Intelligent Design is just intelligent by virtue of irreducible complexity and the undeniable balance and order of life on earth, the complexity of human anatomy and the ecological systems of the earth/atmosphere/moon/sun essential to human existence. Intelligent Design depends only scientific evidence, including the human genome, the DNA blueprint of human existence, which no scientist can create, and it matters not what religious inferences are arrived at by and with and because of scientific knowledge and information. Witness again the words of Francis S. Collins—"It's a happy day for the world. It is humbling for me, and awe-inspiring, to realize that we have caught the first glimpse of our own instruction book, previously known only to God".

And what is humanism? Simply speaking humanism is a secular ideology which believes in reason, ethics, and justice, while specifically rejecting supernatural and religious dogma, as a basis of morality and decision making. And why does humanism exist? Humanism exists because of increasing human intelligence and increasing scientific knowledge and reason. The British Humanistic Religious Association was formed as one of the earliest forerunners of contemporary chartered Humanist organizations in 1853 in London. This early group was democratically organized, with male and female members participating in the election of the leadership, and promoted knowledge of the sciences, philosophy, and the arts.[Morain, Lloyd and Mary (2007). Humanism as the Next Step. Washington, D.C.: Humanist Press] The original signers of the first Humanist Manifesto of 1933, declared themselves to be religious humanists. Because in their view, traditional religions were failing to meet the needs of their day, the signers of 1933 declared it a major necessity to establish a religion that was a dynamic force to meet the needs of the day. Since then two additional Manifestos were written to replace the first. [Wilson, Edwin H. (1995). The Genesis of a Humanist Manifesto. Amherst, NY: Humanist Press; Kurtz, Paul (1995). Living Without Religion: Eupraxophy. Amherst, NY: Prometheus Books]

So, now, what is the problem with Intelligent Design, besides the fact that proponents believe that Intelligent Design infers an intelligent designer, i.e. a supernatural influence. Well, the problem appears to be created by proponents of Intelligent Design. From wikipedia we read that "A key strategy of the intelligent design movement is convincing the general public that there is a debate among scientists about *whether life evolved*. The intelligent design movement creates this controversy in order to convince the public, politicians and cultural leaders that schools should '*Teach the Controversy*'.[Shaw, Linda (Seattle Times) March 31, 2005]"

But, according to scientists, there is no controversy. It does appear that the proponents of Intelligent Design create the controversy. From widipedia we read that "in fact, *there is no such controversy in the scientific community*; the scientific consensus is that life evolved. [National Association of Biology Teachers—2006-09-27][Interacademy Panel on International Issues (67 countries). June 21, 2006][American Association for the Advancement of Science (February 16, 2006).]

From my point of view and my study of life on earth beginning with single cell organisms 3.5 billion years ago, multi-cell organisms 530 million years ago, early amphibians 416 to 360 million years ago, dinosaurs, marine life, avian life, plant life and early mammals 250 to 65 million years ago, early hominids about 6 million years ago, to *Neanderthal man* 230 million years ago, and European *Cro-Magnon* about 40,000 years ago, life on earth does appear to have evolved over a period of time simply because it is incomprehensible that something can be created out of nothing, except for the first *protobionts*, organic molecules from which single cell organisms are thought to have evolved [Wilde SA, Valley JW, Peck WH, Graham CM (January 2001)]. Again, from wikipedia, "However, among a very significant proportion of the general public in the United States the major concern is whether conventional evolutionary biology is compatible with belief in God and in the Bible, and how this issue is taught in schools."[Wallis, Claudia (The Evolution Wars". Time Magazine, August 7, 2005).]

Well, Dr. Francis Collins, director of the Human Genome Project, maintains that "Faith in God and faith in science can be harmonious—combined into one worldview". However, the concept of God does not appear to me to have a place in any science subject, including biology, which deals with humanly observable facts. I continue to maintain that God, a supernatural influence and intelligent designer and creator of the universe, our solar system and earth, and life on earth is a theological concept, that can be logically inferred from the Intelligent Design, balance and order of earth's ecological systems, and our solar system that make life on earth possible, as well the magnificent biological structure not only of human anatomy, but of all animal, plant, aviary, marine, and insect life on earth. The study of God in public schools does appear to me to have a place in sociological and historical studies of diverse religions, so long as it is properly taught objectively without any attempt to proselyte for specific faiths. It seems to me that it is at this point that the concept of Intelligent Designer can be taught, and so long as no one religion is presented as dominant.

Continuing with wikipedia, **"In the Kitzmiller v. Dover case, the court ruled that intelligent design was a religious and creationist position, finding that God and intelligent design were both distinct from the material that should be covered in a science class.[.**" Kitzmiller v. Dover Area School District, 04 cv 2688 (December 20, 2005)., Ruling, p. 24]**"

Well now we come to the crux of the whole matter of Intelligent Design vs Science, principally because of the expert testimony of people like Barbara Forest who successfully associated Intelligent Design with the religious beliefs of the people associated with the Discovery Institute. From wikipedia we read that "Stuart Burgess, Phillip E. Johnson, William Dembski, and Stephen C. Meyer are *evangelical Protestants*, and Michael Behe is a *Roman Catholic*, while Jonathan Wells is a member of the *Unification Church*". Intelligent Design is not a religious and creationist position and, in the face of all the human logic and reason known to man, Intelligent Design is simply a logical conclusion about the obvious balance and order in the universe, the earth's ecological systems that make all life on earth possible, including the human anatomy, as well as the anatomy of all animal, aviary, and plant life on earth, it does not and should not matter that theologians, philosophers, and mathematicians logically infer an intelligent designer, including myself, from the marvels of scientific discovery.

But, that is not all. The real problem with the Discovery Institute Intelligent Design campaign is its agenda, strongly opposed by the scientific community and which opposition I agree with, to replace the nature of science, as taught in the classroom, with theistic realism, as defined by *legal scholar* Phillip Johnson. Again from wikipedia, **"Intelligent design proponents seek to change this fundamental basis of science[154**—Forrest, Barbara (Fall-Winter 2000).] **by eliminating "methodological naturalism" from science[155**—Johnson, Phillip E.

(1995). Reason in the Balance] **and replacing it with what the leader of the intelligent design movement, Phillip E. Johnson, calls "*theistic realism*".[156—**Phillip E. Johnson (Access Research Network, August 31, 1996). " . . . we affirm that God is objectively real as Creator, and that the reality of God is tangibly recorded in evidence accessible to science, particularly in biology"]"

Continuing from wikipedia, we get to the bottom line of the intent of the Discovery Intelligent Design proponents. "Some have called this approach 'methodological supernaturalism', which means belief in a transcendent, nonnatural dimension of reality inhabited by a transcendent, nonnatural deity. [Vuletic, Mark I. (February 1997). "Methodological Naturalism and the Supernatural".] **Intelligent design proponents argue that naturalistic explanations fail to explain certain phenomena and that supernatural explanations provide a very simple and intuitive explanation for the origins of life and the universe.** [Watanabe, Teresa (March 25, 2001). 'Enlisting Science to Find the Fingerprints of a Creator'. Los Angeles Times] **Proponents say that evidence exists in the forms of irreducible complexity and specified complexity that cannot be explained by natural processes.** [What is the theory of intelligent design? Discovery Institute. Retrieved 2007-05-13]"

Here again, while the concept of "theistic realism" or "methodological supernaturalism" may be a logical inference based on scientific evidence, I agree that these concepts are not and should not be either a part of Intelligent Design or replace the scientific process of "methodological naturalism". This concept of "methodological supernaturalism" does appear to me to have a place in public schools in sociological and historical studies of diverse religions, so long as it is properly taught objectively without any attempt to proselyte for specific faiths. It seems to me that it is at this point that the concept of Intelligent Designer can be taught, and so long as no one religion is presented as dominant. However, it is clear to me that Intelligent Design, sans any inference to an Intelligent Designer, can be logically inferred in scientific studies based on the observable balance and order of earth's ecological systems, and our solar system that make life on earth possible, as well the magnificent biological structure not only of human anatomy, but of all animal, plant, aviary, marine, and insect life on earth.

Now comes the question of whether or not Intelligent Design is scientifically observable. *William Dembski, for example, has written that "Intelligence leaves behind a characteristic signature". The characteristics of intelligence are assumed by intelligent design proponents to be observable without specifying what the criteria for the measurement of intelligence should be.* Dembski, instead, asserts that "in special sciences ranging from forensics to archaeology to SETI (the Search for Extraterrestrial Intelligence), appeal to a designing intelligence is indispensable".[Dembski, William A. (April 2002). "Detecting Design in the Natural Sciences". Intelligent Design?. Natural History Magazine.]

From wikipedia now comes the question of "How this appeal is made and what this implies as to the definition of intelligence are topics left largely unaddressed".

Seth Shostak, a researcher with the SETI Institute, disputed Dembski's comparison of SETI and intelligent design, saying that *intelligent design advocates base their inference of design on complexity*—**the argument being that some biological systems are too complex to have been made by natural processes**—while SETI researchers are looking primarily for artificiality. [Shostak, Seth (December 2005). "SETI and Intelligent Design".]

Now we get to the point that I have been making, and that is that Intelligent Design is observable in the balance and order of earth's ecological systems, and our solar system that make life on earth possible, as well the magnificent biological structure not only of human anatomy, but of all animal, plant, aviary, marine, and insect life on earth. All of these things must work together in order to sustain life on earth. Some scientists argue that all of this is the result of a random process. So perhaps Intelligent Design advocates are correct maintaining that intelligence is inferred from irreducible complexity, and here I describe that irreducible complexity as well as the *"criteria for the measurement of Intelligent Design"*:

1. the perfect size and distance from the sun and the perfect heat radiated from the sun;

2. the heliosphere around the solar system which protects the earth from galactic radiation [Richard Gray, www.telegraph.co.uk];

3. the perfect size and distance of the moon from the earth that controls the oceans tides, stabilizes the axial tilt and gradually slows the planet's rotation [wikipedia];

4. the perfect size of earth's oceans which make up about 71% of the earth's surface—Sea water having an important influence on the world's climate, with the oceans acting as a large heat reservoir [Scott, Michon (2006-04-24). "Earth's Big heat Bucket". NASA Earth Observatory];

5. the earth's water cycle. From wikipedia, "The water cycle purifies water, replenishes the land with freshwater, and transports minerals to different parts of the globe". It is estimated that the oceans supply about 90% of the evaporated water that goes into the water cycle. [http://ga.water.usgs.gov/edu/watercycleoceans.html USGS, The Water Cycle: Water Storage in Oceans—Retrieved on 2008-05-14]. The water cycle is powered from solar energy. About 86% of the global evaporation occurs from the oceans, reducing their temperature by evaporative cooling. Without the cooling, the effect of evaporation on the greenhouse effect would lead to a much higher surface temperature of 67 °C (153 °F), and a warmer planet. [Water Cycle — Science Mission Directorate". http://nasascience. nasa.gov/earth-science/oceanography/ocean-earth-system/ ocean-water-cycle. Retrieved 7 January 2009] ;

6. The earth's nitrogen cycle. The majority of Earth's atmosphere (approximately 78%) is nitrogen, [Steven B. Carroll; Steven D. Salt (2004). Ecology for gardeners]. Nitrogen is essential for many processes; it is crucial for any life on Earth. In plants, much of the nitrogen is used in chlorophyll molecules, which are essential for photosynthesis and further growth [Smil, V (2000). Cycles of Life. ScientificAmerican Library, New York., 2000]. Chemical processing, or natural fixation (through processes such as bacterial conversion— rhizobium), are necessary to convert gaseous nitrogen into forms usable by living organisms. This makes nitrogen a crucial part of food production [Nitrogen: The Essential Element. Nancy M. Trautmann and Keith S. Porter. Center for Environmental Research, Cornell Cooperative Extension]. Denitrification is the reduction of nitrates back into the largely inert nitrogen gas (N2), completing the nitrogen cycle. This process is performed by bacterial species such as Pseudomonas and Clostridium in anaerobic conditions.[Smil, V (2000). Cycles of Life. ScientificAmerican Library, New York., 2000];

7. The earth's oxygen cycle. The oxygen cycle is the cycle that moves oxygen between the earth and the atmosphere. 99.5% of Earth's oxygen is within the silicate and oxide minerals of the crust and mantle. Only a 0.01% has been released as free oxygen to the biosphere(the sum of all ecological systems on earth) and 0.36% to the atmosphere The main source of atmospheric oxygen is photosynthesis, which produces sugars and oxygen from carbon

dioxide and water [2]. Oxygen also forms the ozone layer within the stratosphere, which absorbs harmful ultraviolet radiation [2].

8. Photosynthesis—Photosynthesis occurs in plant life on land and phytophlankton and Prochlorococcus in the oceans [1]. Photosynthesis uses carbon dioxide and water and releases oxygen to maintain the normal level of oxygen in the atmosphere. Nearly all life either depends on photosynthesis directly as a source of energy, or indirectly as the ultimate source of the energy in their food [D.A. Bryant & N.-U. Frigaard (2006). "Prokaryotic photosynthesis and phototrophy illuminated". Trends Microbiol 14 (11): 488. doi:10.1016/j.tim.2006.09.001. PMID 16997562] The rate of energy capture by photosynthesis is immense, approximately 100 terawatts [Nealson KH, Conrad PG (1999). "Life: past, present and future". Philos. Trans. R. Soc. Lond., B, Biol. Sci. 354 (1392): 1923-39. doi:10.1098/rstb.1999.0532. PMID 10670014], which is about six times larger than the power consumption of human civilization [World Consumption of Primary Energy by Energy Type and Selected Country Groups, 1980-2004" (XLS). Energy Information Administration. July 31, 2006.]. Photosynthesis is also the source of the carbon in all the organic compounds within organisms' bodies [Field CB, Behrenfeld MJ, Randerson JT, Falkowski P (1998). "Primary production of the biosphere: integrating terrestrial and oceanic components". Science (journal) 281 (5374): 237-40. doi:10.1126/science.281.5374.237. PMID 9657713].

9. The earth's perfect atmosphere which protects the earth and contains the earth's heat. From wikipedia, "The atmosphere of Earth is a layer of gases surrounding the planet Earth that is retained by Earth's gravity. The atmosphere protects life on Earth by absorbing ultraviolet solar radiation, warming the surface through heat retention (greenhouse effect), and reducing temperature extremes between day and night. Earth's atmosphere is mainly composed of nitrogen(78.09%), oxygen(20.95%), argon(0.93%), and carbon dioxide(0.039%), which together constitute the major gases of the atmosphere. The remaining gases are often referred to as trace gases, among which are the greenhouse gases such as water vapor, methane(0.000179%), nitrous oxide(0.00003%), and ozone(0% to $7 \times 10{-6}$%)." Also from wikipedia, Earth's atmosphere can be divided into five main layers where the ionosphere, which influences

radio propagation on Earth, overlaps both the exosphere and the thermosphere and stretches from 31 to 620 mi:

(1) Exosphere, The outermost layer of Earth's atmosphere
(2) Thermosphere about 200 and 240 mi where the International Space Station orbits. The top of the thermosphere, thermopause, is the bottom of the exosphere, called the exobase, and varies in height with solar activity and ranges from about 220 to 500 mi
(3) Mesosphere, protecting the earth, where most meteors burn up upon entering the atmosphere, extends from the stratopause, top of the stratosphere, to 50-53 mi, where the mesopause, the top of the mesosphere, is the coldest place on Earth and has an average temperature around –85 °C.
(4) stratosphere extends from the tropopause to about 32 mi, and the stratopause extends from about 31 to 34 mi. Part of the stratosphere, the *ozone layer* is 9.3-22 mi, with about 90% of the ozone in our atmosphere.
(5) troposphere begins at the surface of the earth and extends between 23,000 ft at the poles and 56,000 ft at the equator,

10. The Earth's perfect axis of rotation, tilted about 23.40° to perfectly divide the earth's 365.26 solar days into four (4) seasons [Staff (2008-07-24). "World". The World Factbook. Central Intelligence Agency]

(A) Planet Earth—*formed 4.54 billion years ago* out of the solar nebula—a disk-shaped mass of dust and gas left over from the formation of the Sun. [Dalrymple, G.B. (1991). The Age of the Earth. California: Stanford University Press. ISBN 0-8047-1569-6.].
(B) Between approximately 3.8 billion and 4.1 billion years ago, numerous asteroid impacts during the Late Heavy Bombardment caused significant changes to the greater surface environment. Both the mineral resources of the planet, as well as the products of the biosphere, contribute resources that are used to support a global human population. [wikipedia]
(C) *Outgassing and volcanic activity* **produced** the *primordial atmosphere.* [wikipedia]

(D) By 3.5 billion years ago, the *Earth's magnetic field* was established, which helped **prevent the atmosphere from being stripped away by the solar wind**.[Staff (March 4, 2010). "Oldest measurement of Earth's magnetic field reveals battle between Sun and Earth for our atmosphere". Physorg.news. *http://www. physorg.com/news186922627.html. Retrieved 2010-03-27*]

(E) Condensing water vapor, augmented by ice and liquid water delivered by asteroids and the larger proto-planets, comets, and trans-Neptunian objects produced the oceans. [Morbidelli, A.; Chambers, J.; Lunine, J. I.; Petit, J. M.; Robert, F.; Valsecchi, G. B.; Cyr, K. E. (2000). "Source regions and time scales for the delivery of water to Earth". Meteoritics & Planetary Science 35 (6)]

(F) Earth's biosphere has significantly altered its atmosphere. **Oxygenic photosynthesis evolved 2.7 billion years ago, forming the primarily nitrogen-oxygen atmosphere of today**. This change **enabled the proliferation of aerobic organisms** as well as the **formation of the ozone layer** which, together with Earth's magnetic field, **blocks** harmful **ultraviolet solar radiation**, permitting life on land. [Harrison, Roy M.; Hester, Ronald E. (2002). Causes and Environmental Implications of Increased UV-B Radiation. Royal Society of Chemistry. ISBN 0854042652 . . .]

(G) Roughly **750 million years ago** (Ma), one of the earliest known supercontinents, Rodinia, began to break apart. The continents later *recombined to form Pannotia, 600-540 Ma*, then finally Pangaea, which broke apart 180 Ma.[Murphy, J. B.; Nance, R. D. (1965). "How do supercontinents assemble?". American Scientist 92: 324-33. doi:10.1511/2004.4.324].

(H) The physical properties of the Earth, as well as its geological history and orbit, have allowed life to persist until today. Planet Earth is expected to continue supporting life for at least another 500 million years. [Britt, Robert (2000-02-25). "Freeze, Fry or Dry: How Long Has the Earth Got?"][Carrington, Damian (2000-02-21). "Date set for desert Earth". BBC News]

(I) **Earth's outer surface** is divided into several rigid segments, or **tectonic plates**, that migrate across the surface over periods of many millions of years. [wikipedia]

(J) The planet's interior remains active, with a thick layer of relatively *solid mantle*, a *liquid outer core* that generates a magnetic field, and a *solid iron inner core*. [wikipedia]

(K) *Cambrian explosion*—530 million years ago, *when multicellular life forms began to proliferate*.[Kirschvink, J. L. (1992). Schopf, J.W.; Klein, C. and Des Maris, D. ed. Late Proterozoic low-latitude global glaciation: the Snowball Earth. The Proterozoic Biosphere: A Multidisciplinary Study. Cambridge University Press. pp. 51-52]

(L) Following the Cambrian explosion, about 535 Ma, there have been *five major mass extinctions* (starting over) [Raup, D. M.; Sepkoski, J. J. (1982). "Mass Extinctions in the Marine Fossil Record". Science 215 (4539): 1501-1503. doi:10.1126/science.215.4539.1501. PMID 17788674.] Extinction events eliminate the old dominant group and makes way for the new one.[Benton, M.J. (2004). "6. Reptiles Of The Triassic". Vertebrate Palaeontology. Blackwell][Van Valkenburgh, B. (1999). "Major patterns in the history of carnivorous mammals". Annual Review of Earth and Planetary Sciences 26: 463-493. doi:10.1146/annurev.earth.27.1.463.]

A. Cretaceous-Tertiary extinction event 70 to 65 Ma (End Cretaceous or K-T extinction—a **meteor impact on the Yucatan Peninsula raised huge clouds of dust, blotting out the sun and causing most of this vegetation to die out**)—75% of species went extinct. [Raup, D.; Sepkoski Jr, J. (1982). "Mass extinctions in the marine fossil record". Science (New York, N.Y.) 215 (4539): 1501-1503. doi:10.1126/science.215.4539.1501. PMID 17788674.] It ended the reign of dinosaurs and opened the way for mammals and birds to become the dominant land vertebrates. In the seas it reduced the percentage of sessile animals to about 33%.

B. Triassic-Jurassic Global warming extinction event 205 Ma (End Triassic)—About 23% of all families and 48% of all genera went extinct. ["extinction". Math.ucr.edu. http://math.ucr.edu/home/baez/extinction. Retrieved 2008-11-09.] Most non-dinosaurian archosaurs, most therapsids, and most of the large amphibians were eliminated, leaving dinosaurs with little terrestrial competition. Non-dinosaurian archosaurs continued to dominate aquatic environments, while non-archosaurian diapsids continued to dominate marine environments. The Temnospondyl lineage of large amphibians also survived until the Cretaceous in Australia (e.g., Koolasuchus).

C. Permian-Triassic cooling event extinction global 251 Ma (End Permian)—Earth's largest extinction killed 57% of all families and 83% of all genera[6] (53% of marine families, 84% of marine genera, about 96% of all marine species and an estimated 70% of land species) including insects. [Labandeira CC, Sepkoski JJ (1993). "Insect diversity in the fossil record". Science 261 (5119): 310-5. doi:10.1126/science.11536548. PMID 11536548]

D. Late Devonian global cooling extinction—360-375 Ma near the Devonian-Carboniferous transition. At the end of the Frasnian Age in the later part(s) of the Devonian Period, a prolonged series of extinctions eliminated about 19% of all families, 50% of all genera ["extinction". Math.ucr. edu. http://math.ucr.edu/home/baez/extinction. Retrieved 2008-11-09] and 70% of all species.

E. Ordovician-Silurian global cooling extinction event 440-450 Ma (End Ordovician)—at the Ordovician-Silurian transition. Two events occurred that killed off 27% of all families and 57% of all genera. ["extinction". Math.ucr. edu. http://math.ucr.edu/home/baez/extinction. Retrieved 2008-11-09] Together they are ranked by many scientists as the second largest of the five major extinctions in Earth's history in terms of percentage of genera that went extinct.

(12) Rainforests of the earth:

Intelligent Design is observable in the balance, order and irreducible complexity of earth's ecological systems, including the rainforests of the Earth.

According to http://www.srl.caltech.edu/personnel/krubal/rainforest/ Edit560s6/www/where.html, rainforests are dense, hot and humid jungles with a high amount of rainfall per year. And, although the rainforests of the earth cover only about 6% of the

Earth's surface, they contain more than one half of the world's plant and animal species. According to www.rain-tree.com, rainforests evolved over millions of years, and represent a store of living and breathing renewable resources that for eons have contributed a wealth of resources for the survival of mankind. However, the World Resources Institute estimates that the demand for wood could double by 2050, but it is still the tropical forests that supply most of the world's demand for wood.

According to Rhett Butler (rainforests.mongabay.com) rainforests of the earth are important to global ecosystems and human existence, not only because they contain about fifty (50%) percent of the (plant and animal) species on Earth, but also because they also contain various indigenous (human) cultures. According to Butler rainforests are also important in regulating global weather, maintaining regular rainfall, buffering against floods, droughts and erosions, as well as storing large quantities of carbon while producing "a significant amount of the world's oxygen".

Where are these rainforests? According to Butler, rainforests exist around the equator between latitudes 22.5^0 North and 22.5^0 South. Rainforests are in Central America; The Amazon (the largest, largely in Brazil); Africa, with the Madagascar being the second largest rainforest in the world; Southern Asia with the rainforests of Java, Borneo and Bangladesh; and Australasia, being Australia, New Zealand and New Guinea.

But, Earth's rainforests are in danger of destruction. According to Butler, just a few thousand years ago, torpical rainforests covered as much as 12% of the Earth's land, about 6 million square miles. But, today, less than 5% of the Earth's land, about 2.4 million square miles, contain these rainforests. Why is this? According to http://www.srl.caltech.edu/personnel/krubal/rainforest/ Edit560s6/ www/where.html, the world's rainforests are currently disappearing at a rate of about 6000 acres every hour. This loss harms life on earth because we need rainforests to produce oxygen and clean the atmosphere to help us breath. Loss of rainforests can also affect the Earth's climate and water cycle, as well as medicinal plants to possibly cure deadly diseases.

Why are our rainforests disappearing? According to rainforests. moongaby.com/20brazil.htm, Brazil's rainforests are being cleared for patureland, construction of the Trans-Amazonian Highway, clearing for agriculture, fires and logging.

Despite massive rainforest deforestation, Brazil has protected rainforest areas under "Amazon Region Protected Areas (ARPA). Brazil has also set aside large land areas and the Amazon basin for the indigenous population, about 450,000 Indians. In addition, the World Land Trust Atlantic Rainforest Project has been established to protect the Brazilian Atlantic Rainforest Project located in the Serra dos Órgãos Mountains, in the state of Rio de Janeiro Brazil.

What is the measure of wasting the rainforests of the Earth? According to www.rain-tree.com (1) clearing rainforests for cattle operation yields the landowner about $60 per acre; (2) clearing rainforests for timber yields about $400 per acre; (3) but, harvesting rainforests for medicinal plants, fruits nuts, oil yields about $2,400 per acre. Also, according to www.rain-tree.com, the U.S. National Cancer Institute has identified 3000 plants that are active against cancer cells, of which 70% of the plants are found in the rainforests.

13. Universe and the Big Bang—According to Dr. Francis Collins, in his book, "The Language of God", the vast majority of physicists and cosmologists conclude that the universe began at a single moment, now referred to as the Big Bang. Calculations suggest that the Big Bang happened approximately 14 billion years ago. Dr. Collins also writes that "the universe began as an infinitely dense, dimensionless point of pure energy" (pp64-65). Dr. Collins further writes that "for the first million years after the Big Bang, the universe expanded, the temperature dropped, and nuclei and atoms began to form. Matter began to coalesce into galaxies under the force of gravity. It acquired rotational motion as it did so, ultimately resulting in the spiral shape of galaxies such as our own. Within those galaxies local collections of hydrogen and helium were drawn together, and their density and temperature rose. Ultimately nuclear fusion commenced" (p67).

Dr. Collins further writes that "This process (nuclear fusion) whereby four hydrogen nuclei fuse together to form both energy and a helium nucleus, provides the major source of fuel for stars" (p67). Dr. Collins further states that as the stars burn out, "they generate within their core even heavier elements such as carbon and oxygen". " . . . some of these stars then went through massive explosions known as super-novae, flinging heavier elements back into the gas in the galaxie" (p68).

On page 71, Dr. Collins explains that, "In the early moments of the universe following the Big Bang, matter and antimatter were created in almost equivalent amounts. At one millisecond of time, the universe cooled enough for quarks and antiquarks to 'condense out'" (p72). **Quarks** are fundamental matter particles that are constituents of neutrons and protons, and they are confined by the strong (or color charge) force fields. [**http://www2.slac. stanford. edu/vvc/theory/quarks.html**] **Antiquarks** have similar properties as a Quark but have opposite and equal charge. [**http://egglescliffe. org. uk/physics/particles/mkquark/quarks.html**]

Continuing, Dr. Collins explains that "for about every billion pair of quarks and antiquarks, there was an extra quark. It is that tiny fraction of the initial potentiality of the entire universe that makes up the mass of the universe as we know it"(p72). "If there had been complete symmetry between matter and antimatter, the universe would quickly have devolved into pure radiation, and people, planets, stars, and galaxies would never have come into existence".

Quoting Stephen Hawking "Brief History of Time", Dr. Collins writes, "If the rate of expansion (of the universe) one second after the Big Bang had been smaller by even one part in 10^{16} (10 to the 16th power) the universe would have recollapsed before it ever reached its present size". "On the other hand, it the rate of expansion had been greater by even one part in a million, stars and planets could not have been able to form".

Now, about the heavier elements of the universe, Dr. Collins writes, "If the strong nuclear force that holds together protons and neutrons had been even slightly weaker, then only hydrogen could have formed in the universe. If, on the other hand, the strong nuclear force had been slightly stronger, all the hydrogen would have been converted to helium, instead of the 25 percent that occurred early in the Big Bang, and thus the fusion furnaces of stars and their ability to generate heavier elements would never have been born" (p73).

Continuing, Dr. Collins further writes that, " . . . the nuclear force appears to be tuned just sufficiently for carbon to form, which is critical for life forms on Earth" (p74).

Concluding, Dr. Collins writes, "Altogether, there are fifteen physical constants whose values current theory is unable to predict. They are givens—(1) the speed of light, (2) the strength of the weak and strong nuclear forces, (3) various parameters associated with electromagnetism, and (4) the force of gravity. The chance that all of these constants would take on the values necessary to result in a stable universe capable of sustaining complex life forms is almost infinitesimal. And yet, those are exactly the parameters that we observe. In sum, our universe is wildly improbable". And, Dr. Collins concludes with the "Anthropic Principle", "that our universe is uniquely tuned to give rise to humans" (p74).

Dr. Collins further writes that "Scientists believe our own sun . . . formed 5 billion years ago by local re-coalescence" (p68), and that "a small proportion of heavier elements . . . collected into the planets that now rotate around our sun" (p68), including planet earth.

13. **Electronic configuration**: Electronic configuration is presented in Chapter 12, but a brief introduction is included in this chapter to tie this subject into "Intelligent Design" and has to do with the order in which electrons fill energy levels in the atoms of the elements of the Atomic Periodic Table, originally defined by the Russian Chemist Dmitri Ivanovich Mendeleev and published in "Principles of Chemistry" in 1869 with only 63 elements. Today the Atomic Periodic Table contains some 114 elements according to the National Institute of Standards and Technology. The periodic table is another exhibit in describing the irreducible complexity, balance and order of the universe, the earth, and life on earth clearly indicating "Intelligent Design". Clearly, this exhibit of the essence of matter of the universe, and the earth is not the result of a random process, natural selection, adaptation, or mutation.

Returning to the point that I have been making, and that is that Intelligent Design is observable in the balance and order of earth's ecological systems, and our solar system that make life on earth possible, as well the magnificent biological structure not only of human anatomy, but of all animal, plant, aviary, marine, and insect life on earth. All of these things must work together in order to sustain life on earth. Some scientists argue that all of this is the result of a random process. But perhaps Intelligent Design advocates are correct maintaining that intelligence is inferred from irreducible complexity, and here I have described 13 major parts of that irreducible complexity as well as the *"criteria for the measurement of Intelligent Design"*. Random process? I have seen no evidence of random process from the formation of the earth, to the beginning and evolution of life on earth. In fact, I have seen only scientific evidence of intelligence, balance and order in the formation of the universe, the earth, and life on earth.

Returning to my earlier pontification, "We could say that God, or the creator of the universe, and earth and life on earth, cooked the primordial soup through many stages, from the beginning of the earth about 4.5 billion years ago, whether by random process, natural selection, adaptation, or mutation, until:", and then I presented scientific evidence of nine (9) phases of the evolution of life on earth, including twenty one (21) phases in the evolution of human beings on earth beginning with **Orrorin tugenensis**, about 6 million years ago, and continuing to **Homo sapiens** (modern humans) about 195,000 years ago, which included (1) **Cro-Magnon**—about 40,000 years ago, (2) **Paleolithic humans,** about 30,000 years ago**, and Mesolithic humans,** about 10,000 years ago.

The question I have insofar as human life on earth is concerned, and that is "how did hominids evolve over a period of 6 million years from the very primitive types to the extremely sophisticated machinery humans are today, with, as Dr. Daniel Amen writes "The brain is the most complicated organ in the universe". Random process? Well, no. Random process doesn't achieve the human sophistication from **Orrorin tugenensis** 6 million years ago to modern man. So then from a scientific point of view that leaves natural selection, adaptation, or mutation. And what is the vehicle for that mutation? Well the DNA code of life imbedded in the chromosomes of the nucleus of the human cell is the only possible way.

Now herein comes the supernatural issue. Did a supernatural influence cause the mutations over billions of years from one cell organisms to modern man? Well, scientists would reject the possibility of a supernatural influence because it is simply not a scientifically provable concept. But there is no other explanation beyond the limitations of natural selection, adaptation, or mutation. So this puts us into the realm of the philosophical

logical inference that only a supernatural influence could cause the mutation over millions and billions of years from one cell organisms to the most sophisticated human machinery in the universe, and this conclusion is based on purely scientific evidence, including, but not limited to, the awesome capability of the human brain, as well as the awesome intelligence imbedded in the "double helix" structure of DNA in the nucleus of the cell of all living things on earth. In his book, "Signature of the Cell", Dr. Meyer presents a different type of logical inference which he terms "abductive logic", as opposed to inductive, which in historical sciences means to infer a past event from a present fact or clue. Dr. Meyer further writes in his book that "Inferences to intelligent design exemplify this abductive and retrodictive logical structure" (p153, p409).

And what is the scientific evidence for the creation of life on earth? Well, not only the eleven (11) phases of the development of the earth and its attendant ecological systems necessary to sustain life on earth which I have already presented, but also nine (9) phases of the evolution of life on earth, including twenty one (21) phases in the evolution of human beings, and the miracle of the Big Bang that created the vast universe, of which the earth and the earth's solar system is only a small part.

And what is the purpose of all of this analysis of the development of the earth and life on earth? Well, now we are back to where we started. The purpose of all of this analysis is to realize that the sophisticated irreducible complexity, balance and order, not only of the universe, but the earth and its attendant ecological systems necessary to sustain life, the earth's solar system, but life on earth, none-the-least of which is human life, equate to nothing less than orderly Intelligent Design, which is in fact a metaphysical conclusion of cause and effect based on scientific evidence. How do I know this? I know this because I am a dyed in the wool metaphysicist and I have been for several decades.

And, I have seen no evidence to support **Oxford naturalist and philosopher A. C. Grayling's dismissal of Intelligent Design as "*a little driblet of childish ignorance; a mark of mankind's infancy*".** [Grayling, A.C. (Web exclusive September/October 2008). "Bolus of nonsense". New Humanist. *http://newhumanist.org.uk/1881. Retrieved 2009-09-19*]. Perhaps Intelligent Design proponents, Dr. William Dembski (mathematics and philosophy), Dr. Michael Behe (biochemistry), Dr. Stephen C. Meyer (history of science), et al, had not as of yet presented scientifically plausible reasoning from a strict scientific perspective for the concept of Intelligent Design, but, in his 2009 book, "Signature in the Cell", Dr. Stephen Meyer does appear to me to present a logical scientific basis for the concept of Intelligent Design. And, while Dr. Francis Collins rejects the concept of Intelligent Design in his 2006 book, "The Language of God", Dr. Collins also presents a logical scientific basis for the concept of Intelligent Design.

And, I have seen no evidence to agree with *Eugenie Scott, along with Glenn Branch* and other critics, that have argued that many points raised by *intelligent design proponents are arguments from ignorance.* [Scott, Eugenie C.; Branch, Glenn (September 2002). "'Intelligent Design' Not Accepted by Most Scientists". National Center for Science Education] I have found Dr. William Dembski, Dr. Michael Behe, and Dr. Stephen C. Meyer to be extremely knowledgeable and intelligent, and certainly not ignorant, albeit they present a nontraditional perspective of science adding the dimension of "intelligence". The problem I have seen for this type of ridicule is simply that Intelligent Design proponents have not published in traditional scientific journals. Well, publishing in scientific journals is about new scientific discoveries, and not about the philosophical perception and inference of intelligence based on existing scientific facts and evidence. The 2009 book, "Signature in the Cell", by Dr. Stephen Meyer, is very intelligently written and scientific about the Human Genome, adding the dimension of Intelligent Design and addressing the scientific community concerns about Intelligent Design.

And, from wikipedia, *"Evolutionary algorithms*, a subfield of machine learning (itself a subfield of artificial intelligence), *have been used to mathematically demonstrate that randomness and selection can be used to "evolve" complex, highly adapted structures* that are *not explicitly designed by a programmer.* Evolutionary **algorithms use the** *Darwinian metaphor of random mutation, selection and the survival of the fittest* **to** *solve diverse mathematical and scientific problems* **that are usually not solvable using conventional methods".** Yes, but while Steffen Schulze-Kremer, wrote a genetic algorithm (GA) to predict the three-dimensional structure of a protein based on the sequence of amino acids that go into it [talkorigins.org/faps/genalg/ genalg.html#mitchell1996, p. 62], I do not see that this algorithm even begins to address the complexity of scientific evidence we have seen in the evolution of life on earth over the past 3.5 billion years. While random processes are a reality in the DNA code of life in terms of mutations causing diseases, I see no evidence that any random process could result in the finely tuned irreducible complexity, balance and order of the creation of the universe, the earth and earth's solar system, earth's ecological systems, and the evolution of life on earth itself.

In his book, "Signature in the Cell, 2009", Dr. Stephen Meyer points out the limitations of evolutionary algorithms to be that they require (1) preexisting sources of information provided by designing minds (p337), and (2) an information rich target sequence (p336), all of which come from intelligent computer programmers.

Now I will present scientific facts and evidence about the finely tuned irreducible complexity, balance and order of the Human Genome and Human Anatomy.

1. **Human Genome**—I have pondered extensively about how to write this section within the scope of this book to include meaningful and understandable information. I have studied Dr. Stephen Meyer's 2009 book on "Signature in the Cell", with 789 note references and 574 Bibliography references; Dr. Francis Collins' 2006 book on "The Language of God", with 74 note references; wikipedia with 35 references on "Human Genome" and wikipedia with 26 references on the human gene and the double helix DNA. So the information in this section is the result of that pondering.

Now let's begin with the fact that the evolutionary branch between the primates and mouse, for example, occurred 70-90 million years ago. So why is this important? Well because identification of regulatory sequences relies in part on evolutionary conservation. [Nei M, Xu P, Glazko G (2001). "Estimation of divergence times from multiprotein sequences for a few mammalian species and several distantly related organisms.". Proc Natl Acad Sci USA 98 (5): 2497-502.doi:10.1073/pnas.051611498. PMID 11226267. PMC 30166.]

So the double helix puzzle begins to develop, and now we have identified something called "regulatory sequences". Well, so what? The so what is that "The human genome has many different **regulatory sequences** which are crucial to controlling **gene expression**. These are typically short sequences that appear near or within genes. Some types of non-coding DNA are genetic **"switches"** that do not encode proteins, but do **regulate when and where genes are expressed**.[Carroll, Sean B. et al. (May 2008). "Regulating Evolution", Scientific American, pp. 60-67]".

And now the account of the human genome begins to get more complicated, and indeed it is. Let's look at some basics, and proceed from there. Dr. Meyer writes (p82) that "On April 25, 1953, a seemingly modest paper appeared in the journal 'Nature'. The article was only nine hundred words long, was signed by a pair of unknowns, biologists J.D. Watson and F.H.C. Crick, and featured the anodyne title 'Molecular Structure of Nucleic Acids: A Structure for Deoxyribose Nucleic Acid (DNA)'" According to Dr. Meyer, "The Watson-Crick model made it clear that DNA had an impressive chemical and structural complexity. It was a very long molecule composed on the outside of a regular arrangement of sugar and phosphate molecules. But on the inside it could contain many potentially different arrangements of the **four bases**" (p83). Dr. Meyer further writes that as Watson and Crick later explained: "The phosphate-sugar backbone of our model is completely regular, but any sequence of the **pairs of the bases** can fit into the structure. It follows that in a long molecule, many different permutations are possible, and it therefore seems likely that the precise sequence of the bases is the code which carries the **genetic information**" [Watson and Crick, "Genetic Implications", 965].

And what are these bases that fit into the backbone structure of the "double helix". Dr. Meyer writes "by the early part of the twentieth century, scientists knew that . . . (Deoxyribose) nucleic acid (DNA) was composed of the four bases adenine, thymine, cytosine, and guanine". These are denoted as A, T, C, and G. [Signature in the Cell, p64]

Next we look at the issues of **"gene"** and **"gene expression**. From wikipedia, "A modern working definition of a **gene** is "a locatable region of genomic sequence, corresponding to a unit of inheritance, which is associated with regulatory regions, transcribed regions, and or other functional sequence regions ".[Pearson H (2006). "Genetics: what is a gene?". Nature 441 (7092): 398-401. doi:10.1038/441398a. PMID 16724031][Elizabeth Pennisi (2007). "DNA Study Forces Rethink of What It Means to Be a Gene". Science 316 (5831): 1556-1557. doi:10.1126/science. 316.5831.1556. PMID 17569836] Colloquial usage of the term gene (e.g. "good genes, "hair color gene") may actually refer to an **allele**: a gene is the basic instruction, a sequence of nucleic acid (DNA or, in the case of certain viruses RNA), while an **allele** is one variant of that gene". Also from wikipedia, "A **gene** is a unit of heredity in a living organism. It normally resides on a stretch of DNA that codes for a type of **protein** or for an **RNA (ribonucleic acid) chain** that has a function in the organism. All living things depend on genes, as they specify all proteins and functional RNA chains. Genes hold the information to build and maintain an organism's cells and pass genetic traits to offspring".

Ok, now let's look at the bigger picture. Where does this complicated DNA double helix reside in a living cell? Well, DNA is packaged into **chromosomes**, which reside in the nucleus of every cell. [The Language of God, fig 4.1] Oh no! Now enters another entity into the Human Genome story, the **chromosome**. From wikipedia, "human cells are diploid and have 22 different types of autosome (not a sex chromosome), each present as two copies, and two sex chromosomes (X and Y—two copies of the X-Chromosome in females, but males have a single X chromosome and a Y-chromosome)". The Gene (information in the DNA double helix) is the unit of hereditary information that occupies a fixed position (locus) on a chromosome. Genes achieve their effects by directing the synthesis of proteins.[www.britannica.com/ EBchecked/topic/228226/gene]

Now what "gene expression"? From "Signature in the Cell" (p103), "Gene expression begins as long chains of nucleotide bases are copied during a process known as 'transcription'. During this process, the genetic assembly instructions stored on a strand of DNA are reproduced on another molecule called '**messenger RNA—mRNA**'. The resulting single-stranded copy or 'transcript' contains a sequence of **RNA bases** precisely matching the sequence of bases on the **original DNA strand**". [Alberts, et al., Molecular Biology of the Cell, 106-8; Wolfe, Molecular and Cellular Biology, 48]

Well now, we have 2 new entities in the story of the Human Genome—**RNA and protein. RNA** also uses chemicals called bases to store genetic information, but it uses a slightly different chemical alphabet than DNA. RNA substitutes a base called "**uracil**" for the base "**thymine**" in the DNA". The messenger RNA moves from the nucleus of the cell to the "**cytoplasm**" of the cell and to a protein factory called the "**ribosome**", where the RNA is converted into a **specific protein** made up of **amino acids**. It is the **proteins** that do the work of the cell and provide its structural integrity. [The Language of God, p104] The work of Nirenburg and Ochoa showed that "groups of three nucleotides (called codons) on the mRNA specify the addition of one of the twenty protein-forming amino acids during the process of protein synthesis". "Other scientists discovered that the cell uses a set of adapter molecules to help convert the information on mRNA into proteins". [Signature in the Cell, p119] Random process; Natural Selection; Adaptation; Mutation—Not a chance! This process is nothing short of intelligent design by virtue of the balance and order and irreducible complexity of the process.

Not complicated enough you say. Well, there is more. The question now is "how does the mRNA convert gene information from the huge DNA sequence inside the nucleus of the cell to the "protein structures" the cell needs to function? Well, the conversion occur in two (2) phases know as **Transcription** (phase 1) and **Translation** (phase 2).

From Dr. Meyer's book, Signature in the Cell (p122), "During **transcription**, a copy, or transcript of the DNA text is made by a large protein complex, known as **RNA polymerase**, that moves down the DNA chain and reads the original DNA text. As RNA polymerase proceeds, it makes an identical copy of the DNA transcript in an RNA format". Then Dr. Meyer quotes biologist Stephen Wolfe (123-124), "The structure of the RNA polymerases reflects the complexity of their activities in RNA transcription. The enzymes have sites that recognize promoters, react with initiation, elongation and termination factors, recognize DNA bases for correct pairing, bind and hydrolyze RNA nucleotides, form phosphor-diester linkages, terminate transctiption and perhaps unwind and rewind DNA". [Wolfe, Molicular and Cellular Biology, 580-81, 639-48]

Now, from Dr. Meyer's book (p127-129), "many biologists . . . think of the process of protein synthesis as a process of **translating**, information from the four-character alphabets of DNA and RNA into the twenty-character amino-acid alphabet; hense the name 'translation' ". In the ribosome, "a group of three (3) RNA bases on a transfer-RNA (tRNA) molecule binds to the first triplet of RNA bases on the mRNA molecule". "The groups of three bases . . . on the mRNA are called codons. The groups of three bases to which they bind on the tRNA are called antidodons. The sequence AUG constitutes the 'initiator codon' at the head of the mRNA transcript". [Watson, et al, Molecular Biology of the Gene, vol. 1:443] Then subunits of ribosome join, "forming a large complex of molecules, including . . . the mRNA, and the tRNA. The protein chain can now begin to form". " . . . the process repeats itself until the signal for termination is reached on the mRNA, . . . and the newly assembled protein then detaches".

Again, from Dr. Meyer's book (p131), "Besides transcribing and translating, the cells information-processing system also replicates DNA. This happens whenever cells divide and copy themselves. As with transcription and translation, the process of DNA replication depends on many separate protein catalysts to unwind, stabilize, copy, edit, and rewind the original DNA message". " . . . further, proteins must catalyze formation of the basic building blocks of cellular life such as sugars, lipids, blycollipids, nucleotides, and ATP (adenosine triphosphate, the main energy molecule of the cell)".

Dr. Meyer concludes by quoting from biochemist David Goodsell, "The key molecular process that makes modern life possible is protein synthesis, since proteins are used in nearly every aspect of living. The synthesis of proteins requires a tightly integrated sequence of reactions, most of which are themselves performed by proteins". [**Goodsell, The Machinery of Life, 45**] Random process; Natural Selection; Adaptation; Mutation—Not a chance! This process is nothing short of intelligent design by virtue of the balance and order and irreducible complexity of the process. (Signature in the Cell, p133)

Dr. Stephen Meyer addresses the issue of chance in chapter 10 of his book, Signature in the Cell. Dr. Meyer writes that using 10^{80} as the number of elementary particles in the observable universe, 10^{16} as the number of seconds since the Big bang, the Plank length of $10^{-33 \text{ cm}}$, Plank time of 10^{-43} seconds, the number of times elementary particles can interact with each other, 10^{43}, Bill Dembski "fixed the total number of event that could have taken place in the observable universe since the origin of the universe at 10^{139} ". (p217) Further, "the probability of producing a single 150-amino-acid functional protein by chance stands at about 1 in 10^{164}. Thus, for each functional sequence of 150 amino acids, there are at least 10^{164} other possible nonfunctional sequences of the same length. Therefore, to have a good (better than 50-50) chance of producing a single functional protein of this length by chance, a random process would have to generate (or sample) more than one-half of the 10^{164} nonfunctional sequences corresponding to each functional sequence of that length. Unfortunately, that number vastly exceeds the most optimistic estimate of the probabilistic resources of the entire universe—that is, the number of events that could have occurred since the beginning of it's existence". (p217) Then, Dr. Meyer points out that .5X10^{164} exceeds10^{139} by more than a trillion trillion times, meaning, the 150-amino-acid functional protein will never. be produced, which is what I meant by "Random process; Natural Selection; Adaptation; Mutation—Not a chance! This process is nothing short of intelligent design by virtue of the balance and order and irreducible complexity of the process". And Dr. Meyer concludes that "the universe itself does not possess the probabilistic resource necessary to render probable the origin of biological information by chance alone".

And finally, Dr. Meyer quotes from British philosopher, Sir Karl Popper, "What makes the origin of life and the genetic code a disturbing riddle is this: the code cannot be translated except by using certain products of its translation. This constitutes a really baffling circle: a vicious circle it seems, for any attempt to form a model, or a theory, of the genesis of the genetic code". [Popper, "Scientific Reduction"] (Signature in the Cell, p134)

Now we get even more complicated. Now comes the issue of "Junk DNA". The evolutionary conservation across the mammalian genomes of much more sequence than can be explained by protein-coding regions indicates that many, and perhaps most, functional elements in the genome remain unknown.[Mouse Genome Sequencing Consortium (2002). "Initial sequencing and comparative analysis of the mouse genome.". Nature 420 (6915): 520-62. doi:10.1038/nature01262. PMID 12466850]

But, from Dr. Meyer's book, Signature in the Cell, " . . . portions of the genome that many biologists previously regarded as 'junk DNA' are now known to perform many important functions, including the regulation and expression of the information for building proteins. In this respect, the nonprotein coding regions of the genome function much like an operating system in a software program, directing and regulating how other information in the system is processes" (p367). "In any case, the cell's information processing system has three key elements: (1) digital storage and encoding of information, (2) machinery for processing that information to produce a functional outcome, and (3) encoding of higher-order (hierarchically arranged) regulatory information". (p367-368)

Then, Dr. Meyer quotes Richard Dawkin's observation that "the machine code of the genes is uncannily computer-like", and Bill Gates that "DNA is like a computer program". (Signature in the Cell, p368) And, Dr. Meyer also relates the account of a software engineer at the biologic Institute studying how the cell processes information, "He showed me a book called Design Patterns, a standard text for software engineers. The text was full of different design strategies for processing, storing, copying, organizing, accessing, and correcting digitally encoded strings of information". The software engineer, Dr. Meyer writes, "told me that he recognized many of these specific design patterns and strategies at work in the cell. He expressed his awe at the 'sophistication of its design logic' and its resemblance to that used in the software industry. He said the cell often employs a functional logic that mirrors our own, but exceeds it in the elegance of its execution. When I see how the cell processes information, it gives me an eerie feeling that someone else figured this out before we got here". (Signature in the Cell, p369)

Dr. Stephen Meyers writes, " . . . at nearly the same time that computer scientist were beginning to develop machine languages, molecular biologists were discovering that living cells had been using something akin to machine code [Dawkins, River Out of Eden, 17] or software [Gates, The Road ahead, 188] all along". (Signature in the Cell, p110)

2. **Human Anatomy**—Up to this point, I have presented scientific evidence for intelligent design for many of the necessary systems required to be in place in the universe, and on earth, for the existence of human life, and all other life on earth. As if this irreducible complexity, balance and order were not enough, we still have the tremendously irreducible complexity, balance and order of the human anatomy, let alone the Human Genome which I have just presented. What then are some of the complex systems of the human anatomy necessary for human existence, also obviously exhibiting intelligent design by virtue of complex interrelated functionality, irreducible complexity, balance and order, and possibly mutation, but certainly and obviously not the result of random process, natural selection, or adaptation? All of theses systems, and more, are necessary for normal human existence, but now I am adding one more characteristic, and that is the characteristic of specificity, which Dr. Stephen Meyer has already identified in his book, "Signature in the Cell".

Specificity, that is specific design and purpose, has been and is present in all of the universe, the ecological systems of the earth, the earth itself, the human genome, and now human anatomy. The human genome is complex and specific enough, but when we look at the functional product in the systems in the human anatomy, especially the human brain, then the evidence of specificity in the systems of the human anatomy, together with irreducible complexity, balance and order clearly point to Intelligent Design.

And, as if that were not enough, from available scientific and medical knowledge, it appears to me that the human brain developed, evolved, grew itself, over a period of millions of years, from older more primitive versions to the modern version we know today. And, we have yet to see the full potential of the human brain and telepathic abilities, which we already have, but are not aware of, or know how to use. For example, brain electrical activity can be measured by electroencephalography (EEG), and the brain's magnetic field can be measured by magnetoencephalography (MEG).

Today electrodes can be connected to the skull of a human being and calibrated to respond to specific electromagnetic signals to operate complex games and equipment. [Dr. Eric Leuthardt, assistant professor of neurosurgery at the Washington University's School of Medicine—AP, 26Oct, 2006]

So now witness the following systems of the human anatomy exhibiting complex interrelated functionality, irreducible complexity, balance and order, specificity, and possibly mutation,—A. **Auditory system**; B. **Inner Ear**; C. **Cochlear nerve**; D. **Cochlear nuclei**; E. **Human brain**; F. **Human Eye**; G. **Metabolism**; H. **Circulatory system** ; I. **Human gastrointestinal tract**

A. **Auditory system**—the sensory system for the sense of hearing [wikipedia—the following are exact quotes, and although a considerable amount of study went into the collection and understanding of this information, is not intended to be tutorial, but merely identifying and expository] The irreducible complexity of the human auditory system, is clearly intelligent design, without implications about an intelligent designer, and is clearly not the result of a random process. In these brief descriptions we will see that the incredibly complex human auditory system not only collects sound and converts it to digital electronic signals sent to the brain, does binaural computations (both ears), does sound source localization, senses pitch and rhythm, and detects amplitude (level) and time differences.

(1) **Outer ear**—"The folds of cartilage surrounding the ear canal are called the pinna. Sound waves are reflected and attenuated when they hit the pinna, and these changes provide additional information that will help the brain determine the direction from which the sounds came."

"The sound waves enter the auditory canal, a deceptively simple tube. The ear canal amplifies sounds that are between

3 and 12 kHz. At the far end of the ear canal is the eardrum (or tympanic membrane), which marks the beginning of the middle ear."

(2) **Middle ear**—"Sound waves traveling through the ear canal will hit the tympanic membrane, or eardrum. This wave information travels across the air-filled middle ear cavity via a series of delicate bones: the malleus (hammer), incus (anvil) and stapes (stirrup). These ossicles act as a lever and a teletype, converting the lower-pressure eardrum sound vibrations into higher-pressure sound vibrations at another, smaller membrane called the oval (or elliptical) window."

(3) **Inner ear**—"The inner ear consists of the cochlea and several non-auditory structures. The cochlea has three fluid-filled sections, and supports a fluid wave driven by pressure across the membrane separating two of the sections. Strikingly, one section, called the cochlear duct or scala media, contains an extracellular fluid similar in composition to endolymph, which is usually found inside of cells. The organ of Corti is located at this duct, and transforms mechanical waves to electric signals in neurons. The other two sections are known as the scala tympani and the scala vestibuli; these are located within the bony labyrinth which is filled with fluid called perilymph. The chemical difference between the two fluids (endolymph & perilymph) is important for the function of the inner ear."

(4) **Organ of Corti**—"The organ of Corti forms a ribbon of sensory epithelium which runs lengthwise down the entire cochlea. The hair cells of the organ of Corti transform the fluid waves into nerve signals. The journey of a billion nerves begins with this first step; from here further processing leads to a panoply of auditory reactions and sensations."

(5) **Hair cells**—"Hair cells are columnar cells, each with a bundle of 100-200 specialized cilia at the top, for which they are named. These cilia are the mechanosensors for hearing. Lightly resting atop the longest cilia is the tectorial membrane, which moves back and forth with each cycle of sound, tilting the cilia and allowing electric current into the hair cell."

(6) **Neurons**—"Afferent neurons innervate cochlear inner hair cells, at synapses where the neurotransmitter glutamate

communicates signals from the hair cells to the dendrites of the primary auditory neurons."

"There are far fewer inner hair cells in the cochlea than afferent nerve fibers. The neural dendrites belong to neurons of the auditory nerve, which in turn joins the vestibular nerve to form the vestibulocochlear nerve, or cranial nerve number VIII. [**Meddean—CN VIII. Vestibulocochlear Nerve**]"

(7) **Central auditory system**—"This sound information, now re-encoded, travels down the **vestibulocochlear nerve**, through intermediate stations such as the **cochlear nuclei** and **superior olivary complex** of the brainstem and the **inferior colliculus** of the midbrain, being further processed at each waypoint. The information eventually reaches the *thalamus*, and from there it is relayed to the cortex. In the human brain, the **primary auditory cortex** is located in the **temporal lobe**."

(8) **Cochlear nucleus**—"The cochlear nucleus is the first site of the neuronal processing of the newly converted "digital" data from the inner ear. This region is anatomically and physiologically split into two regions, the **dorsal cochlear nucleus (DCN)**, and **ventral cochlear nucleus (VCN)**."

(9) **Trapezoid body**—"The Trapezoid body is a bundle of decussating fibers in the **ventral pons** that carry information used for binaural computations in the brainstem"

(9) **Superior olivary complex**—"The **superior olivary complex** is located in the **pons**, and receives projections predominantly from the **ventral cochlear nucleus**, although the **posterior cochlear nucleus** projects there as well, via the ventral acoustic stria. Within the superior olivary complex lies the **lateral superior olive (LSO)** and the **medial superior olive (MSO)**. The former is important in detecting interaural level differences while the latter is important in distinguishing interaural time difference."

(10) Lateral lemniscus—"The **lateral lemniscus** is a tract of axons in the brainstem that carries information about sound from the **cochlear nucleus** to various brainstem nuclei and ultimately the **contralateral inferior colliculus** of the midbrain."

(11) Inferior colliculi—"The IC are located just below the visual processing centers known as the superior colliculi. The central

nucleus of the IC is a nearly obligatory relay in the ascending auditory system, and most likely acts to integrate information (specifically regarding sound source localization from the superior olivary complex and dorsal cochlear nucleus) before sending it to the thalamus and cortex"

(12) Medial geniculate nucleus—"The **medial geniculate nucleus** is part of the **thalamic relay system.**"

(13) Primary auditory cortex—"The **primary auditory cortex** is the first region of cerebral cortex to receive auditory input."

"Perception of sound is associated with the **right posterior superior temporal gyrus** (STG). The **superior temporal gyrus** contains several important structures of the brain, including **Brodmann areas** 41 and 42, marking the location of the **primary auditory cortex**, the cortical region responsible for the sensation of basic characteristics of sound such as pitch and rhythm"

B. Inner Ear [wikipedia—the following are exact quotes or almost exact quotes, and although a considerable amount of study went into the collection and understanding of this information, is not intended to be tutorial, but merely identifying and expository]
"The inner ear includes both the organ of hearing (the cochlea) and a sense organ that is attuned to the effects of both gravity and motion (labyrinth or vestibular apparatus). The balance portion of the inner ear consists of three semi-circular canals and the vestibule. The inner ear is encased in the hardest bone of the body."

(1) Vestibular System (the human gyroscope)—"The vestibular system is important in maintaining balance, or equilibrium. The vestibular system includes the saccule, utricle, and the three semicircular canals. The vestibule is the name of the fluid-filled, membranous duct than contains these organs of balance. The vestibule is encased in the temporal bone of the skull"

a. Superior semicircular ear canal—"it is 15 to 20 mm in length, is vertical in direction, and is placed transversely to the long axis of the petrous portion of the temporal bone, on the anterior surface of which its arch forms a round projection. As part of the vestibular system it detects rotation of the head around a rostral-caudal (anterior-posterior) axis.

b. Posterior semicircular ear canal—"It is the longest of the three canals, measuring from 18 to 22 mm, and is vertical, like the superior. It is directed backward, nearly parallel to the posterior surface of the petrous bone. It is part of the bony labyrinth and is used by the vestibular system to detect rotations of the head in the sagittal plane.

c. Horizontal semicircular ear canal—"It measures from 12 to 15 mm, and its arch is directed horizontally backward and lateralward; thus each semicircular canal stands at right angles to the other two. Movement of fluid within this canal corresponds to **rotation of the head around a vertical axis** (i.e. the neck)".

d. **Utricle**—"The cavity of the utricle communicates behind with the semicircular ducts by five orifices. The utricle contains mechanoreceptors called hair cells that distinguish between degrees of tilting of the head, thanks to their apical cilia set-up. These are covered by otolith which, due to gravity, pull on the cilia and tilt them. Depending on whether the tilt is in the direction of the kinocilium or not, the resulting hair cell polarisation is excitatory (depolarising) or inhibitory (hyperpolarisation), respectively. This signal to the vestibular nerve (which takes it to the brainstem) does not adapt with time. The effect of this is that, for example, an individual lying down to sleep will continue to detect that they are lying down hours later when they awaken".

e. **Vestibule**—"On its medial wall, at the forepart, is a small circular depression, the recessus sphæricus, which is perforated, at its anterior and inferior part, by several minute holes (macula cribrosa media) for the passage of filaments of the acoustic nerve to the saccule; and behind this depression is an oblique ridge, the crista vestibuli, the anterior end of which is named the pyramid of the vestibule".

"The apertures in the pyramid transmit the nerves to the utricle; those in the recessus ellipticus are the nerves to the ampullæ of the superior and lateral semicircular ducts".

"Behind, the five orifices of the semicircular canals can be found".

"There is, in the frontal view, an elliptical opening, which communicates with the scala vestibuli of the cochlea"

f. **Saccule**—"The saccule is a bed of sensory cells situated in the inner ear. . . . (and) translates head movements into neural impulses which the brain can interpret. The saccule is sensitive to linear translations of the head, specifically movements up and down (think about moving on an elevator). When the head moves vertically, the sensory cells of the saccule are disturbed and the neurons connected to them begin transmitting impulses to the brain. These impulses travel along the vestibular portion of the eighth cranial nerve to the vestibular nuclei in the brainstem".

"The anterior part of the saccule exhibits an oval thickening, the macula acustica sacculi, or macula, to which are distributed the saccular filaments of the vestibular branch of the vestibulocochlear nerve, also known as the acoustic nerve or cranial nerve VIII."

"Within the macula are hair cells, each having a hair bundle on the apical aspect. The hair bundle is composed of a single kinocilium and many (at least 70) stereocilia. Stereocilia are connected to mechanically-gated ion channels in the hair cell plasma membrane via tip links."

(2) **Cochlea**—"Within the cochlea are three fluid filled spaces: the tympanic canal, the vestibular canal, and the middle canal. The eighth cranial nerve comes from the brain stem to enter the inner ear. When sound strikes the ear drum, the movement is transferred to the footplate of the stapes, which presses into one of the fluid-filled ducts of the cochlea. The fluid inside this duct is moved, flowing against the receptor cells of the Organ of Corti, which fire. These stimulate the spiral ganglion, which sends information through the auditory portion of the eighth cranial nerve to the brain."

C. Cochlear nerve—[wikipedia—the following are exact quotes or almost exact quotes, and although a considerable amount of study went into the collection and understanding of this information, is not intended to be tutorial, but merely identifying and expository] "The cochlear nerve (also auditory or acoustic nerve) is a nerve in the head that carries signals from the cochlea of the inner ear to the brain. It is part of the vestibulocochlear nerve, the 8th cranial nerve which is found in higher vertebrates; the other portion of the 8th cranial nerve is the vestibular nerve which carries spatial orientation information from the semicircular canals. The cochlear nerve is a sensory nerve, one which conducts to the brain information about the environment, in this case acoustic energy impinging on the tympanic membrane. The cochlear nerve arises from within the cochlea and extends to the brainstem, where its fibers make contact with the cochlear nucleus, the next stage of neural processing in the auditory system."

"In humans, the number of nerve fibers within the cochlear nerve averages around 30,000.[1] The number of fibers varies significantly across species—for example, the domestic cat has some 50,000 fibers. Auditory nerve fibres provide synaptic connections between the hair cells of the cochlea and the cochlear nucleus within the brainstem."

"(The) central axons (of the cochlear nerve) exit the cochlea at its base, where it forms a nerve trunk. In humans, this aspect of the nerve is roughly one inch in length. It projects centrally to the brainstem, where its fibers synapse with the cell bodies of the cochlear nucleus."

D. Cochlear nuclei—[wikipedia—the following are exact quotes or almost exact quotes, and although a considerable amount of study went into the collection and understanding of this information, is not intended to be tutorial, but merely identifying and expository] "The cochlear nucleus is the first 'relay station' of the auditory nervous system and receives mainly ipsilateral afferent input."

"The three major components of the cochlear nuclear complex are: (see figure below)"

* the dorsal cochlear nucleus (DCN)
* the anteroventral cochlear nucleus (AVCN)
* the posteroventral cochlear nucleus (PVCN)

"Each of the three cochlear nuclei are tonotopically organised. The axons from the lower frequency area of the cochlea innervate the ventral portion of the dorsal cochlear nucleus and the ventrolateral portions of the anteroventral cochlear nucleus, while the higher frequency axons project into the dorsal portion of the anteroventral cochlear nucleus and the uppermost dorsal portions of the dorsal cochlear nucleus. The mid frequency projections end up in between the two extremes, in this way the frequency spectrum is preserved."

Reference:

Spoendlin H, Schrott A (1989). "Analysis of the human auditory nerve". Hear Res 43 (1): 25-38.

E. Human brain—[wikipedia—the following are exact quotes or almost exact quotes, and although a considerable amount of study went into the collection and understanding of this information, is not intended to be tutorial, but merely identifying and expository]

"The human brain is the center of the human nervous system and is a highly complex organ. Enclosed in the cranium, it has the same general structure as the brains of other mammals, but is over three times as large as the brain of a typical mammal with an equivalent body size. [Andrews, DG (2001). Neuropsychology. Psychology Press. ISBN 9781841691039. http://books.google.com] Most of the expansion comes from the cerebral cortex, a convoluted layer of neural tissue that covers the surface of the forebrain. Especially expanded are the frontal lobes, which are associated with executive functions such as self-control, planning, reasoning, and abstract thought. The portion of the brain devoted to vision is also greatly enlarged in human beings."

"The human brain has been estimated to contain 50-100 billion neurons, of which about 10 billion are cortical pyramidal cells. These cells pass signals to each other via as many as 1000 trillion synaptic connections. [Buxton, RB (2002). An Introduction to Functional Magnetic Resonance Imaging: Principles and Techniques. Cambridge University Press. ISBN 9780521581134. *http://books.google.com/?id=FordF5AN9vwC*.]"

"The adult human brain weighs on average about 3 lb (1.5 kg) [4] with a size (volume) of around 1130 cubic centimetres (cm3) in women and 1260 cm3 in men, although there is substantial individual variation.[Fisch, BJ; Spehlmann R (1999). Fisch and Spehlmann's

EEG Primer: Basic Principles of Digital and Analog EEG, Elsevier Health Sciences.] Men with the same body height and body surface area as women have on average 100g heavier brains,[Gray, Peter (2002). Psychology (4th ed.). Worth Publishers] although these differences do not correlate in any simple way with gray matter neuron counts or with overall measures of cognitive performance. [Kandel, ER; Schwartz JH, Jessel TM (2000). Principles of Neural Science. McGraw-Hill Professional] Neanderthals had larger brains at adulthood than present-day humans.[Parent, A; Carpenter MB (1995). Carpenter's Human Neuroanatomy. Williams & Wilkins] The brain is very soft, having a consistency similar to soft gelatin or firm tofu. [Preissl, H (2005). Magnetoencephalography. Academic Press] Despite being referred to as "grey matter", the live cortex is pinkish-beige in color and slightly off-white in the interior. At the age of 20, a man has around 176,000 km and a woman, about 149,000 km of myelinated axons in their brains. [Seymour (1999). The Brain. HarperTrophy. ISBN 0-688-17060-9]"

Psychologist Michael Gurian, and author of "What Could He Be Thinking?", believes there are about a hundred structural differences that have been identified between the male and female brain.   [cnn.com/2005/TECH/science/02/14/gender.brain,   15 Feb, 2005]

Gurian believes, "Men, because we tend to compartmentalize our communication into a smaller part of the brain, we tend to be better at getting right to the issue".

Gurian further believes, "The more female brain (will) gather a lot of material, gather a lot of information, feel a lot, hear a lot, sense a lot".

According to the 15 Feb, 2005 CNN report on the brain, "Scientists say males have more activity in mechanical centers of the brain, whereas females show more activity in verbal and emotional centers".

And, According to the 15 Feb, 2005 CNN report on the brain, "MRI scans show that in most women, the corpus callosum area, which handles communication between the brain's two "hemispheres", is larger. In layman's terms, it means that the two sides of the female brain "talk" better to each other — which could explain why studies show women tend to multi-task better. On the other hand, the scans show men tend to move information more easily within each hemisphere."

According to Dr. Daniel Goleman, "Emotional Intelligence, 1995", [p9] "Over millions of years of evolution, the brain has grown from the bottom up, with its higher centers developing as elaborations of lower, more ancient parts." 'The most primitive part of the brain", Dr. Goleman writes [p10], is the brainstem surrounding the top of the spinal cord." "From the most primitive root, the brainstem," Dr. Goleman further writes, "emerged the emotional centers. Millions of years later in evolution, from these emotional areas evolved the thinking brain or 'neocortex'"

Dr. Goleman also writes that, "The most ancient root of our emotional life is in the sense of smell, or, more precisely, in the olfactory lobe . . ." Then, Dr. Goleman writes, "From the olfactory lobe the ancient centers for emotion began to evolve eventually growing large enough to encircle the top of the brainstem, . . . called the 'limbic system'." [p10]

(1) **Brain Monitors and Regulates**—"The brain monitors and regulates the body's actions and reactions. It continuously receives sensory information, and rapidly analyzes this data and then responds, controlling bodily actions and functions."

    a. "The *brainstem* controls breathing, heart rate, and other autonomic processes that are independent of conscious brain functions."

    b. The *neocortex* is the center of higher-order thinking, learning, and memory."

    c. "The **cerebellum** is responsible for the body's balance, posture, and the coordination of movement."

(2) **Functional areas of the brain:**

    a. **"One** consists of the **primary sensory areas**, which receive signals from the sensory nerves and tracts by way of **relay nuclei in the thalamus.** Primary sensory areas include the visual area of the occipital lobe, the auditory area in parts of the temporal lobe and insular cortex, and the somatosensory area in the parietal lobe."

    b. "A **second** category is the **primary motor area**, which **sends axons down to motor neurons in the brainstem** and spinal cord. This area occupies the rear portion of the frontal lobe, directly in front of the somatosensory area."

c. The **third** category consists of the remaining parts of the cortex, which are called the **association areas**. These areas **receive input from the sensory areas** and lower parts of the brain and are involved in the complex process that we call **perception, thought, and decision making**.

(3) **Brodmann Areas**—"Several anatomists have constructed maps of cortical areas on the basis of variations in the appearance of the layers as seen with a microscope. One of the most widely used schemes came from Brodmann, who split the cortex into 51 different areas and assigned each a number (anatomists have since subdivided many of the Brodmann areas). For example, Brodmann area 1 is the primary somatosensory cortex, Brodmann area 17 is the primary visual cortex, and Brodmann area 25 is the anterior cingulate cortex."

(4) **Primary Motor Cortex**—"In a number of cases, brain areas are organized into "topographic maps", where adjoining bits of the cortex correspond to adjoining parts of the body, or of some more abstract entity. A simple example of this type of correspondence is the primary motor cortex, a strip of tissue running along the anterior edge of the central sulcus, shown in the image to the right. Motor areas innervating each part of the body arise from a distinct zone, with neighboring body parts represented by neighboring zones. Electrical stimulation of the cortex at any point causes a muscle-contraction in the represented body part. This "somatotopic" representation is not evenly distributed, however. **The head**, for example, is represented by a region about three times as large as the zone for the **entire back and trunk**. The size of a zone correlates to the precision of motor control and sensory discrimination possible. The areas for the **lips**, **fingers**, and **tongue** are particularly large, considering the proportional size of their represented body parts."

(5) **Visual Areas**—"In visual areas, the maps are retinotopic—that is, they reflect the topography of the retina, the layer of light-activated neurons lining the back of the eye. In this case too the representation is uneven: the fovea—the area at the center

of the visual field—is greatly overrepresented compared to the periphery. The visual circuitry in the human cerebral cortex contains several dozen distinct retinotopic maps, each devoted to analyzing the visual input stream in a particular way. The primary visual cortex (Brodmann area 17), which is the main recipient of direct input from the visual part of the thalamus, contains many neurons that are most easily activated by edges with a particular orientation moving across a particular point in the visual field. Visual areas farther downstream extract features such as color, motion, and shape."

(6) **Auditory Areas**—"In auditory areas, the primary map is tonotopic. Sounds are parsed according to frequency (i.e., high pitch vs. low pitch) by subcortical auditory areas, and this parsing is reflected by the primary auditory zone of the cortex. As with the visual system, there are a number of tonotopic cortical maps, each devoted to analyzing sound in a particular way."

(7) *Visual input*—"Visual input follows a more complex rule: the **optic nerves from the two eyes come together at a point called the *optic chiasm*, and half of the fibers from each nerve split off to join the other. The result is that *connections from the left half of the retina, in both eyes, go to the left side of the brain*, whereas *connections from the right half of the retina go to the right side of the brain*. Because each half of the retina receives light coming from the opposite half of the visual field, the functional consequence is that visual input from the left side of the world goes to the right side of the brain, and vice versa. Thus, the right side of the brain receives somatosensory input from the left side of the body, and visual input from the left side of the visual field—an arrangement that presumably is helpful for **visuomotor coordination**."

(8) *Language*—"In human beings, it is the left hemisphere that usually contains the specialized language areas. While this holds true for 97% of right-handed people, about 19% of left-handed people have their language areas in the right hemisphere and as many as 68% of them have some language abilities in both the left and the right hemisphere. The two hemispheres are thought to contribute to the processing and understanding of language: the left hemisphere processes the

linguistic meaning of prosody (or, the rhythm, stress, and intonation of connected speech), while the right hemisphere processes the emotions conveyed by prosody. [Manlove, George (February 2005). *"Deleted Words"*. UMaine Today Magazine] Studies of children have shown that if a child has damage to the left hemisphere, the child may develop language in the right hemisphere instead. The younger the child, the better the recovery. So, although the "natural" tendency is for language to develop on the left, human brains are capable of adapting to difficult circumstances, if the damage occurs early enough."

"The first language area within the left hemisphere to be discovered is Broca's area. named after Paul Broca, who discovered the area while studying patients with aphasia . . .".

"The second language area to be discovered is called Wernicke's area, after Carl Wernicke, a German neurologist who discovered the area while studying patients who had similar symptoms to Broca's area patients . . .".

(9) **Corpus Callosum**—"The two ***cerebral hemispheres are connected by a very large nerve bundle*** called the ***corpus callosum***, which crosses the midline above the level of the thalamus. There are also two much smaller connections, the anterior commisure and hippocampal commisure, as well as many subcortical connections that cross the midline. The ***corpus callosum is the main avenue of communication between the two hemispheres***, though. It connects each point on the cortex to the mirror-image point in the opposite hemisphere, and also connects to functionally related points in different cortical areas."

(10) **Left and Right Sides**—"In ***most respects, the left and right sides of the brain are symmetrical in terms of function***. For example, the counterpart of the left-hemisphere motor area controlling the right hand is the right-hemisphere area controlling the left hand. There are, however, several very important ***exceptions, involving language and spatial cognition***. In most people, the left hemisphere is "dominant" for language: a stroke that damages a key language area in the left hemisphere can leave the victim unable to speak or

understand, whereas equivalent damage to the right hemisphere would cause only minor impairment to language skills."

(11) *Neocortex*—"The neocortex is a part of the brain of mammals. It is the outer layer of the cerebral hemispheres, and made up of six layers, labelled I to VI (with VI being the innermost and I being the outermost). The **neocortex is part of the cerebral cortex** (along with the archicortex and paleocortex, which are cortical parts of the limbic system). It is involved in **higher functions** such as **sensory perception**, generation of **motor commands**, **spatial reasoning**, **conscious thought and language**."

According to Dr. Daniel Goleman, "Emotional Intelligence, 1995", the **neocortex** is the emotional center of the human brain, which Dr. Goleman terms "the thinking brain". [p10] Dr. Goleman further writes that, "The neocortex is the seat of thought; it contains the centers that put together and comprehend what the senses perceive. It adds to a feeling that we think about it—and allows us to have feelings about ideas, art, symbols, imaginings." [p11] And, Dr. Goleman continues, "The addition of the neocortex and its connections to the limbic system allowed for the mother-child bond that is the basis of the family unit and the long-term commitment to childrearing that makes human development possible." Dr. Goleman also writes that, "The neocortex allows for the subtlety and complexity of emotional life, such as the ability to have feelings (emotions) about our feelings." [p13]

(12) *Cerebellum*—The cerebellum is a region of the brain that plays an important role in motor control. It is also involved in **some *cognitive functions* such as attention and language**, and probably in some **emotional functions** such as regulating **fear and pleasure responses**,[1] but it is its function in movement that is most clearly understood. The cerebellum does not initiate movement, but it **contributes to coordination, precision, and accurate timing**. It receives input from sensory systems and from other parts of the brain and spinal cord, and integrates these inputs to **fine tune motor activity**.[2] Because of this fine-tuning function, damage to the cerebellum does not cause paralysis, but instead produces disorders in fine movement, equilibrium, posture, and motor learning.[2]

1. Wolf U, Rapoport MJ, Schweizer TA (2009). "Evaluating the affective component of the cerebellar cognitive affective syndrome". J. Neuropsychiatry Clin. Neurosci. 21 (3): 245-53. doi:10.1176/appi.neuropsych.21.3.245. PMID 19776302.

2. a b c d Fine EJ, Ionita CC, Lohr L (2002). "The history of the development of the cerebellar examination". Semin Neurol 22 (4): 375-84. doi:10.1055/s-2002-36759. PMID 12539058.

(13) **Basal ganglia**—"The basal ganglia (or basal nuclei) are a group of nuclei in the brains of vertebrates. They are situated at the base of the forebrain and strongly connected with the cerebral cortex, thalamus and other areas. The basal ganglia are associated with a variety of functions, including motor control and learning."

"Experimental studies show that the basal ganglia exert an inhibitory influence on a number of motor systems, and that a release of this inhibition permits a motor system to become active. The "behavior switching" that takes place within the basal ganglia is influenced by signals from many parts of the brain, including the prefrontal cortex, which is widely believed to play a key role in executive functions."

"The **main components of the basal ganglia** are the *striatum, pallidum,* **substantia nigra**, and *subthalamic nucleus.*"

"The **basal ganglia** also have **a limbic sector** whose components are assigned distinct names: the *nucleus accumbens* (NA), *ventral pallidum,* **and** *ventral tegmental area* (VTA)."

"**VTA efferents** provide dopamine to the **nucleus accumbens** (ventral striatum) in the same way that the **substantia nigra** provides dopamine to the **dorsal striatum**. Because there is much evidence that it plays a central role in reward learning, the VTA→NA **dopaminergic** projection has attracted a great deal of attention. For example, a number of **highly addictive drugs**, including cocaine, amphetamines, and nicotine, are thought to work by **increasing the efficacy of the VTA→NA dopamine signal**. There is also evidence implicating overactivity of the VTA dopaminergic projection in schizophrenia."

"The flow of neural signals through the basal ganglia is strongly directional. The striatum is the primary recipient of input from other brain areas, most notably the cerebral cortex. The internal segment of the globus pallidus (GPi), together with the reticular part of the substantia nigra (SNr), give rise to the primary output, most notably to the thalamus. The striatum projects to the pallidum both directly and indirectly via the subthalamic nucleus, which also receives cortical input. The substantia nigra consists of two parts, one of which functions similarly to the pallidum, the other of which sends a modulatory dopaminergic input to the striatum and other structures."

Basal Ganglia Main components dscriptions:

a. **striatum**—"The **striatum receives input from many brain areas** but sends **output only to other components of the basal ganglia.**"
b. **pallidum**—"The **pallidum receives its most important input from the** *striatum* (either directly or indirectly), and sends **inhibitory output to a number of motor-related areas, including the part of the thalamus** that projects to the motor-related areas of the cortex."
c. **substantia nigra**—"The **substantia** *nigra* consists of two parts, one that functions **similarly to the pallidum**, and another that **provides the source of dopamine input to the striatum.**"
d. **subthalamic nucleus**—The **subthalamic nucleus receives input mainly from** *the* **striatum and cortex, and projects to the pallidum.**

Basal Ganglia role in Eye movements—"One of the most intensively studied functions of the BG is their role in controlling eye movements.[**Hikosaka, O; Takikawa, Y; Kawagoe, R (1 July 2000).** "**Role of the basal ganglia in the control of purposive saccadic eye movements**] Eye movement is influenced by an extensive network of brain regions that converge on a midbrain area called the superior colliculus (SC). The SC is a layered structure whose layers form two-dimensional retinotopic maps of visual space. A "bump" of neural activity in the deep layers of the SC drives an eye movement directed toward the corresponding point in space."

"The SC receives a strong inhibitory projection from the BG, originating in the substantia nigra pars reticulata (SNr).[**Hikosaka, O; Takikawa, Y; Kawagoe, R (1 July 2000). "Role of the basal ganglia in the control of purposive saccadic eye movements"**] Neurons in the SNr usually fire continuously at high rates, but at the onset of an eye movement they "pause", thereby releasing the SC from inhibition. Eye movements of all types are associated with "pausing" in the SNr; however, individual SNr neurons may be more strongly associated with some types of movements than others. Neurons in some parts of the caudate nucleus also show activity related to eye movements. Since the great majority of caudate cells fire at very low rates, this activity almost always shows up as an increase in firing rate. Thus, eye movements begin with activation in the caudate nucleus, which inhibits the SNr via the direct GABAergic projections, which in turn disinhibits the SC."

Basal Ganglia role in motivation—"The role in motivation of the "limbic" part of the basal ganglia—the nucleus accumbens (NA), ventral pallidum, and ventral tegmental area (VTA)—is particularly well established. Thousands of experimental studies combine to demonstrate that the dopaminergic projection from the VTA to the NA plays a central role in the brain's reward system."

Basal Ganglia Disorders:

a. **Parkinson's disease**—"Parkinson's disease involves major loss of dopaminergic cells in the substantia nigra. Parkinson's disease is characterized by gradual loss of the ability to initiate movement"

b. **Huntington's disease**—"Huntington's disease involves massive loss of medium spiny neurons in the striatum. Huntington's disease is characterized by an inability to prevent parts of the body from moving unintentionally."

c. **Hemiballismus**—"A different movement disorder, called hemiballismus, may result from damage restricted to the subthalamic nucleus. Hemiballismus is characterized by violent and uncontrollable flinging movements of the arms and legs."

(14) **Brainstem**—"In vertebrate anatomy the brainstem (or brain stem) is the posterior part of the brain, adjoining and structurally continuous with the spinal cord. The brain stem provides the **main motor and sensory innervation to the face** and neck via the cranial nerves. Though small, this is an extremely important part of the brain as the **nerve connections of the motor and sensory systems from the main part of the brain to the rest of the body pass through the brain stem**. This includes the *corticospinal* tract (motor), the posterior *column-medial lemniscus pathway* (fine touch, vibration sensation and proprioception) and the *spinothalamic tract* (pain, temperature, itch and crude touch). The brain stem also plays an important role in the *regulation of cardiac and respiratory function*. It also *regulates the central nervous system*, and is pivotal in *maintaining consciousness and regulating the sleep cycle*."

Proprioception—means "one's own perception, and is the sense of the relative position of neighbouring parts of the body. Unlike the exteroceptive senses by which we perceive the outside world, and interoceptive senses, by which we perceive the pain and movement of internal organs, proprioception is a third distinct sensory modality that provides feedback solely on the status of the body internally. It is the sense that indicates whether the body is moving with required effort, as well as where the various parts of the body are located in relation to each other."

Brainstem components are:

a. *medulla oblongata* (myelencephalon)—"The *medulla oblongata* is the lower half of the brainstem. In discussions of neurology and similar contexts where no ambiguity will result, it is often referred to as simply the medulla. The medulla contains the cardiac, respiratory, vomiting and vasomotor centers and deals with autonomic functions, such as breathing, heart rate and blood pressure."

b ***pons*** (part of metencephalon)—"This *white matter* includes tracts that conduct signals from the *cerebrum* down to the cerebellum and medulla, and tracts that carry the sensory signals up into the *thalamus*. The pons contains nuclei that relay signals from the forebrain to the cerebellum, along with nuclei that deal primarily with sleep, respiration, swallowing, bladder control, hearing, equilibrium, taste, eye movement, facial expressions, facial sensation, and posture." [Saladin Kenneth S.(2007)]

c. ***midbrain*** (mesencephalon). [Dorland's Medical Dictionary]—"The mesencephalon (or midbrain) comprises the tectum (or corpora quadrigemina), tegmentum, the ventricular mesocoelia (or "iter"), and the cerebral peduncles, as well as several nuclei and fasciculi. Caudally the ***mesencephalon adjoins the pons*** (metencephalon) and rostrally it ***adjoins the diencephalons***"

d. **diencephalon** (Less frequently, parts of the diencephalon are included)—"The diencephalon **("interbrain")** is the region of the brain that includes the thalamus, metathalamus, hypothalamus, epithalamus, prethalamus **or** subthalamus, pretectum, and the posterior portion of the pituitary gland. The diencephalon and the telencephalon both derive from the prosencephalon **(forebrain).** The diencephalon is located near the midline of the brain, above the mesencephalon **(midbrain)."** [Dorland's Medical Dictionary]

"The hypothalamus performs numerous vital functions, most of which relate directly or indirectly to the regulation of visceral activities (heart rate, digestion, respiration rate, salivation, perspiration, diameter of the pupils, micturition (urination), and sexual arousal. Breathing works in tandem with the conscious mind) by way of other brain regions and the autonomic nervous system." [Dorland's Medical Dictionary]

(15) **Cerebral cortex**—"The ***cerebral cortex*** is a sheet of neural tissue that is outermost to the cerebrum of the mammalian

brain. It plays a key role in memory, attention, perceptual awareness, thought, language, and consciousness. It is constituted of up to six horizontal layers, each of which has a different composition in terms of neurons and connectivity. The human cerebral cortex is 2-4 mm (0.08-0.16 inches) thick."

"The phylogenetically (evolutionary relatedness) most recent part of the cerebral cortex, the **neocortex** (also called isocortex), is differentiated into six horizontal layers; the more ancient part of the cerebral cortex, the hippocampus (also called archicortex), has at most three cellular layers, and is divided into subfields."

"The cerebral cortex is connected to various subcortical structures such as the *thalamus* and the *basal ganglia*, **sending information to them along *efferent connections* and receiving information from them via *afferent connections*.** Most sensory information is routed to the cerebral cortex via the thalamus."

"Olfactory information, however, passes through the *olfactory bulb to the olfactory cortex* (piriform cortex)."

The **cortex** is commonly described as comprising *three parts*:

a. *sensory*—"The sensory areas are the areas that receive and process information from the senses. The senses of *vision*, *audition*, and *touch* are served by the *primary visual cortex*, *primary auditory cortex* and *primary somatosensory cortex*."

b. *Motor*—"The motor areas are very closely related to the control of voluntary movements, especially fine fragmented movements performed by the hand. The right half of the motor area controls the left side of the body, and vice versa."

c. *association areas.*—"Association areas function to produce a meaningful perceptual experience of the world, enable us to interact effectively, and support abstract thinking and language. They are involved in higher mental functions such as learning, remembering, thinking, and speaking." [David G Meyers Publisher: Catherine Woods Title: Exploring Psychology seventh edition pages: 55]

(16) **Thalamus** [wikipedia]—The thalamus "is situated between the cerebral cortex and midbrain", and, "is perched on top of the brainstem, near the center of the brain, in a position to send nerve fibers out to the cerebral cortex in all directions. Its function includes relaying sensation, spatial sense and motor signals to the cerebral cortex, along with the regulation of consciousness, sleep and alertness".

"The thalamus comprises a system of lamellae (made up of myelinated fibers) separating different thalamic subparts. Other areas are defined by distinct clusters of neurons, such as the periventricular gray, the intralaminar elements, the 'nucleus limitans', and others." [Jones Edward G.(2007) "The Thalamus" Cambridge Uni. Press]

"The thalamus has multiple functions. It is generally believed to act as a relay between a variety of subcortical areas and the cerebral cortex. In particular, every sensory system (with the exception of the olfactory system) includes a thalamic nucleus that receives sensory signals and sends them to the associated primary cortical area."

For the visual system, for example, inputs from the retina are sent to the lateral geniculate nucleus of the thalamus, which in turn projects to the primary visual cortex (area V1) in the occipital lobe."

"The thalamus is believed to both process sensory information as well as relaying it—each of the primary sensory relay areas receives strong 'back projections' from the cerebral cortex."

"Similarly the medial geniculate nucleus acts as a key auditory relay between the inferior colliculus of the midbrain and the primary auditory cortex, and the ventral posterior nucleus is a key somatosensory relay, which sends touch and proprioceptive information to the primary somatosensory cortex."

"The thalamus also plays an important role in regulating states of sleep and wakefulness. [Steriade, M. and Llinas, R. (1988) "The functional states of the thalamus and the associated neuronal interplay". Physiological Reviews 68: 699-742] Thalamic nuclei have strong reciprocal connections with the cerebral cortex, forming thalamo-cortico-thalamic circuits that are believed to be involved with consciousness. The thalamus plays a major role in regulating arousal, the level of awareness, and activity. Damage to the thalamus can lead to permanent coma."

"Many different functions are linked to various regions of the thalamus. This is the case for many of the sensory systems (except for the olfactory system), such as the auditory, somatic, visceral, gustatory and visual systems where localized lesions provoke specific sensory deficits. A major role of the thalamus is devoted to "motor" systems."

(17) **Vestibular nerve** [wikipedia]-
"The vestibular nerve is one of the two branches of the Vestibulocochlear nerve (the cochlear nerve being the other). It goes to the semicircular canals via the vestibular ganglion. It receives positional information."

"Axons of the vestibular nerve synapse in the vestibular nucleus on the lateral floor and wall of the fourth ventricle in the **pons** and **medulla**."

"It (Vestibular nerve) arises from bipolar cells in the vestibular ganglion, ganglion of Scarpa, which is situated in the upper part of the outer end of the internal auditory meatus."

(18) **Hippocampus and the amygdala** [Dr. Daniel Goleman, psychologist, "Emotional Intelligence", 1995]—

a. **Amygdala**—"In humans the amygdala is an almond shaped cluster of interconnected structures perched above the brainstem near the bottom of the limbic ring. There are two amygdalas, one on each side of the brain, nestled toward the side of the head. The human amygdala is relatively large compared to that in any of our closest evolutionary cousins, the primates." [p15]

b. **Hyppocampus** [wikipedia]—The **hippocampus** is a major component of the brains of humans and other mammals. It belongs to the limbic system and plays important roles in long-term memory and spatial navigation. Like the cerebral cortex, with which it is closely associated, it is a paired structure, with mirror-image halves in the left and right sides of the brain. In humans and other primates, the hippocampus is located inside the medial temporal lobe, beneath the cortical surface. It contains two main interlocking parts: Ammon's horn and the dentate gyrus.

"The hippocampus and the amygdala were the two key parts of the primitive 'nose brain' that, in evolution, gave rise to the cortex and then the neocortex. These limbic structures do much or most of the brain's learning and remembering; the amygdala is the specialist for emotional matters. If the amygdala is severed from the rest of the brain, the result is a striking inability to gauge the emotional significance of events." [p15]

"The amygdala acts as a storehouse of emotional memory, and thus of significance itself; life without the amygdala is a life stripped of personal meanings." [p15]

"Animals that have their amygdala removed or severed lack fear and rage, lose the urge to compete or cooperate, and no longer have any sense of the place in their kind's social order." [p15]

"The brain gives the amygdale a privileged position as an emotional sentinel, able to hijack the brain." [Joseph LeDoux, "The shooting of Matilda Crabtree", The New York time, Nov. 11, 1994] LeDoux's research has shown that, "sensory signals from eye or ear travel first in the brain to the thalamus, and then—across a single synapse—to the amygdale; a second signal from the thalamus is routed to the neocortex—the thinking brain. This branching allows the amygdala to begin to respond before the neocortex, which mulls information through several levels of brain circuits before it fully perceives and finally initiates its more finely tailored response. This circuit does much to explain the power of emotion to overwhelm rationality." [p17]

"The amygdala can trigger an emotional response via this emergency route even as a parallel reverberating circuit begins between the amygdale and the neocortex. The amygdala can have us spring to action while the slightly slower—but more fully informed—neocortex unfolds its more refined plan for reaction." [p18]

"The amygdala can house memories and response repertoires that we enact without quite realizing why we do so because the shortcut from thalamus to amygdala completely bypasses the neocortex." [LeDoux, p18]

"While the hippocampus remembers the dry facts, the amygdala retains the emotional flavor that goes with those facts." [p20]

"Under stress a nerve running from the brain to the adrenal glands atop the kidney triggers a secretion of the hormones epinephrine and norepinephrine, which surge through the body priming it for an emergency. These hormones activate receptors on the vagus nerve; while the vagus nerve carries messages from the brain to regulate the heart, it also carries signals back into the brain, triggered by epinephrine and norepinephrine. The amygdala is the main site in the brain where these signals go; they activate neurons within the amygdale to signal other brain regions to strengthen memory for what is happening." [pp20-21]

(19) **Brain metabolism**—"Brain metabolism normally is completely dependent upon blood glucose as an energy source, since fatty acids do not cross the blood-brain barrier.[MedBio. info > Integration of Metabolism, Professor em. Robert S. Horn, Oslo, Norway] During times of low glucose (such as fasting), the brain will primarily use ketone bodies for fuel with a smaller requirement for glucose. The brain does not store any glucose in the form of glycogen, in contrast, for example, to skeletal muscle."

(20) **Blood-brain barrier**—"The blood-brain barrier (BBB) is a *separation of circulating blood and cerebrospinal fluid (CSF)* in the *central nervous system (CNS)*. It occurs along all capillaries and consists of tight junctions around the capillaries that do not exist in normal circulation. Endothelial cells restrict the diffusion of microscopic objects (e.g. bacteria) and large or hydrophilic molecules into the CSF, while allowing the diffusion of small hydrophobic molecules (O_2, hormones, CO_2). Cells of the barrier actively transport metabolic products such as glucose across the barrier with specific proteins."

(21) **Brain Disorders:**

    a. **Nurodegenerative diseases**—"**Nurodegenerative diseases**, such as Alzheimer's disease, Parkinson's disease, motor neurone disease, and Huntington's disease are caused by the gradual death of individual neurons, leading to diminution in movement control, memory, and cognition."

b. **Infectious Diseases**—"Some **infectious diseases** affecting the brain are caused by viruses and bacteria. Infection of the meninges, the membrane that covers the brain, can lead to meningitis. Bovine spongiform encephalopathy (also known as "mad cow disease") is deadly in cattle and humans and is linked to prions. Kuru is a similar prion-borne degenerative brain disease affecting humans. Both are linked to the ingestion of neural tissue, and may explain the tendency in human and some non-human species to avoid cannibalism. Viral or bacterial causes have been reported in multiple sclerosis and Parkinson's disease, and are established causes of encephalopathy, and encephalomyelitis."

c. **Genetic and Chromosomal Errors**—"Many brain disorders are congenital, occurring during development. Tay-Sachs disease, fragile X syndrome, and Down syndrome are all linked to genetic and chromosomal errors. Many other syndromes, such as the intrinsic circadian rhythm disorders, are suspected to be congenital as well. Normal development of the brain can be altered by genetic factors, drug use, nutritional deficiencies, and infectious diseases during pregnancy."

F. **Human Eye** [Dr. Ted Montgomery, *http://www.tedmontgomery.com/the_eye*]—All quotations in this section are from Dr. Montgomery's website. There is of course much more to human eyesight in Dr. Montgomery's website than I have presented here. I have just presented here the highlights as expository identification to show the irreducible complexity, and very specific design which equivocates to intelligent design. As I near the end of my discussion on "Intelligent Design", I get the eerie feeling that the human brain evolved over a period of millions of years by modifying (mutating) the human genome to build the human brain as it exists today and all of its attendant human anatomy, as I have described in these sections on human anatomy. As scientists have concluded this evolution appears to have happened by (1) natural selection, (2) adaptation, and (3) mutation. However, I have seen no evidence into my investigations for Intelligent Design for human existence on this earth, nor for the creation of the universe, nor for the creation of the earth and all of the ecosystems necessary to sustain life on earth to have evolved by "random processes".

And now for the scientific facts about human eyesight quoting from Dr. Montgomery's website.

"The eye allows us to see and interpret the shapes, colors, and dimensions of objects in the world by processing the light they reflect or emit. The eye is able to detect bright light or dim light, but it cannot sense objects when light is absent."

"Several structures compose the human eye. Among the most important anatomical components are the **cornea, conjunctiva, iris, crystalline lens, vitreous humor, retina, macula, optic nerve, and extraocular muscles**."

"Light waves from an object (such as a tree) enter the eye first through the cornea, which is the clear dome at the front of the eye. The light then progresses through the **pupil**, the circular opening in the center of the **colored iris**."

"Fluctuations in incoming light change the size of the eye's **pupil**. When the light entering the eye is bright enough, the pupil will constrict (get smaller), due to the pupillary light response."

"Initially, the **light waves are bent or converged first by the cornea**, and then further by the **crystalline lens** (located immediately behind the **iris** and the **pupil**), to a nodal point (N) located immediately behind the back surface of the lens. At that point, the image becomes reversed (turned backwards) and inverted (turned upside-down)."

"The light continues through the **vitreous humor**, the clear gel that makes up about 80% of the eye's volume, and then, ideally, back to a clear focus on the **retina**, behind the vitreous. The small central area of the retina is the **macula**, which provides the best vision of any location in the **retina**."

"Within the layers of the **retina**, light impulses are changed into **electrical signals**. Then they are sent through the **optic nerve**, along the visual pathway, to the **occipital cortex** at the posterior (back) of the brain. Here, the electrical signals are interpreted or "seen" by the brain as a visual image."

According to Dr. Montgomery, "The eyeball is set in a protective cone-shaped cavity in the skull called the '**orbit**' or 'socket'. The orbit is surrounded by layers of soft, fatty tissue (**extraocular muscles**). These layers protect the eye and enable it to turn easily."

Also according to Dr. Montgmoery, "The **cornea** is composed of 5 layers, from the front to the back" These layers are:

1. epithelium,
2. Bowman's (anterior limiting) membrane,
3. stroma (substantia propria),
4. Descemet's (posterior limiting) membrane, and
5. endothelium (posterior epithelium).

Dr. Montgomery also writes that, "Along its circumference, the cornea is continuous with the **sclera**: the white, opaque portion of the eye. The **sclera** makes up the back five-sixths of the eye's outer layer. It provides protection and serves as an attachment for the **extraocular muscles**, which move the eye.

"The **conjunctiva** is a clear mucous membrane that lines the inner surfaces of the eyelids and continues on to cover the front surface of the eyeball, except for the central clear portion of the outer eye (the cornea). The entire conjunctiva is transparent."

"The **iris**, visible through the clear cornea as the colored disc inside of the eye, is a thin diaphragm composed mostly of connective tissue and smooth muscle fibers. It is situated between the cornea and the crystalline lens. The iris is composed of 3 layers, from the front to the back":

1. endothelium,
2. stroma, and
3. epithelium.

"The transparent **crystalline lens** of the eye is located immediately **behind the iris**. It is composed of fibers that come from epithelial (hormone-producing) cells. In fact, the cytoplasm of these cells makes up the transparent substance of the lens. The lens capsule is a clear, membrane-like structure that is quite elastic, a quality that keeps it under constant tension. As a result, the lens naturally tends towards a rounder or more globular configuration, a shape it must assume for the eye to focus at a near distance. The crystalline lens is composed of 4 layers, from the surface to the center":

1. capsule,
2. subcapsular epithelium,
3. cortex, and
4. nucleus.

Also, according to Dr. Montgomery, "Light entering the eye is converged first by the cornea, then by the crystalline lens. This focusing system is so powerful that the light rays intersect at a point just behind the lens (inside the vitreous humor) and diverge from that point back to the retina. This diverging light passes through 9 (clear) layers of the retina and, ideally, is brought into focus in an upside-down image on the first (outermost) retinal layer (pigmented epithelium). Then, amazingly, the image is reflected back onto the adjacent second layer, where the rods and cones are located."

Then, Dr. Montgomery writes about the real magic of eyesight and that is the **photoreceptors (cones and rods).**

"Rods and cones actually face away from incoming light, which passes by these photoreceptors before being reflected back onto them. Light causes a **chemical reaction with "iodopsin" in cones** (activated in photopic or bright conditions) and with **"rhodopsin" in rods** (activated in scotopic or dark conditions), *beginning the visual process.*"

"Activated **photoreceptors stimulate bipolar cells, which in turn stimulate ganglion cells. The impulses continue into the axons of the ganglion cells, through the optic nerve, and to the visual center at the back of the brain,** where the image is perceived as right-side up. The brain actually can detect one photon of light (the smallest packet of energy available) being absorbed by a photoreceptor."

"There are about **6.5 to 7 million cones in each eye**, and they are sensitive to bright light and to color. The highest concentration of cones is in the macula. The fovea centralis, at the center of the macula, contains only cones and no rods."

"There are about **120 to 130 million rods in each eye**, and they are sensitive to dim light, to movement, and to shapes. The highest concentration of rods is in the peripheral retina, decreasing in density up to the macula."

"The optic nerve (also known as cranial nerve II) is a continuation of the axons of the ganglion cells in the retina. There are approximately **1.1 million nerve cells in each optic nerve. The optic nerve, which acts like a cable connecting the eye with the brain**, actually is more like brain tissue than it is nerve tissue."

G. **Metabolism** [wikipedia]—"Metabolism involves a vast array of chemical reactions, but most fall under a few basic types of reactions that involve the transfer of functional groups". [Mitchell P (1979). "The Ninth Sir Hans Krebs Lecture. Compartmentation and communication in living systems. Ligand conduction: a general catalytic principle in chemical, osmotic and chemiosmotic reaction systems". *Eur J Biochem* **95** (1): 1-20]

"This common chemistry allows cells to use a small set of metabolic intermediates to carry chemical groups between different reactions". [Wimmer M, Rose I (1978). "Mechanisms of enzyme-catalyzed group transfer reactions". *Annu Rev Biochem* **47**: 1031-78.]

"These group-transfer intermediates are called coenzymes. Each class of group-transfer reaction is carried out by a particular coenzyme, which is the substrate for a set of enzymes that produce it, and a set of enzymes that consume it. These coenzymes are therefore continuously being made, consumed and then recycled". [Dimroth P, von Ballmoos C, Meier T (March 2006). "Catalytic and mechanical cycles in F-ATP synthases Fourth in the cycles Review Series"]

One central coenzyme is adenosine triphosphate (ATP), the universal energy currency of cells. This nucleotide is used to transfer chemical energy between different chemical reactions. There is only a small amount of ATP in cells, but as it is continuously regenerated, the human body can use about its own weight in ATP per day. [Dimroth P, von Ballmoos C, Meier T (March 2006). "Catalytic and mechanical cycles in F-ATP synthases Fourth in the cycles Review Series"] ATP acts as a bridge between catabolism and anabolism, with catabolic reactions generating ATP and anabolic reactions consuming it. It also serves as a carrier of phosphate groups in phosphorylation reactions.

F. **Circulatory system** [wikipedia]—"The cardiovascular system and the lymphatic system collectively make up the circulatory system. Two types of fluids move through the circulatory system: blood and lymph. The blood, heart, and blood vessels form the cardiovascular system. The lymph, lymph nodes, and lymph vessels form the lymphatic system."

(1) Human cardiovascular system—"The main components of the human cardiovascular system are the heart and the blood vessels. It includes: the pulmonary circulation, a "loop" through the lungs where blood is oxygenated; and the systemic circulation, a "loop" through the rest of the body to provide oxygenated blood. An average adult contains five to six quarts (roughly 4.7 to 5.7 liters) of blood, which consists of plasma, red blood cells, white blood cells, and platelets. Also, the digestive system works with the circulatory system to provide the nutrients the system needs to keep the heart pumping."

(2) Pulmonary circulation—"The Pulmonary circulation is the portion of the cardiovascular system which transports oxygen-depleted blood away from the heart, to the lungs, and returns oxygenated blood back to the heart."

(3) "Oxygen deprived blood from the vena cava enters the right atrium of the heart and flows through the tricuspid valve into the right ventricle, from which it is pumped through the pulmonary semilunar valve into the pulmonary arteries which go to the lungs. Pulmonary veins return the now oxygen-rich blood to the heart, where it enters the left atrium before flowing through the mitral valve into the left ventricle. Then, oxygen-rich blood from the left ventricle is pumped out via the aorta, and on to the rest of the body."

(4) Systemic circulation—"Systemic circulation is the portion of the cardiovascular system which transports oxygenated blood away from the heart, to the rest of the body, and returns

oxygen-depleted blood back to the heart. Systemic circulation is, distance-wise, much longer than pulmonary circulation, transporting blood to every part of the body."

(5) Coronary circulation—"The coronary circulatory system provides a blood supply to the heart. As it provides oxygenated blood to the heart, it is by definition a part of the systemic circulatory system."

(6) Heart—"The heart pumps oxygenated blood to the body and deoxygenated blood to the lungs. In the human heart there is one atrium and one ventricle for each circulation, and with both a systemic and a pulmonary circulation there are four chambers in total: left atrium, left ventricle, right atrium and right ventricle. The right atrium is the upper chamber of the right side of the heart. The blood that is returned to the right atrium is deoxygenated (poor in oxygen) and passed into the right ventricle to be pumped through the pulmonary artery to the lungs for re-oxygenation and removal of carbon dioxide. The left atrium receives newly oxygenated blood from the lungs as well as the pulmonary vein which is passed into the strong left ventricle to be pumped through the aorta to the different organs of the body."

(7) Closed cardiovascular system—"The cardiovascular systems of humans are closed, meaning that the blood never leaves the network of blood vessels. In contrast, oxygen and nutrients diffuse across the blood vessel layers and enters interstitial fluid, which carries oxygen and nutrients to the target cells, and carbon dioxide and wastes in the opposite direction. The other component of the circulatory system, the lymphatic system, is not closed. The heart is located in the center of the body between the two lungs. The reason that the heart beat is felt on the left side is because the left ventricle is pumping harder."

(8) Oxygen transportation—"About 98.5% of the oxygen in a sample of arterial blood in a healthy human breathing air at sea-level pressure is chemically combined with haemoglobin molecules. About 1.5% is physically dissolved in the other blood liquids and not connected to Hgb. The haemoglobin molecule is the primary transporter of oxygen in mammals and many other species."

I. **Human gastrointestinal tract** [wikipedia]—"The Human gastrointestinal tract refers to the stomach and intestine, [gastrointestinal tract at Dorland's Medical Dictionary] and sometimes to all the structures from the mouth to the anus. [MeSH Gastrointestinal+tract] (The "digestive system" is a broader term that includes other structures, including the accessory organs of digestion)." [MeSH Gastrointestinal+tract]

"In an adult male human, the gastrointestinal (GI) are 5 metres (20 ft) long in a live subject, or up to 9 metres (30 ft) without the effect of muscle tone, and consists of the upper and lower GI tracts. The tract may also be divided into foregut, midgut, and hindgut, reflecting the embryological origin of each segment of the tract."

"The GI tract releases hormones as to help regulate the digestion process. These hormones, including gastrin, secretin, cholecystokinin, and grehlin, are mediated through either intracrine or autocrine mechanisms, indicating that the cells releasing these hormones are conserved structures throughout evolution." [Nelson RJ. 2005. Introduction to Behavioral Endocrinology. Sinauer Associates: Massachusetts. p 57.]

The GI tract can be divided into four concentric layers:

a. **Mucosa**—"This layer comes in direct contact with food (or bolus), and is responsiblefor absorption and secretion, important processes in digestion."

b. **Submucosa**—"The submucosa consists of a dense irregular layer of connective tissue with large blood vessels, lymphatics, and nerves branching into the mucosa and muscularis externa. It contains Meissner's plexus, an enteric nervous plexus, situated on the inner surface of the muscularis externa."

c. **Muscularis externa** (the external muscle layer)—"The muscularis externa consists of an inner circular layer and a longitudinal outer muscular layer. The circular muscle layer prevents food from traveling backward and the longitudinal layer shortens the tract. The coordinated contractions of these layers is called peristalsis and propels the bolus, or balled-up food, through the GI tract."

d. **Adventitia or serosa**—"The adventitia consists of several layers of epithelia."

(1) **Upper gastrointestinal tract**—"The upper gastrointestinal tract consists of the esophagus, stomach, and duodenum." [MeSH Upper+Gastrointestinal+Tract]

(2) **Lower gastrointestinal tract**—"The lower gastrointestinal tract includes most of the small intestine and all of the large intestine." [MeSH Lower+Gastrointestinal+Tract]

Small intestine, which has three parts:

+ Duodenum—Here the digestive juices from pancreas and liver mix together, where most chemical digestion takes place

The duodenum is largely responsible for the breakdown of food in the small intestine, using enzymes. Brunner's glands, which secrete mucus, are found in the duodenum. The duodenum wall is composed of a very thin layer of cells that form the muscularis mucosae. The duodenum is almost entirely retroperitoneal.

The duodenum also regulates the rate of emptying of the stomach via hormonal pathways. Secretin and cholecystokinin are released from cells in the duodenal epithelium in response to acidic and fatty stimuli present there when the pylorus opens and releases gastric chyme into the duodenum for further digestion. These cause the liver and gall bladder to release bile, and the pancreas to release bicarbonate and digestive enzymes such as trypsin, lipase and amylase into the duodenum as they are needed.

+ Jejunum—It is the midsection of the intestine, connecting duodenum to ileum.
+ Ileum— where all soluble molecules are absorbed into the blood.

Large intestine, which has three parts:

+ Cecum (the vermiform appendix is attached to the cecum).
+ Colon (ascending colon, transverse colon, descending colon and sigmoid flexure)
+ Rectum

(3) **Immune function**—"The gastrointestinal tract also is a prominent part of the immune system. [Richard Coico, Geoffrey Sunshine, Eli Benjamini (2003). Immunology: a short course. New York: Wiley-Liss. ISBN 0-471-22689-0] The surface area of the digestive tract is estimated to be the surface area of a football field. With such a large exposure, the immune system must work hard to prevent pathogens from entering into blood and lymph." [Animal Physiology textbook]

"The low pH (ranging from 1 to 4) of the stomach is fatal for many microorganisms that enter it. Similarly, mucus (containing IgA antibodies) neutralizes many of these microorganisms. Other factors in the GI tract help with immune function as well, including enzymes in saliva and bile. Enzymes such as Cyp3A4, along with the antiporter activities, also are instrumental in the intestine's role of detoxification of antigens and xenobiotics, such as drugs, involved in first pass metabolism."

"Health-enhancing intestinal bacteria serve to prevent the overgrowth of potentially harmful bacteria in the gut. These two types of bacteria compete for space and "food," as there are limited resources within the intestinal tract. A ratio of 80-85% beneficial to 15-20% potentially harmful bacteria generally is considered normal within the intestines. Microorganisms also are kept at bay by an extensive immune system comprising the gut-associated lymphoid tissue (GALT)."

Oxygen Cycle References

1. Steve Nadis, The Cells That Rule the Seas, Scientific American, Nov. 2003 [1]
2. Walker, J. C. G. (1980) The oxygen cycle in the natural environment and the biogeochemical cycles, Springer-Verlag, Berlin, Federal Republic of Germany (DEU)

*   Cloud, P. and Gibor, A. 1970, The oxygen cycle, Scientific American, September, S. 110-123
*   Fasullo, J., Substitute Lectures for ATOC 3600: Principles of Climate, Lectures on the global oxygen cycle, http://paos.colorado.edu/~fasullo/pjw_class/oxygencycle.html
*   Morris, R.M., OXYSPHERE—A Beginners' Guide to the Biogeochemical Cycling of Atmospheric Oxygen, http://seis.natsci.csulb.edu/rmorris/oxy/Oxy.htm

Auditory References

1. Greinwald, John H. Jr MD; Hartnick, Christopher J. MD The Evaluation of Children With Hearing Loss. Archives of Otolaryngology — Head & Neck Surgery. 128(1):84-87, January 2002
2. Stenström, J. Sten: Deformities of the ear; In: Grabb, W., C., Smith, J.S. (Edited): "Plastic Surgery", Little, Brown and Company, Boston, 1979, ISBN 0-316-32269-5 (C), ISBN 0-316-32268-7 (P)
3. Deborah S. Sarnoff, Robert H. Gotkin, and Joan Swirsky (2002). Instant Beauty: Getting Gorgeous on Your Lunch Break. St. Martin's Press. ISBN 031228697X. http://books.google.com/books?id=ljeY_Tvyl_MC&pg=PA60&ots=pt_I8xjg9k&dq=earlobe+tear+earring&sig=YBnRJSoIUiA1Kjhrzpq_Odd_0yk.
4. Lam SM. Edward Talbot Ely: father of aesthetic otoplasty. [Biography. Historical Article. Journal Article] Archives of Facial Plastic Surgery. 6(1):64, 2004 Jan-Feb.
5. Siegert R. Combined reconstruction of congenital auricular atresia and severe microtia. [Evaluation Studies. Journal Article] Laryngoscope. 113(11):2021-7; discussion 2028-9, 2003 Nov.
6. Trigg DJ. Applebaum EL. Indications for the surgical repair of unilateral aural atresia in children. [Review] [33 refs] [Journal Article. Review], American Journal of Otology. 19(5):679-84; discussion 684-6, 1998 September
7. Anson and Donaldson, Surgical Anatomy of the Temporal Bone, 4th Edition, Raven Press, 1992
8. Senate Public Works Committee, Noise Pollution and Abatement Act of 1972, S. Rep. No. 1160, 92nd Cong. 2nd session.
9. a b Darwin, Charles (1871). The Descent of Man, and Selection in Relation to Sex. John Murray: London.
10. Yack, JE, and JH Fullard, 1993. What is an insect ear? Ann. Entomol. Soc. Am. 86(6): 677-682.
11. Piper, Ross (2007), Extraordinary Animals: An Encyclopedia of Curious and Unusual Animals, Greenwood Press.
12. Scoble, MJ. 1992. The Lepidoptera: Form, function, and diversity. Oxford University Press.

HUMAN BRAIN REFERENCES:

1. Andrews, DG (2001). Neuropsychology. Psychology Press. ISBN 9781841691039. http://books.google.com/?id=kiCtU8wBTfwC.

2. Buxton, RB (2002). An Introduction to Functional Magnetic Resonance Imaging: Principles and Techniques. Cambridge University Press. ISBN 9780521581134. http://books.google.com/?id=FordF5AN9vwC.
3. Campbell, Neil A. and Jane B. Reece. (2005). Biology. Benjamin Cummings. ISBN 0-8053-7171-0
4. Cosgrove, KP; Mazure CM, Staley JK (2007). "Evolving knowledge of sex differences in brain structure, function, and chemistry.". Biol Psychiat 62 (8): 847-55. doi:10.1016/j.biopsych.2007.03.001. PMID 17544382. PMC 2711771. http://linkinghub.elsevier.com/retrieve/pii/S0006322307001989.
5. Fisch, BJ; Spehlmann R (1999). Fisch and Spehlmann's EEG Primer: Basic Principles of Digital and Analog EEG . . . Elsevier Health Sciences. ISBN 9780444821485. http://books.google.com/?id=YMHsluy4QygC.
6. Gray, Peter (2002). Psychology (4th ed.). Worth Publishers. ISBN 0716751623.
7. Kandel, ER; Schwartz JH, Jessel TM (2000). Principles of Neural Science. McGraw-Hill Professional. ISBN 9780838577011.
8. Parent, A; Carpenter MB (1995). Carpenter's Human Neuroanatomy. Williams & Wilkins. ISBN 9780683067521. http://books.google.com/?id=IJ5pAAAAMAAJ.
9. Preissl, H (2005). Magnetoencephalography. Academic Press. ISBN 9780123668691. http://books.google.com/?id=ElTJAAAACAAJ.
10. Simon, Seymour (1999). The Brain. HarperTrophy. ISBN 0-688-17060-9
11. Thompson, Richard F. (2000). The Brain: An Introduction to Neuroscience. Worth Publishers. ISBN 0-7167-3226-2
12. Toro, R; Perron M, Pike B, Richer L. Veillette S, Pausova Z, Paus T (2008). "Brain size and folding of the human cerebral cortex.". Cerebral cortex (New York, N.Y. : 1991) 18 (10): 2352-7. doi:10.1093/cercor/bhm261. PMID 18267953. http://cercor.oxfordjournals.org/cgi/content/abstract/18/10/2352.
13. Vanderwolf, CH; Kolb, B; Cooley, RK (Feb 1978). "Behavior of the rat after removal of the neocortex and hippocampal formation". Journal of comparative and physiological psychology 92 (1): 156-75. doi:10.1037/h0077447. ISSN 0021-9940. PMID 564358.

Basal Ganglia References:

1. Soltanzadeh, Akbar (2004). Neurologic Disorders. Tehran: Jafari. ISBN 964-6088-03-1.
2. Percheron et al. (1991)
3. Parent and Parent (2005)

4. Mena-Segovia et al. (2004)
5. Hikosaka, O; Takikawa, Y; Kawagoe, R (1 July 2000). "Role of the basal ganglia in the control of purposive saccadic eye movements" (Free full text). Physiological reviews 80 (3): 953-78. ISSN 0031-9333. PMID 10893428. http://physrev.physiology.org/cgi/pmidlookup?view=long&pm id=10893428. edit
6. Niv, Y.; Rivlin-Etzion, M. (Oct 2007). "Parkinson's disease: fighting the will?" (Free full text). The Journal of neuroscience : the official journal of the Society for Neuroscience 27 (44): 11777-11779. doi:10.1523/ JNEUROSCI.4010-07.2007. ISSN 0270-6474. PMID 17978012. http:// www.jneurosci.org/cgi/pmidlookup?view=long&pmid=17978012. edit
7. Parent A (1986). Comparative Neurobiology of the Basal Ganglia. Wiley. ISBN 9780471803485.
8. Grillner, S; Ekeberg,; El, Manira; Lansner, A; Parker, D; Tegnér, J; Wallén, P (May 1998). "Intrinsic function of a neuronal network—a vertebrate central pattern generator". Brain research. Brain research reviews 26 (2-3): 184-97. doi: 10.1016/S0165-0173(98)00002-2. PMID 9651523. edit
9. Radua, Joaquim; Mataix-Cols, David (November 2009). "Voxel-wise meta-analysis of grey matter changes in obsessive-compulsive disorder". British Journal of Psychiatry 195 (5): 393-402. doi:10.1192/bjp.bp.108.055046. PMID 19880927.
10. Radua, Joaquim; van den Heuvel, Odile A.; Surguladze, Simon; Mataix-Cols, David (5 July 2010). "Meta-analytical comparison of voxel-based morphometry studies in obsessive-compulsive disorder vs other anxiety disorders". Archives of General Psychiatry 67 (7): 701-711. doi:10.1001/ archgenpsychiatry.2010.70. PMID 20603451.
11. Alm PA (2004). "Stuttering and the basal ganglia circuits: a critical review of possible relations". Journal of communication disorders 37 (4): 325-69. doi:10.1016/j.jcomdis.2004.03.001. PMID 15159193. http://theses.lub. lu.se/scripta-archive/2005/02/02/med_1035/part2/Per_Alm_Paper_II.pdf.
12. Andrew Gilies, A brief history of the basal ganglia, retrieved on 27 June 2005
13. Vieussens, 1685
14. Percheron et al. (1994)

Thalmus References:

1. Jones Edward G.(2007) "The Thalamus" Cambridge Uni. Press
2. Percheron, G. (2003) "Thalamus". In Paxinos, G. and May, J.(eds). The human nervous system. 2d Ed. Elsevier. Amsterdam. pp.592-675

3. Percheron, G. (1982) The arterial supply of the thalamus. In Schaltenbrand and Walker, A.E.(eds) Stereotaxy of the human brain. Thieme. Stuttgart. pp.218-232

4. Steriade, M. and Llinas, R. (1988) "The functional states of the thalamus and the associated neuronal interplay". Physiological Reviews 68: 699-742 PMID 2839857

5. Your Brain Boots Up Like a Computer | LiveScience

6. Dejerine, J. and Roussy. G.(1906) Le syndrome thalamique. Rev. Neurol. 14: 521-532

7. Kuhlenbeck, H. (1937). The ontogenetic development of diencephalic centres in the bird's brain (chick) and comparison with the reptilian and mammalian diencephalon. J. Comp. Neurol. 66

8. Shimamura, K., Hartigan, D. J., Martinez, S., Puelles, L. and Rubenstein, J. L. (1995). Longitudinal organization of the anterior neural plate and neural tube. Development 121,3923-3933.

9. Scholpp S, Lumsden A Building a bridal chamber: development of the thalamus. Trends Neurosci. 2010 Aug;33(8):373-380. Epub 2010 Jun 11. [1]

10. 8 Hirata, T., et al. (2006) Zinc-finger genes Fez and Fez-like function in the establishment of diencephalon subdivisions. Development 133, 3993-4004[2]

11. Jeong JY, Einhorn Z, Mathur P, Chen L, Lee S, Kawakami K, Guo S. Patterning the zebrafish diencephalon by the conserved zinc-finger protein Fezl. Development. 2007 Jan;134(1):127-36. [3]

12. Acampora D, Avantaggiato V, Tuorto F, Simeone A. Genetic control of brain morphogenesis through Otx gene dosage requirement. Development. 1997 Sep;124(18):3639-50. [4]

13. Scholpp S, Foucher I, Staudt N, Peukert D, Lumsden A, Houart C. Otx1, Otx2 and Irx1b establish and position the ZLI in the diencephalon. Development. 2007 Sep;134(17):3167-76. [5]

13. Puelles, L. and Rubenstein, J. L. (2003). Forebrain gene expression domains and the evolving prosomeric model. Trends Neurosci. 26,469-476.

14. Ishibashi, M. and McMahon, A. P. (2002). A sonic hedgehog-dependent signalling relay regulates growth of diencephalic and mesencephalic primordia in the early mouse embryo. Development 129, 4807-4819.

15. Kiecker, C. and Lumsden, A. (2004). Hedgehog signalling from the ZLI regulates diencephalic regional identity. Nat. Neurosci. 7, 1242-1249.

16. Scholpp S, Wolf O, Brand M, Lumsden A. Hedgehog signalling from the zona limitans intrathalamica orchestrates patterning of the zebrafish diencephalon'. Development. 2006 Mar;133(5):855-64[6]

17. Scholpp S, Delogu A, Gilthorpe J, Peukert D, Schindler S, Lumsden A. Her6 regulates the neurogenetic gradient and neuronal identity in the thalamus. Proc Natl Acad Sci U S A. 2009 Nov 24;106(47):19895-900[7]

18. Vue TY, Bluske K, Alishahi A, Yang LL, Koyano-Nakagawa N, Novitch B, Nakagawa Y. Sonic hedgehog signaling controls thalamic progenitor identity and nuclei specification in mice. J Neurosci. 2009 Apr 8;29(14):4484-97[8]

19. Scholpp S, Lumsden A Building a bridal chamber: development of the thalamus. Trends Neurosci. 2010 Aug;33(8):373-380. Epub 2010 Jun 11. [9]

20. Young KA, Holcomb LA, Yazdani U, Bonkale W, Hicks PB and German DC (2007). "5HTTLPR polymorphism and enlargement of the pulvinar: Unlocking the backdoor to the limbic system". Biol Psychiatry 61 (6): 813-8. doi:10.1016/j.biopsych.2006.08.047. PMID 17083920.

Circulatory system References:

1. cardiovascular system at Dorland's Medical Dictionary

2. circulatory system at Dorland's Medical Dictionary

3. MeSH Cardiovascular+System

4. Dwivedi, Girish & Dwivedi, Shridhar (2007). History of Medicine: Sushruta—the Clinician—Teacher par Excellence. National Informatics Centre (Government of India).

5. Anatomy—History of anatomy

6. Mohammadali M. Shojaa, R. Shane Tubbsb, Marios Loukasc, Majid Khalilid, Farid Alakbarlie, Aaron A. Cohen-Gadola; Tubbs, RS; Loukas, M; Khalili, M; Alakbarli, F; Cohen-Gadol, AA (29 May 2009), "Vasovagal syncope in the Canon of Avicenna: The first mention of carotid artery hypersensitivity", International Journal of Cardiology (Elsevier) 134 (3): 297-301, doi:10.1016/j. ijcard.2009.02.035, PMID 19332359

7. Rachel Hajar (1999), "The Greco-Islamic Pulse", Heart Views 1 (4): 136-140 [138]

8. Chairman's Reflections (2004), "Traditional Medicine Among Gulf Arabs, Part II: Blood-letting", Heart Views 5 (2), p. 74-85 [80].

9. West, John B. (October 9, 2008), "Ibn al-Nafis, the pulmonary circulation, and the Islamic Golden Age", Journal of Applied Physiology 105 (6): 1877-80, doi:10.1152/japplphysiol.91171.2008, PMID 18845773

10. Peter E. Pormann and E. Savage Smith, Medieval Islamic medicine Georgetown University, Washington DC, 2007, p. 48.

Human gastrointestinal tract References:

1. gastrointestinal tract at Dorland's Medical Dictionary
2. MeSH Gastrointestinal+tract
3. digestive system at Dorland's Medical Dictionary
4. Nelson RJ. 2005. Introduction to Behavioral Endocrinology. Sinauer Associates: Massachusetts. p 57.
5. MeSH Upper+Gastrointestinal+Tract
6. MeSH Lower+Gastrointestinal+Tract
7. David A. Warrell (2005). Oxford textbook of medicine: Sections 18-33. Oxford University Press. pp.511-. ISBN 9780198569787. http://books.google.com/books?id=hL1NKQJlY1IC&pg=PA511. Retrieved 1 July 2010.
8. Bruce M. Carlson (2004). Human Embryology and Developmental Biology (3rd ed.). Saint Louis: Mosby. ISBN 0-323-03649-X.
9. Colorado State University > Gastrointestinal Transit: How Long Does It Take? Last updated on May 27, 2006. Author: R. Bowen.
10. Richard Coico, Geoffrey Sunshine, Eli Benjamini (2003). Immunology: a short course. New York: Wiley-Liss. ISBN 0-471-22689-0.
11. Animal Physiology textbook
12. Abraham L. Kierszenbaum (2002). Histology and cell biology: an introduction to pathology. St. Louis: Mosby. ISBN 0-323-01639-1.

CHAPTER 11

Quotations and Rules to Live By

"Quotations to live by" includes both those that are legend, and those defined by **Dionysius the Divine (DtD)**. I have attempted to give credit to the originator of the legendary quotes where I could identify the originator. Otherwise, I just label the quote as "legend".

1. You can go far if you don't care who gets the credit—[Ronald Reagan]
2. No man is an island—[English poet John Donne]
3. If you don't love life, you don't know love—[DtD]
4. A brave man dies only once;
   A coward dies many deaths. [William Shakespeare]
5. I think, therefore I am.
   I am therefore I think. [René Descartes]
6. The cumulative subconscious is the essence of God. [possibly Carl Jung]
7. A word to the wise is sufficient. [legend]
8. A fool and his money are soon separated. [Thomas Tusser (1524-1580), an English poet]
9. I think of God, therefore God exists
   God exists, therefore I think of God—[DtD]
10. True love is unconditional.—[DtD]
11. Journey of a thousand miles begins with the first step.—[Confucius]
12. I'm stupid, but my brain is smart.—[DtD]
13. The spirit is willing, but the flesh is weak.—[Christian Bible—Matthew 26:41]
14. A stitch in time saves nine.—[English astronomer Francis Baily—1797]
15. A penny saved is a penny earned.—[Ben Franklin]

16. To err is human, to forgive is divine. [Alexander Pope]
17. If at first you don't succeed try and try again. [Charlie Sheen]
18. Winners never quit and quitters never win. [Vince Lombardi]
19. What's good for the goose is good for the gander. [American Proverb]
20. An apple a day keeps the doctor away. [legend]
21. The only thing to fear is fear itself. [Winston Churchill, Rosevelt]
22. Give a man to fish, you feed him a meal.
    Teach a man to fish, your feed him for a lifetime. [Chinese Proverb]
23. Before you criticize me, walk a mile in my shoes. [original by Mahatma Gandhi]
24. Thinking—shut the mouth, turn on the brain. Let your brain do your work for you. [DtD]
25. Until you are perfect don't point fingers at others faults;
    It might backfire. [DtD]
26. The human spirit—the combination of beliefs, emotions, self image, belonging. [DtD]
27. Success [DtD]
    Respect (earn it)
    Discipline (do it)
    Think (turn on the brain)
    Understand—(put it all together)
28. Your level of existence is your level of Awe-inspiration [DtD]
29. The biggest form of worship is self worship [DtD]
30. Without the human existence, the concept of good and evil,
    God and the Devil, have no meaning. [DtD]
31. If the shoe fits, wear it. [old proverb]
32. An idle mind is the workshop of the Devil. [legend]
33. The mind of good is the dwelling place of God;
    The mind of evil is the dwelling place of the Devil. [DtD]
34. Universally applicable truth: Love, the human connection. [DtD]
35. Universal religion:
    Brotherhood of all mankind, past, present and future. [DtD]
36. You always miss 100% of the shots you don't take. [Larry Bird]
37. Organization is the key to success. [DtD]
38. Definition of the problem is 90% of the solution. [DtD]
39. God helps him who helps himself. [Aeschylus—ancient Greek playwright]
40. [reserved]
41. If you can't say anything good about someone, don't say anything at all. [legend]

42. Might makes right. [Plato's The Republic]
43. An ounce of prevention is worth a pound of cure. [Benjamin Franklin]
44. Golden Rule (Secular): He who has the gold, makes the rules. [legend]
45. The buck stops here. [Harry S. Truman]
46. A bird in hand is worth two in the bush [legend]
47. Don't count your chickens before the hatch. [Aesop—around 570 B.C]
48. He who lives by the sword, dies by the sword. [English dramatist Anthony Munday]
49. The pen is mightier than the sword. [English author Edward Bulwer-Lytton—play Richelieu]
50. If you have doubt about doing something, then don't do it at all. [legend]
51. Where there is smoke there is fire. [legend]
52. A picture is worth a thousand words. [possiblly Frederick R. Barnard]
53. If you always tell the truth, then you won't have to remember your lies. [legend]
54. The only love I ever got, was the love I gave, except for Mother's love. [DtD]
55. A rolling stone gathers no moss.
56. Either you are self serving or God serving. [DtD]
57. It is better to have loved and lost, then never to have loved at all. [Alfred Lord Tennyson's poem In Memoriam]
58. Youth is wasted on the young. [George Bernard Shaw]
59. Be careful who you step on the way up the corporate ladder, they might re4member you on your way down. [legend]
60. Garbage in, garbage out. [legend for computer programming and learning]
61. You cannot be gentle if you are not strong; weak is just weak. [DtD]
62. A real man will not harm you without provocation. [DtD]
63. You should never turn your back to a coward. [DtD]
64. All bullies are cowards. [DtD]
65. My father used to tell me when playing checkers think long, think wrong. [DtD]
66. Always trust your 1st instinct. [DtD]
67. He who hesitates is lost. [adaptation from Joseph Addison's play Cato]
68. For want of a nail, the shoe was lost;
    For want of a shoe the horse was lost;
    For want of a horse the man was lost;
    For want of a man, the battle was lost;
    For want of a battle, the war was lost;
    For want of a war, the city was lost.
69. Never turn back; always go forward. [DtD]

70. Whatever a woman has to give she is giving. [DtD]
71. If you learned from you mistakes, you have not failed. [DtD]
72. Ignorance is bliss. [Thomas Gray's poem, "Ode on a Distant Prospect of Eton College" (1742)]
73. If you can't stand to be by yourself, maybe you bore other people too. [legend]
74. The only dumb question is the question you don't ask. [legend]
75. If you're asking questions you are learning. [DtD]
76. If you're not learning you are dying. [original by Dr. Daniel Amen]
77. The 10 senses to/from Brain: [DtD]
    Input:
    1. Smell (oldest)
    2. Sight
    3. Taste
    4. Touch
    5. Hearing
    Output:
    6. Gut feeling (subconscious experience)
    7. Instinct (survival, mating, birth, nesting)
    8. Emotions (fear, happiness, anger, sadness, hate/love)
    9. Natural (breathing, cardiovascular, digestion)
    10. Telepathic (subconscious)
78. purpose of life: Enjoy life, living and being alive [legend]
79. If you love someone, turn them loose; If they return they love you. [legend]
80. In order to win love, you must be willing to lose love. [DtD]
81. No news is good news, if your son is at war. [DtD]
82. He who laughs last, laughs loudest. [original by Sir John Vanbrugh (1664-1726) in his play 'The Country House]
83. Two wrongs don't make a right. [1783 B. Rush]
84. No news is bad news, if your loved one is far away. [DtD]
85. The highest level of existence is intellectual/spiritual. [DtD]
86. The lowest level of existence is primordial self gratification. [DtD]
87. The proof of your religion is what you do with it. [DtD]
88. You cannot love and hate at the same time. [DtD]
89. The highest level of life is serving your fellow man, especially those in need. [DtD]
90. Where there is a will, there is a way. [legend]
91. When you flaunt decency, you have nothing left to respect. [DtD]
92. Cleanliness is next to Godliness [original—Sir Francis Bacon, "Advancement of Learning", 1605]

93. The lowest level of life is serving only yourself through vice, greed and lust. [DtD]
94. You get out of life what you put into it. [DtD]
95. Nothing is free. [DtD]
96. Pay me now, or pay me later.
    (service your machinery, or pay more after breakdown/crash). [legend]
97. Train a child the way he should go, and when he is old, he will not depart from it.—[Christian Bible]
98. Toilet training is the most important training a child can receive for behavior—unknown
99. Beauty is in the eye of the beholder. [3rd century BC in Greek]
100. All girls are pretty, but some are prettier than others. [legend]
101. Honey draws more flies than vinegar. [legend]
102. A boy models his father's strength and courage, and learns love from his mother. [DtD]
103. A girl models her mother's nurturing and learns love from her father. [DtD]
104. Let sleeping dogs lie (Do not instigate trouble). [legend]
105. Don't stir the pot (you might find trouble you don't want) [legend].
106. Spare the rod, spoil the child. [Samuel Butler, in "Hudibras"]
107. The best investment you can make is in yourself (education) [legend]
108. Close only counts in horseshoes. [legend]
109. Don't rock the boat (you might start trouble you don't want) [legend].
110. If you fear death, you haven't lived, and you don't know love. [DtD]
111. If you do me wrong once, shame on you.
     If you do me wrong twice, shame on me. [legend]
112. Elements of Religion: [DtD]
     1. Belief in an unseen provider that is everywhere and controls the elements of earth and the fate of all life on earth.
     2. Belief in life after death.
     3. Male virility and strength
     4. Female fertility and beauty
     5. Human connection (church/community, society, love/hate, nurturing, belonging.)
113. If you can't stand the fire, get out of the kitchen. [Harry S. Truman]
114. I cannot teach you what you are not willing to learn. [DtD]
115. Birds of a feather flock together. [original—1545, William Turner—"The Rescuing of Romish Fox"]
116. Your lack of planning does not constitute an emergency on my part. [legend]

117. Turn about is fair play. [original—1755 "Life of Captain Dudley Bradstreet" p338]
118. What goes around comes around. [legend]
119. Possession is nine-tenths of the law. [original—Roman law, John Duncan (2007)]
120. A friend in need is a friend indeed. [original—Quintus Ennius, 3rd century BC]
121. Too many chiefs, not enough Indians. [legend]
122. Too many cooks spoil the soup. [legend]
123. I never met a man I didn't like.—Will Rogers
124. Don't bite the hand that feeds you. [legend]
125. Early to bed, early to rise makes a man healthy, wealthy and wise.—[Treatise of Fishing with Angle, 1496]
126. What goes up must come down. [gravity, investments, career]
127. A lover may come and go, but, a friend is forever. [DtD]
128. A Friend [DtD]
      Is happy when you are happy;
      Is sad when you are sad;
      Cares about you and for you come rain or shine,
         through thick and thin, through good times,
         and bad times.
      Rejoices in your successes and sorrows in your pain.
129. You cannot well raise children without cookies, milk and puppies. [DtD]
130. Anything worth doing is worth doing right. [Hunter S. Thompson]
131. You can take the boy out of the country, but, you can't take the country out of the boy. [legend]
132. You can fool some of the people some of the time; But, you can't fool all the people all the time. [Abraham Lincoln]
133. If you haven't failed, then you haven't tried anything hard. [legend]
134. Practice makes perfect. [legend]
135. In romance "don't rob the cradle". [legend]
136. In love "out of sight, out of mind". [legend]
137. "that's the way the cookie crumbles". or, that's the way the ball bounces". In life whatever happens, happens [legend]
138. "It all come out in the wash", or "What goes around comes around". In life, when someone is unfair to us, [legend]
139. "get off the treadmill from time-to-time" and "smell the roses", and "feed the ducks and pigeons" and, "play with puppies and babies". [DtD]
140. "two peas in a pod", When two people are in like mind,. [legend]
141. Happy as a bug in a rug. [legend]

142. Education begins in the home. [legend]
143. Keep your chin up (have hope; look forward when life is discouraging). [Pennsylvania newspaper *The Evening Democrat*, October 1900]
144. Heaven—the spiritual nature of heaven is the peace that results from the balance of beliefs (God and Love), emotions, society, and the environment. [DtD]
145. Hell—the spiritual nature of hell is the pain and torment that results from the extreme lack of balance of beliefs, emotions, society and the environment. [DtD]
146. Sin—anything we say, do or think to altienate oneself, or others, from the spiritual nature of Heaven. [DtD]
147. Evil—anything or anyone that sins or otherwise tempts anyone to sin. [DtD]
148. When you assume, you make an ASS out of you and me. [legend]
149. Faith, hope, courage, charity—without these you have no life. [DtD]
150. Strike while the iron is hot. [1386 Chaucer, "Tale of Melibee"]
151. In order to win in social conflict, always take the last blow. [DtD]
152. Winners find solutions, losers make excuses. [DtD]
153. A woman in love cannot be stopped from pursuing her love, unless she gives up. [DtD]
154. Hell has no fury like a woman scorned (in love) [William Congreve, in "The mourning bride", 1697]
155. People who live in glass houses shouldn't throw rocks. [Geoffrey Chaucer's "Troilus and Criseyde" (1385).]
156. Discretion is the better part of valor. [Shakespeare, in "Henry IV, Part One", 1596]
157. There is a thin line between genius and insanity. [Oscar Levant, composer, pianist, actor, author, actor]
    (Be careful with this one. Insanity is mental and/or emotional and/or cognitive dysfunction, but can display genius. Genius is accelerated mental function (high IQ—150+) that can appear to be insanity if the genius becomes socially withdrawn and dysfunctional. The successful genius has both a high IQ and a high EQ (emotional intelligence), and seeks approval from no one.)
158. The squeaky wheel gets the grease. [Josh Billings, American humorist (1818-1885) poem, "The Kicker"]
159. Nothing ventured, nothing gained. [legend]
160. No pain no gain. [1577 N. Breton, "Works of Young Wit"]

161. Absence makes the heart grow fonder. [original—Roman poet Sextus Propertius, "Elegies"]
162. Only love can break a heart, only love can mend it again. [Gene Pitney, singer-songwriter—1962]
163. Feather your nest. [legend—negotiate gain for yourself]
164. Buyer beware. [original—Chief Justice John Marshall, 1817, in Laidlaw v. Organ] (buy at your own risk without an express warranty)
165. In work, to survive and succeed, give more than you get paid for. [legend] (note: I Dionysius the Divine have survived and succeeded many decades by this principal in spite of many disadvantages)
166. Everybody loves somebody sometime. [Dean Martin]
167. Love and hate are the only emotions that are not natural. They have to be taught/learned and you can only do one at a time. [DtD]
168. Hate self destructs; Love self nourishes and heals. [DtD]
169. Beware the calm before the storm. [legend]
170. When life seems dark, look for the light at the end of the tunnel. [DtD]
171. Sometimes it is darkest before dawn of a new and better day. [legend] (note: This legend has nothing to do with the light of day. It simply means, and I have seen it to be true, that many times just when it seems we have no hope, we find a way)
172. Don't carry a chip on your shoulder. Someone might knock it off. [DtD]
173. Don't wear your problems like a badge, people will shun you. [DtD]
174. Some people can read you like a book. [DtD]
175. You can't judge a book by it's cover. [legend]
176. Clothes don't make the man. [legend]
177. The best offence is a good defense. [legend]
178. Success and/or political power are dangerous aphrodisiacs. ["The Ultimate Aphrodisiac", Dr. Ruth Westheimer, Dr. Steven Kaplan]
179. Conquer the world: take everything the world has to dish out without striking back. [DtD]
180. Dare to be different; be a target, or set a trend. [legend—also quoted by Harry Millner, Wilfred Peteson]
181. Like father, like son. [legend]
182. A good leader makes himself look good.
    A great leader makes others look good. [legend]
183. Some people aren't worth the powder it takes to blow them away. [DtD]
184. Some people are so good, they are worth their weight in gold. [DtD]
188. When the going gets tough, the tough get going. [original—Joseph P. Kennedy (1888-1969)]

186. Sometimes, we can't win for losing. [1950's American legend]
187. Sometimes, if it weren't for bad luck we wouldn't have any luck at all. [legend]
188. Sometimes people helping other people is like "the blind leading the blind". [legend]
189. Sometimes we get so focused on detail we "can't see the forest for the trees". (the whole picture) [legend]
190. Sometimes we get so involved with detail we can't finish a project, so "we get wrapped around the axle". [legend]
191. Don't let the cat out of the bag. [legend]
192. Curiosity killed the cat. [legend]
193. A chain is only as strong as it's weakest link. [original—Thomas Reid's "Essays on the Intellectual Powers of Man", 1786]
194. A team is only as strong as it's weakest member. [legend]
195. If you do good deeds, like helping people expecting nothing in return, you are a good person. [DtD]
196. If you do great deeds, like serving many sacrificially, expecting nothing in return, you are a great person. [DtD]
197. The statement, "There are no absolutes" is not only an absolute, but also a COPOUT. [DtD]
198. If you are afraid of failure, you may never have success. [DtD]
199. Put your best foot forward. [original—Sir Thomas Overbury's poem "A Wife", 1613]
200. Life is not always a bed of roses. [original—Christopher Marlowe's poem "The Passionate Shepherd to His Love", 1599]
201. Life is not always peaches and cream. [legend]
202. Haste makes waste. [original—Chaucer "Tale of Melibee", 1386]
203. A man went back in time to drill for oil and become rich, but, he had not the technology to drill so Deep.
204. A man had been depressed for a long time.
    A Psychologist told him to get cleaned up, shave, put on clean clothes.
    The man saw himself in a new light and recovered. [unknown]
205. I would rather be a live chicken than a dead hero. [legend]
206. The family that prays together, stays together. [original—Al Scalpone, writer, 1942]
207. Necessity is the mother of invention. [original—Plato's "The Republic"]
208. Nirvana—any place or condition of great peace or bliss [unknown]
209. Sex without dating is the lowest form of human existence with total lack of respect for human value. [DtD]

(apparently a 21st century college fad)

210. Marriage, who needs it? Those who are willing to make a public lifetime commitment and mutual promise of faithfulness, fidelity, caring and responsibility, and present themselves publicly and legally as man and wife. [DtD]

211. Formula for success:
    1. set goals
    2. Disciple and respect
    3. Listen to instruction and directions
    4. Think and understand
    5. Read and understand
    6. Understand English grammar and Literature
    7. Express thoughts in writing.
    8. Know basic math
    9. Understand yourself and your needs
    10. Understand others and their needs
    11. Understand basic biology, chemistry and physics (optional)
    12. Understand basic history, government and politics (optional)
    13. Understand basic morals and religious concepts
    14. Care about and help others
    15. Plan, prioritize and schedule your work/obligations
    16. Budget your time and finances

212. Discipline
    1. Follow directions
    2. Obey rules
    3. Plan your work
    4. Work your plan
    5. Be on time
    6. Do your work
    7. Do your best
    8. Care about your work
    9. Be neat
    10. Write clear
    11. Prioritize and schedule your work

CHAPTER 12

Electronic Configuration

Electronic configuration has to do with the order in which electrons fill energy levels in the atoms of the elements of the Atomic Periodic Table, originally defined by the Russian Chemist Dmitri Ivanovich Mendeleev and published in "Principles of Chemistry" in 1869 with only 63 elements. The periodic table is another exhibit in describing the irreducible complexity, balance and order of the universe, the earth, and life on earth clearly indicating "Intelligent Design". Clearly, this exhibit of the essence of matter of the universe, and the earth is not the result of a random process, natural selection, adaptation, or mutation.

Today the Atomic Periodic Table contains some 114 elements according to the National Institute of Standards and Technology. The 7 atomic energy levels are filled up with electrons either completely (the first two levels, helium and Beryllium through Neon) or partially before the higher energy levels begin to be filled. From the third through the seventh energy level after an energy level is partially filled, electrons begin to fill higher energy levels before completely filling up the lower energy levels.

The electronic configuration chart is a way of describing how the energy levels of atoms are filled. This configuration chart is further defined algorithmically element by element, i.e. Ne = $1s^2 2s^2 2p^6$; Ar = [Ne]$3s^2 3p^6$; and K = [Ar] 4s. Here you see that the electronic configuration definition of the elements of each energy level builds on the electronic configuration definition of the previous energy level, where "s" and "p" are energy sublevels.

The energy sublevels contain a specific number of electrons and are the same at all 7 energy levels, and must be filled before electrons begin filling the next energy level. The electron capacity of the energy sublevels is as follows: $s(2)$, $p(6)$, $d(10)$, $f(14)$.

The 7 energy levels contain energy sublevels as follows: $1(s^2)$, $2(s^2, p^6)$, $3(s^2, p^6 d^{10})$, $4(s^2, p^6 d^{10} f^{14})$, $5(s^2, p^6 d^{10} f^{14})$, $6(s^2, p^6 d^{10})$, $7(s^2, p^6)$.

And, as if that were not enough, the quantum number of an element in the Atomic Periodic Table can also be specified. The quantum number of an element indicates the last energy level, the last energy sublevel, and the spin ($+\frac{1}{2}$-positive,—$\frac{1}{2}$-negative) of the last electron to fill an energy level. The electrons first fill up an energy sublevel with positive spinning electrons, and then begin to fill up the energy sublevel with negative spinning electrons. For example, the quantum number for K = **4, 0, 0, + ½**; Fe = **3, 2, -2, -½**; N = **2, 1, 1, + ½** ; Sn = **5, 1, 0, + ½**. Here, for K, 4 is the 4th energy level, 0 is the first energy sublevel (s), and 0 is the orbital group within the sublevel, and + ½ indicates a positive spin for the last electron to fill the last energy sublevel, s.

In my substitute experience with high achiever high school chemistry students I found that they had a great deal of difficulty understanding electronic configuration from their textbook mathematical definition. So, one night on 23 January, 2006, I came up a chart, instructions and examples to help the students understand electronic configuration. The students I shared this chart with used it successfully, and told me they continued to use it in future years. I also shared this chart with chemistry professor, Dr. Bruce Harris, and he confirmed the accuracy and usefulness of my chart. So, I thought it helpful, and important to include this chart in this book. So here I offer this chart for the benefit of all future chemistry students.

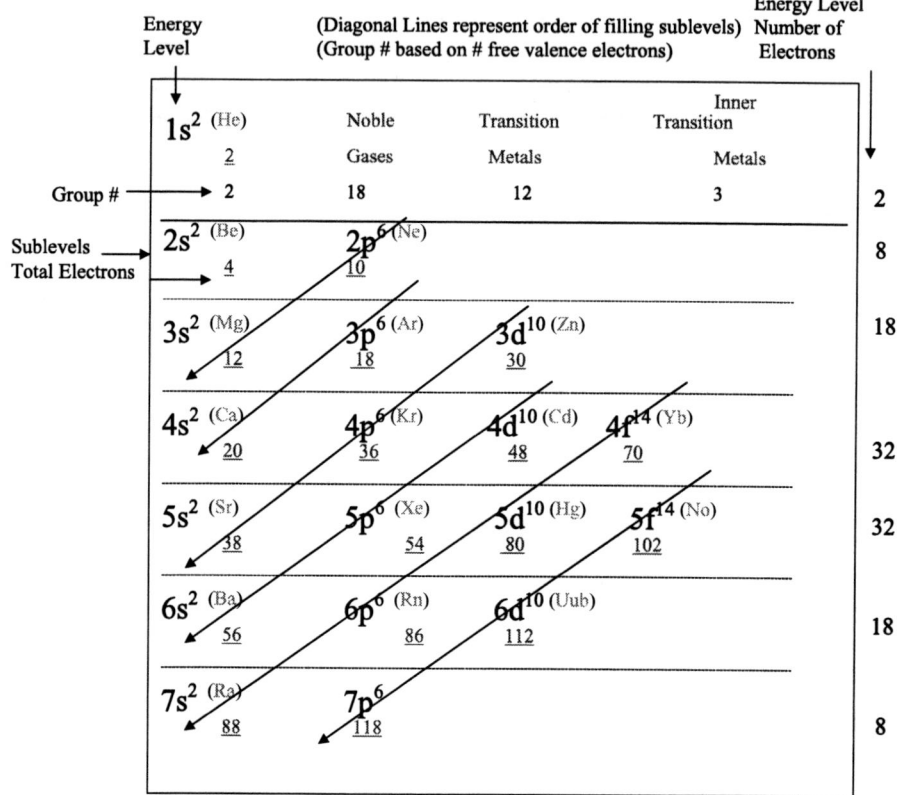

<u>Quantum Numbers Definition</u>:

Level (1-7), sublevel (0-3), orbital, spin ($\uparrow 1^{st}$ + ‰ $\downarrow 2^{nd}$ - ‰)

		s (0),	p (1),		d (2)
sublevel	→				
filling order	→	1 2	1 4 2 5 3 6		1 6 2 7 3 8 4 9 5 10

spin →

Orbitals → 0   -1 0 +1   -2 -1 0 +1 +2

- -

Electron Configuration, Orbital Notation, Quantum Numbers   Work Sheet

Element	Config	Orbital Notation	Quantum Numbers Last Electron to fill
K	[Ar] 4s		4, 0, 0, + ‰
Fe	[Ar] $3d^6 4s^2$		3, 2, -2, - ‰
N	$1s^2 2s^2 2p^3$		2, 1, 1, + ‰
Sn	[Kr] $5s^2 4d^{10} 5p^2$		5, 1, 0, + ‰

CHAPTER 13

Advise to Presidents of the United States
By William J.H. Boetcker

These quotes have been attributed to Abraham Lincoln, but were probably written by William Boetcker in the early 20th century. William Boetcker was born in Hamburg, Germany on July 17, 1873, and was sent to America at age 18 after being recognized for his book, "Neuester Rätzelschatz", a collection of puzzles and mind problems. In America, Boetcker studied for the ministry at Chicago Theological Seminary and Bloomfield Seminary in New Jersey. (dkgoodman.com) Then, Boetcker was ordained a Presbyterian minister.

I include these wise quotes from "theamericans.us" in view of today's runaway Democratic deficit spending on social programs for what appears to me to be pure political gain. However, I am not aware that Boetcker specifically directed these quotes to any president or legislature.

"You cannot bring about prosperity by discouraging thrift."
"You cannot help small men by tearing down big men."
"You cannot strengthen the weak by weakening the strong."
"You cannot lift the wage earner by pulling down the wage payer."
"You cannot help the poor man by destroying the rich."
"You cannot keep out of trouble by spending more than your income."
"You cannot further the brotherhood of man by inciting class
    hatred."

"You cannot establish security on borrowed money."

"You cannot build character and courage by taking away men's initiative and independence."

"You cannot help men permanently by doing for them what they could and should do for themselves."

CHAPTER 14

I'm Just A Substitute

As a child, and as a young man, my nickname was Dion. I remember when I started the first grade in 1948, at Travis Elementary School in San Antonio, Tx, that I was the only child who went happy. All of the other children were crying and holding on to their mothers. I was happy that I was going to learn.

Then, when I started the first grade, people my mother worked for worked with me to learn the famous "Dick and Jane" reading primer—I loved it. Now, 55 years, 5 universities, 2 colleges, 285 college credit hours, 3 degrees, and 3 certifications later, I still have my enthusiasm for learning.

However, in the process of getting to where I am today, and working for 5 major companies, I have had experiences that convinced me that I wanted to be a teacher. But, not only that, I wanted to make a difference in young people's lives. I remember a bad experience in the third grade where a teacher was always getting annoyed with me because I always raised my hand to answer questions. Then one day she said something that really set me back for many years. This teacher told me "You think you're so smart. I can find somebody to beat you". And she did.

Despite the setback with this third grade, most of my teachers through the 12th grade were extremely helpful to help me learn and grow, especially in the honors courses. Back then, we didn't have, PreAP, and AP courses (AP refers to advanced placement).

Then, as I went on to my college career, while I had many good instructors and professors, I never understood why some instructors made their courses so difficult to understand, and I always enjoyed simplifying my college courses.

My experience in industry was the same as in college. In industry I never understood why engineers made their work seem so difficult and I always enjoyed solving problems and explaining designs.

When I was laid off from my good paying job in March of 2002, as a Computer Software Engineer, I started looking for other employment. When I found no employment opportunities as an engineer, I started considering substitute teaching. In August of 2002, I filled out complicated applications and provided references, and transcripts of my college work, and I was accepted to do substitute teaching. In the past I could not afford to teach because industry paid me much more than I could make teaching. In addition, I had looked down on teachers from the snobbishness of my technical credentials and accomplishments in industry.

Then, I started substitute teaching in September of 2002, for grades 6 to 12. What an eye opener I had as I encountered many students with serious behavior, attitude, and learning problems. I found that many students were clueless about their subject matter. I realized that many students were just not being reached. I talked to the principal at a high school, and he said that he had the same concerns. However, I began to marvel when I realized that I was making a difference in student's lives, and that I could reach them.

I knew I was making a difference because many students asked me not to leave them, and to return. Sadly though, time after time I did leave them, realizing that teaching is a sacred responsibility. In the process I began to change. While I am a stern disciplinarian, I am also more gentle, kind, and sensitive than most people. I remember a girl asking me at a middle school asking me "why do you hate us". I responded that I loved them, and that I didn't hate them. I still remember that girl responding that from then on she was going to start doing her best in school. This scene was repeated many times as I repeatedly left the students at the end of the day with tears in my eyes hoping they wouldn't see. With experiences like this I noticed myself becoming even more gentle.

Then, I remember another inspiring experience at a high school with 10th and 11th grade AP Chemistry students. One of the classes challenged me about my credentials, and my IQ, and I was pleased to satisfy their curiosity. I also told them that Emotional Intelligence (Goldman, 1996) was equally important, if not more important, as IQ. These same students saw that I had a good physical build, and they started showing me their physiques. At first they had been reluctant to do their assignment, but after coaxing from me, most of them completed their assignments.

At that very same school, and the very same day, I had another 10th and 11th grade AP Chemistry class, and the students did such good work with very little coaxing, that I was overwhelmed with amazement, and left school that day grateful that I had had the opportunity to work with such high quality students.

In another assignment that lasted for 5 weeks, I was asked to take an ESL-1 class (English as a Second Language) at a middle school. This class was extremely challenging because many spoke very little English, and some spoke no English at all. Worse than that most had attention spans of no more than 5 seconds, and could remember no more that 2 words at a time. However, with my stern, caring, intellectual approach I had great success teaching these students not only English, but eighth grade level Texas History. For this work I received great appreciation not only from the principal, but also from the teacher for whom I was substituting, and I was grateful for the opportunity to make a difference.

At the same time that I had changed this year because of my substitute teaching experience, I began to see the teachers in a different light, as I worked in close proximity with them. I began to admire and respect the teachers I met, and began to see them as saints, as I saw how important their work was in the lives of the students they taught and cared for.

Today, nine plus years later, I am a seasoned substitute teacher having been exposed to many experiences, such as teachers and principals blocking me because I wrote office referrals on favored students, or even worse, students from affluent families getting me blocked from substituting at their school because I wrote office referrals on them for disruptive behavior. For you see, I am just a substitute.

But now I enjoy Working with many fine schools and students as a substitute teacher. How long will I be allowed to continue substituting? I don't know, for you see, I am just a substitute.

CHAPTER 15

I Need A Pastor

There are many pastors that would like for me to sit in a pew at their church for one hour on Sunday. But, after that, they don't really want to be bothered.

Many pastors have paid and volunteer staff to care about, teach and even counsel people, but that isn't the same, for you see a pastor is an angel of God.

I need a pastor who cares about his whole congregation, individual by individual, young and old, rich or poor, married or single, professional, trade, or office worker, even though he can't see everyone very often, but he knows them and reaches for them sincerely when he sees them.

I need a pastor that's well educated, but down to earth, who can reach from the highest intellectual levels to the most modest of intellects for you see intellectuals need God too.

I need a pastor who reminds me of Jesus when I
see him, and who will patiently remind me
when I have erred, and who will congratulate
me when I've done well, for you see sometimes
you might be ashamed of me, and sometimes you
might be proud of me.

But, the pay isn't very good, because sometimes
I may not have very much to put in the fancy
offering plate on Sunday after paying all of
my bills.

And, I don't have a fancy car to take you to
lunch in at a fancy restaurant, or a fancy
home to invite you to supper like some of your
parishioners, but I need a pastor.

What I can offer is myself, and my caring, and
my children at the alter of your church, and
the Throne of Grace, even though our salvation
was assured a long time ago. And, I can extend
a warm and friendly greeting to your parishioners
and visitors.

I have been to many churches and many pastors
who were willing to preach to me, but they didn't
really want to be my pastor for I am a product
of many cultures, intellects, religions and ethics,
but belong to none, for born in poverty, I have not
acquired great wealth to impress any one with,
even though I have many degrees, but I need a pastor.

For you see I haven't had a pastor for over 50 years
since I left home. I conquered the world, found
God, found love, became an intellectual, found
universally applicable truth, and respect, but
I need a pastor.

I need a pastor who tells me what I need to hear
from God not just what I want to hear.

So, you see, the job is tough, and the pay is poor,
but if you would like to be my pastor, the job is open.

CPSIA information can be obtained
at www.ICGtesting.com
Printed in the USA
FSOW01n1020110216
16825FS